A SHORT HISTORY OF THE
KOREAN WAR

A SHORT HISTORY OF THE KOREAN WAR

James L. Stokesbury

QUILL
WILLIAM MORROW
NEW YORK

Library of Congress Cataloging-in-Publication Data

Stokesbury, James L.
    A short history of the Korean War/James L. Stokesbury.
        p.   cm.
    Reprint. Originally published: New York: W. Morrow, c1988.
    Includes bibliographical references.
    ISBN 0-688-09513-5
    1. Korean War, 1950–1953. I. Title.
DS918.S79   1990
951.904′2—dc20   89-39419
                                                              CIP

Printed in the United States of America

First Quill Edition

1   2   3   4   5   6   7   8   9   10

BOOK DESIGN BY PHIL REDISCH

For Seymour and Leone Dickinson, whose fortitude in the face of adversity equals any of war's more dramatic courage

ACKNOWLEDGMENTS

This study, like one of my earlier ones, was completed while I was on sabbatical leave, and it is again a pleasure to acknowledge the support given me by Acadia University in granting release time for writing. My colleagues in the Department of History have been generously supportive of my work, and I have equally appreciated the assistance afforded by the staff of the Vaughan Memorial Library at Acadia.

I wish especially to acknowledge the help of Truman R. Strobridge of Washington, D.C., who provided me with extremely valuable material of which, but for him, I should have remained unaware.

The final draft of this manuscript was typed by Carolyn Bowlby and Joy Cavizzi, both of Acadia, neither of whom could ever be replaced by a machine—even if it *could* learn to make cookies.

I must add the usual disclaimer that none of the above are responsible for errors of fact or interpretation, which are solely my own. Finally, as always and for everything, thanks to Liz.

CONTENTS

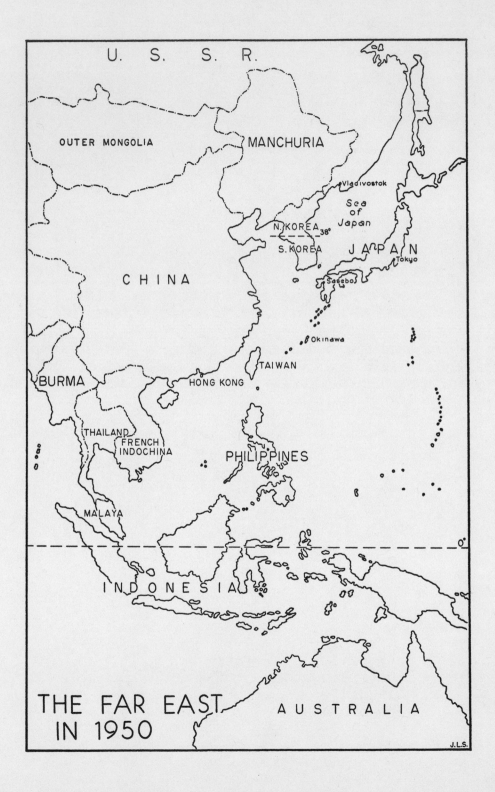

U. S. S. R.

OUTER MONGOLIA

MANCHURIA

Vladivostok

Sea
of
Japan

N. KOREA 38°

S. KOREA

JAPAN

Tokyo

CHINA

Sasebo

Okinawa

TAIWAN

BURMA

HONG KONG

THAILAND

FRENCH
INDOCHINA

PHILIPPINES

MALAYA

0°

I N D O N E S I A

THE FAR EAST
IN 1950

AUSTRALIA

J.L.S.

PROLOGUE

The summer monsoons had begun; scattered but heavy rain swept across the sky, dropping from the thick clouds that blackened the night. On the eastern rim of Asia, it was the early hours of Sunday, June 25, 1950, and most of the oriental world was asleep. Here and there, in the jungles of Malaya or the hills of Indochina, there was furtive movement where British soldiers or French Legionnaires tried to stay awake and alert for attack by Communist guerrillas. But it was quiet in the Philippines, where the Communist Hukbalahap guerrillas—Huks as they were called—had temporarily settled down. The British garrison watched the Communists over the border of the New Territories from Hong Kong, but having just won a civil war, the new Chinese regime did not wish to disturb one of their major channels for supplies from the western world. In Japan, the American occupation forces were asleep, except for those unfortunate few who had drawn duty for the weekend.

On the other side of the Sea of Japan, in the southern part of the Korean peninsula, an area styled the Republic of Korea, all was serene. The republic extended northward to an artificial line, the 38th parallel of latitude. Along its southern edge, the few soldiers on front-line duty huddled in their bunkers or under their ponchos, waited for the rain to stop or dawn to break or their reliefs to arrive, thought of home or girlfriends and wished they were somewhere else.

North of the parallel, it was another country, the Democratic People's Republic of Korea, and here, of all places on that warm, dark summer night, it was not quiet at all. The north, in contrast to the somnolent south, was a beehive of last-minute activity. Infantrymen checked their weapons and shuffled forward to their assault positions; gunners looked at watches, studied firing coordinates, and glanced at their watches again. Inside their steamy tanks, drivers revved engines, listening to the throaty roar; the tanks squatted on their heavy treads, waiting to be unleashed.

Finally the waiting was over. Starting about 0400, the dying hour of the night, the artillery roared out. From west to east along the parallel there was a rippling line of gunfire, so that it took about an hour before the action was general. Beneath the hurtling umbrella of shells, the Communist tanks and infantry surged forward. In the west they hit first, against isolated units on the Ongjin peninsula, cut off by water from the rest of South Korea. To the east, as the attack gathered momentum, the North Koreans met only scattered resistance. Nothing but outposts held the positions immediately below the parallel; the main South Korean line was something from ten to thirty miles back, and even then it was not held with any real strength. The South Koreans had no tanks of their own, few heavy weapons, and, most important as events developed, nothing that would stop a North Korean tank.

In Seoul, the capital of South Korea, there was a small American military advisory group; it received word of the attack on the Ongjin peninsula about 0600, two hours after it had begun. More bad news soon followed, and by 1000 it was clear that a full-scale invasion was in progress. Messages began to flicker back up the chain of command. At midmorning, American Ambassador to Korea John J. Muccio sent a report to the Department of State in Washington; an hour earlier his military attaché had sent a similar message to the Department of the Army, and then throughout the day amplifying calls and telegrams went out, many of them from the U.S. Air Force control group stationed at Kimpo airport near Seoul. At the same time as the first official alarms reached Washington, press reports of the invasion began to arrive over the wire services of the news agencies. It was early Saturday evening on the East Coast of the United States, just in time to make the Sunday papers.

Washington was caught by surprise. As is often the case, government intelligence agencies had been trapped between the rock of capabilities and the hard place of intentions. They knew North Korea possessed the capability to attack South Korea, but that meant relatively little, particularly since most other Communist countries had similar capabilities with respect to their non-Communist neighbors.

The important question had not been whether they could do it but rather whether they intended to do it. In June 1950 there seemed to be far more likely trouble spots than Korea, for at that time, the western world had a lot to worry about, most if it more pressing than an out-of-the-way country on the edge of Asia.

Now, suddenly here was where the action was, where, in the constantly repeated phrase of the day, the Cold War had turned hot. President Harry S. Truman was away from Washington, at his hometown of Independence, Missouri. He flew back to the capital on the afternoon of the 25th, and at a conference that night at Blair House, across the street from the White House, which was being redecorated, he and his advisers began the series of decisions that would ultimately commit American ground troops to fight in Korea. The same day, the Security Council of the United Nations declared North Korea a disturber of the peace and called upon member nations to assist the Republic of Korea in resisting invasion. In response to this, American planes and ships were soon in action over and around the Korean peninsula. It was almost inevitable that they would shortly be followed by American ground forces.

The United Nations peace action—for it never was declared to be a war—so suddenly begun lasted for three years and one month, until July 1953. In it served troops from the Republic of Korea, the United States, and seventeen other member states of the United Nations, on the one side; and troops from North Korea and Communist China and almost certainly some advisers from Soviet Russia on the other side. Billions of dollars were spent, hundreds of thousands of lives lost or altered forever, in a conflict of shadowy nuances, subtle and infuriating limitations, and ambiguous results. A generation after it ended, the question students most often ask of it is: Was this really necessary? But in 1950 the questions were more naive than that. Americans, greeted with the advent of war for the second time in a decade, were asking: Why are there U.S. troops in Korea, and how did they get there? Indeed, most Americans, including many who would die there, did not even know where Korea was.

PART
I
WAR OF MANEUVER

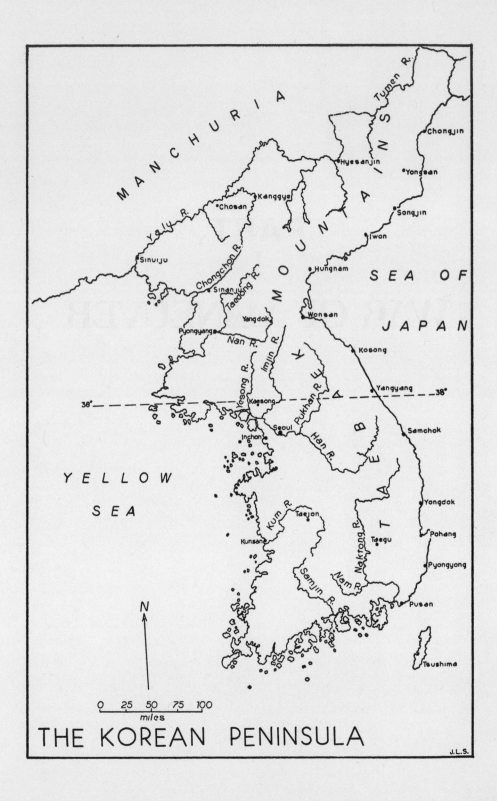

MANCHURIA

Tumen R.

Chongjin

Hyesanjin

Yongsan

Kanggye

Songjin

Chosan

Iwon

Yalu R.

M O U N T A I N S

Sinuiju

Chongchon R.

Hungnam

SEA OF

Sinanju

Taedong R.

Wonsan

JAPAN

Yangdok

Pyongyang

Nan R.

Kosong

Imjin R.

Yesong R.

38°   38°

Yanyang

Kaesong

Pukhan R.

Samchok

Seoul

Inchon

Han R.

YELLOW

Yongdok

SEA

Kum R.

Taejon

Pohang

Naktong R.

Kunsan

Taegu

Pyongyong

Samjin R.

Nam R.

Pusan

N

Tsushima

0   25   50   75   100
miles

THE KOREAN PENINSULA

J.L.S.

CHAPTER 1
THE LAND OF THE
MORNING CALM

For an area that prides itself on being known as "the land of the morning calm," Korea is singularly ill placed on the earth's surface. It consists of the peninsula that separates the Sea of Japan from the Yellow Sea, and its neighbors are the three great powers of East Asia: Japan to the east and south across the Sea of Japan, Russia, latterly the Soviet Union, to the northeast, and China and Manchuria to the north and west.

In the last hundred years, this has put Korea right at the focus of imperial rivalry between the three. In the late nineteenth century the accelerating decline of Manchu China turned the shores of the Yellow Sea into a fertile hunting ground for all the rising imperial powers of both Europe and Asia. The British, French, and Germans all forced concessions from China, but the two countries nearest the scene, Japan and Russia, squeezed hardest. Korea was caught right in the middle of this, and from then until now there has been little peace in the land of the morning calm.

Korea itself is desirable real estate, though few who served there during the Korean War would be able to understand why. The peninsula stretches for nine parallels of latitude, from the 34th to the 43rd, making it almost 600 miles long; its width varies from a narrow waist of about 90 miles to nearly 200. Total area is roughly 85,000 square miles, with some 5,600 miles of coastline, and its shape resembles an elongated New Jersey.

The only land boundary is in the north, an item of considerable significance in a war where one side totally dominated the water; one has only to compare American command of the sea around Korea with the enormous difficulties of containing the later war in Vietnam, half of which has land boundaries, to illustrate how vital this factor was. The northern boundary consists, for the most part, of the Yalu River between North Korea and Manchuria; this major river runs in a generally southwesterly direction for about 350 air miles—nearer 500 on the ground—before emptying into the northeast corner of the Yellow Sea. The remainder of the land boundary is formed mostly by the Tumen River, which rises in the same mountain mass as the Yalu, and it makes a 100-mile inverted V before reaching the Sea of Japan. This again is a boundary with Manchuria, except for the last twelve miles or so, where the Soviet Union holds the coastal area. The northeastern tip of North Korea is about ninety miles from the Russian port of Vladivostok, established in the late nineteenth century and not at all accidentally given a name meaning "Dominion over the East."

The infantryman's view of Korea is of a land of barren, craggy hills, endless ridges always held by someone else, and few amenities. This is not entirely myopic. Relatively little of the country is fit for farming, only about one-fifth, and much of that is under water in the form of rice paddies. The major topographical feature is the Taebaek Range of mountains, which runs down the eastern side of the peninsula, virtually isolating a narrow east-coast shelf from the rest of the country. This range, with its few lateral roads, would do to Korea what the Appenines had done to the Italian campaign in World War II—transform one battle into two interconnected but almost independent ones. Most of the country slopes to the west from the Taebaeks to the Yellow Sea, with successive rivers rising in the mountains and running off in a southwesterly direction. Again as in Italy, the river lines thus become important for defensive positions.

Communications were sparse in 1950. In South Korea a double-track rail line ran from the capital, Seoul, near the west coast, southeast through to Pusan, the major port on the east coast. There were

numerous single-track rail lines in North Korea. Both countries together could not claim fifty miles of paved road; even major road
arteries were only improved gravel surface, which under heavy traffic
conditions meant mud in the winter, dust in the summer.

The population of 30 million was very unevenly divided. North
Korea had about 60 percent of the peninsula, but less than one-third
of the population, 9 million versus 21 million in South Korea; it had
most of the minerals, most of the electric power, and therefore most
of the heavy industry, while the south was largely agricultural.

Finally, a word about the climate, since no one who was in Korea
will ever forget it. An ocean peninsula might be expected to be
reasonably moderate, but Korea was not. The summer was dominated by the monsoons and was usually hot, rainy, and humid; 1950
was an exception, and it was hot, rainless, and humid. Temperatures
could reach 110 degrees or even higher, with humidity up in the 90
percent range; climbing the steep hills with a rifle, pack, and ammunition in that kind of weather finished off many a young soldier. But
the winters were equally extreme. United Nations troops did not get
much farther north than the 40th parallel of latitude, which runs, in
the United States, for example, from Philadelphia to Denver to Reno.
Yet in Korea the winter winds seem to come straight from the heart
of Siberia, funneled down the Yellow Sea and whipped through the
mountains as if by some malignant frost giant. To snuggle down in
a sleeping bag or foxhole was to risk being killed by the ubiquitous
enemy, and to stay out in the cold was to court frostbite. Barren
though it often is, Korea still has aspects of unsurpassed beauty, but
no non-Korean has ever been heard to say a good word about its
climate.

To westerners, Korea, like all of Asia, gave the impression of
having been there forever. A patina of age and infinite use was
everywhere. The peoples of the peninsula were exporting bronze
goods to Japan two centuries before the Christian era, and were
invaded by China at the time of the Han dynasty, in 108, a decade
before Hadrian built his wall in Britain. For the next 1,500 years
Korea was divided up among, and occasionally united by, successive
series of kingdoms. Most of this time the country acknowledged the
cultural superiority of China, and accepted a sort of younger-brother
relationship with the larger civilization. Yet Korea, though perhaps
derivative, was not subservient; the Koreans were able to accept and

adapt, studying Buddhism, for example, and giving it their own interpretations, which were studied in turn in China and Japan. There were always certain continuities. Pyongyang, capital of North Korea, was also the capital of the kingdom of Koguryo in the fifth century, while Seoul and Kaesong were capital cities equally early.

The rulers of the state of Koryo intermarried with the Mongol emperors of China and Manchuria, but when the Mongols collapsed, the Koreans produced their own native line, the I or Li dynasty. It lasted from 1392 to 1910, having a long and unfortunately complicated history; few of the reigning monarchs died in bed of natural causes. There were family faction feuds; Confucianism replaced Buddhism, and then Confucians fell to fighting among themselves. Though there were Japanese invasions in the 1590s, the Koreans preferred to look westward, tying themselves to China, and as that great empire declined in the eighteenth and nineteenth centuries, so did Korea. In the 1860s, French, German and American expeditions all tried to open up Korea, just as the Americans had recently done with Japan, but they met with little success. The French burned a seaport and were driven away, the Germans hoped to rob the royal tombs but were also chased off, and a landing party of U.S. Marines was fired upon and withdrew in 1871.

However, the Japanese succeeded in getting a treaty with Korea in 1876, opening ports and providing for diplomatic relations, and that proved to be the fatal foot in the door. Treaties with the United States, Great Britain, and Russia followed in the 1880s, but the Japanese were both the closest and the most avaricious of Korea's new friends, and they were determined to replace China as the paramount power in the Yellow Sea area.

In the 1890s, Japan's imperial expansion gained momentum, and it rolled right over Korea. The Sino-Japanese War of 1894–95 was a direct result of rivalry between the two powers for control of the peninsula. It was triggered by plots and riots among pro-Japanese and pro-Chinese factions in Seoul, and was fought largely around the Yellow Sea. The Japanese, with their European-trained army and navy, won hands down, and the resulting Treaty of Shimonoseki recognized the independence of Korea from China, a euphemism for replacing any possible Chinese influence with a very real Japanese presence.

The Koreans themselves reacted against this and, denied their traditional reliance on China, turned for support to the third great power player in the region, the Russians. In 1896, King Kojong fled to the Russian embassy, where he stayed for a year; the Russians were delighted to fish in troubled waters, and there was soon a Russian-Korean bank, a flood of Russian advisers, and a series of mining and business concessions.

For the next several years the two powers traded off bits and pieces of Korea's sovereignty and economic life. In 1902, Japan succeeded in gaining great face when she signed the Anglo-Japanese Naval Agreement, and this plus further friction in Korea led in 1904 to the Russo-Japanese War. Again the Japanese gained a clear victory, if not quite as easy a one as they had enjoyed over the Chinese, and this time the Koreans could find no further friends to bail them out. The war was officially ended by the Treaty of Portsmouth, and it explicitly acknowledged Japan's predominant interest in Korea and its right to intervene in the internal life of the country.

The new Japanese resident-general, Prince Ito, set to work with a will to "reform" and "modernize" Korea, which it in fact needed—otherwise it would not have fallen into this situation—but which had the effect of turning the Koreans into slaves in their own country. There were widespread risings, and a guerrilla war against the occupiers that went on for years. None of this worked, though, and in 1910, Korea, given the ancient name of Chosen, was annexed to Japan.

Korea had little history of its own for the next thirty-five years. Japanese exploitation was harsh and effective. In 1919 there was a rebellion among the Koreans, but the occupiers put it down with extreme brutality. The Japanese did substitute civil for military government, but the difference was hardly noticeable. Beyond that, they brought twentieth-century industrialization. Technologically backward Korea had long lost the kind of enterprise that had produced the world's first movable type and early armored ships. The northern mountains of the peninsula were rich in minerals, and the Japanese built dams for hydroelectric power, railroads, and manufacturing facilities. Korea became a major contributor to Japan's drive toward the Greater East Asia Co-Prosperity Sphere; indeed, in the hills behind Hungnam, on the east coast, the Japanese worked to build their first atomic bomb, an effort that marginally ran out of time in 1945.

The Koreans themselves remained hewers of wood and drawers of water. The more independent-minded of them were imprisoned, often tortured or killed, or fled abroad into exile. One such was Syngman Rhee. Born in 1875, a fiery young activist, he was imprisoned from 1897 to 1904 for advocating internal reform. Soon after his release he left the country for the United States, where he tried unsuccessfully to get the American government to protect Korea's interests during the Treaty of Portsmouth negotiations. He went back to Korea in 1910, with the first Ph.D. ever awarded to a Korean student in America, a doctorate from Princeton, where he met Woodrow Wilson, still a university president at the time. There was exile again, in 1919 after the rising of that year was crushed, and Rhee did not finally return home until World War II ended. For years he was president of the Korean Provisional Government, waiting hopefully but fruitlessly in diplomatic anterooms, trying to get anyone he could interested in the fate of his country.

Not all the exiles went to the western world. A young man from northern Korea named Kim Sung Chu adopted the *nom de guerre* of a famous Korean hero, Kim Il Sung. After leading guerrilla forces against Japan, he too left the country, in the late thirties. His official biography says he organized the Anti-Japanese Guerrilla Army in Manchuria, but there have been suggestions that he went instead to the Soviet Union and fought in the Red Army, and even that he was at Stalingrad in 1942. Whichever is true, he too returned home at the end of World War II, a convinced Communist and part of the Soviet occupation forces for northern Korea.

The partition of the Korean peninsula in 1945 was the unfortunate result of one of those ad hoc decisions, taken in the midst of far more pressing concerns, that seem to make sense at the time. In December 1943, President Roosevelt, Prime Minister Churchill, and Generalissimo Chiang Kai-shek issued the Cairo Declaration, promising, among other things, a free and independent Korea "in due course." The qualifier was largely Roosevelt's, for he had considerable doubts about the abilities of colonial peoples to rule themselves and did not allow his constant suspicion of British imperialism to contradict his feeling that a great many areas of the world would need ongoing tutelage in democracy.

It was not until the Potsdam Conference in July 1945 that anyone got down to brass tacks. By then, Germany was already defeated, the Americans were courting Russian entry into the war in the Far East, and time was growing shorter than leaders realized to make concrete agreements. The Americans unilaterally decided that the handiest way to treat Korea would be for them to occupy the southern part of it and the Russians, who a month later would swarm over Japanese-held Manchuria, should occupy the northern portion. That was in late July. Within three weeks, two atomic bombs had been dropped on Japan, the Soviet Union had declared war, and the country was on the verge of surrender. Against this backdrop of far more exciting events, the Russians agreed to the proposition as casually as the Americans offered it. In General Order No. 1, issued by the Allied commander in the Pacific, General of the Army Douglas MacArthur, on September 2, the rules for surrender of Japanese forces were set out, and the Russians were to occupy Korea down to the 38th parallel, while the Americans moved into the south.

There was no real problem with this at the moment. The Russians were closer than the Americans, and they flooded over Manchuria and into Korea. By August 26 they had closed up to the demarcation line on the 38th parallel, and there, except for a couple of minor incursions over the line, they stopped. The Americans were far slower. The U.S. Army had designated Lt. Gen. John R. Hodge as commander in Korea, but his XXIV Corps was still loading aboard ship in Okinawa, 600 miles south of Korea, ten days after the Soviets had already reached the parallel. It was September 9 before the Americans reached Seoul and accepted the surrender of the Japanese forces in the southern part of the country.

To this point and for a few days thereafter, no one paid much attention to the Koreans themselves. They were simply ecstatically happy to see the last of the hated Japanese occupiers; few of them thought much beyond that, and those who did simply expected the liberators to go home now and leave them alone. After thirty-five years of occupation, they did not want any more of it, even if it were well-intentioned. But seeds of dissension were already sprouting. The Americans did not know too much about Korea, but they and the Russians both had an idea what they wanted. The Americans wanted a stable, democratic government, and to go home. The Russians had had a longer and closer association with Korea, and they wanted, as they did all along their now engorged periphery, a government that would be friendly to them, and that meant a Communist government. In each area, the occupiers set up provisional advisory councils to help run the territory. The Americans turned to Dr. Rhee, now approaching seventy, increasingly autocratic, violently anti-Communist, and genuinely afraid both of what he saw as American courting of Soviet Russia and of what that courtship might cost his own country. The Soviets in their zone turned to Kim Il Sung and other Communists of similar background. From the expediencies of 1945, the stage was set for confrontation and tragedy in the future.

To understand that confrontation, it is necessary to do two things: first, to look at Korea itself in the crucial five years between the end of one war and the start of another; second, to place those local tensions in the larger context of an increasingly antagonistic world scene. For what actually happened in Korea was very much conditioned by what might have happened in Berlin or elsewhere.

The initial impasse soon hardened into permanency. At the end of 1945 a big-power conference at Moscow called for a five-year period of trusteeship by Britain, the United States, the Soviet Union, and China, and the establishment of a provisional democratic government. But when the executive agency of the trustees, the Soviet Union and the United States, met in Seoul in March of the new year, it was obvious that it would not work. All the Korean political parties except the Communists demanded immediate and complete independence and refused to cooperate. The Soviets then insisted that the Communists were the only legitimate party in Korea, and that it form the government. The United States was equally insistent that that was not democracy, so from the first the overseers fell out.

For better or worse, both sides now set up their own governments in their own zones. The Soviets passed control over to a Provisional People's Committee, and in the summer all of the parties of the north coalesced into the Korean National Democratic Front; in November this won the standard whopping 97 percent of the vote in a popular election, and over the next two years, the northern part of the peninsula made a predictable, if by no means painless for individuals, transition into the People's Democratic Republic, the standard Marxist-Leninst one-party state modeled after the Soviet Union.

Things went less smoothly in the south. In December 1946 a legislative assembly was set up, half of it elected and half of it nominated. The elected half was almost solidly behind the right-wing Syngman Rhee; the appointed half was an attempt by the American military authorities to balance the scales with what it perceived to be moderates and liberal-leftists. General Hodge, still the military governor, transformed the assembly into a South Korean Interim Government, but it was clear from the start that it lacked any real popular support. The country was in near chaos, hundreds of thousands were hungry, unemployed, and homeless, but the Koreans wanted their independence, and since the Russian, American, and Korean views of what that meant and how to get it simply could not be reconciled, the country just floundered on.

In May 1947 the Joint Commission of the trustee powers had one more try. The Americans proposed free elections throughout the entire peninsula; the Russians rejected the idea. They countered by proposing a meeting of equal numbers of representatives of all the parties of the south, which would have meant all the parties of the south, and all the parties of the north, which would have meant the Communists, since they were the only one. The Americans rejected that.

In September the United States took the problem to the infant United Nations. Two months later the United Nations agreed that Korea ought to be independent, and voted to set up a temporary commission to bring that about. The members from eastern Europe boycotted the vote, and when a UN commission reached Korea early in 1948, with the task of supervising elections, it was refused admission to North Korea. With no recourse, it then recommended free elections in the south; these were held on May 10, and the conservative rightist parties gained a large majority. On August 15, 1948, Syngman Rhee became the first president of the Republic of Korea; four months later the republic was recognized by the UN as the only free state in Korea. But it was given diplomatic recognition just by the western powers, as the People's Democratic Republic received recognition solely from the eastern bloc.

The UN then set up a permanent commission to try to unify the country. The Americans ended their military government of the south and agreed to provide advisers and training for defense forces. The Russian occupation forces left the north. Both countries left behind a government which the other denounced as illegitimate and which claimed to represent all of Korea, not just the half over which it held temporary sway. Within six months there was occasional raiding across the 38th parallel, and major exchanges of gunfire. Rhee was vigorously calling for war against the north, perhaps to take people's minds off the real failure of his government to improve their lives substantially, and off the strongly authoritarian tactics he employed to keep himself in power. Kim Il Sung was equally busy fomenting trouble, and openly boasting of the thousands of guerrillas North Korea was supporting in South Korea. Both constantly wallowed in the tiresome rhetoric of the day, calling each other "reactionary imperialist traitor" or "Communist terrorist revolutionary" or rather less complimentary terms. In early 1950, Rhee's government lost control of the Assembly, when large numbers of moderates were returned. A perfectly objective observer might well have concluded that one side was not worth supporting at all, and the other was only marginally better.

Unfortunately, the state of the world from 1945 to 1950 was such that there were few objective observers around. Ever since the Russian Revolution, the democratic and capitalist system of the western European and North American states had been opposed by the totalitarian approach adopted by the Communists in the Soviet Union. Lenin in power in Russia had preached world revolution, and his successor, Joseph Stalin, had combined the revolutionary claims of Communism with traditional Russian expansionism and fear of its neighbors. The basic antagonism of these two systems had been submerged by the common danger of Nazi Germany, and the temporary necessity of alliance to defeat Hitler and his followers in World War II. Under the stress of that cataclysm, Russia and the West had helped each other survive. But once the menace was removed, the old differences surfaced again, and within a tragically short time after 1945, it was obvious that the world had entered on the old and dangerous paths once more.

In fact, they were even more perilous in the late forties than they had been in the thirties. For now most of the earlier players had been swept from the board; now instead of a series of "great powers" and potential balances among them, there were really only two, the "superpowers," the United States and the Soviet Union. Great Britain, France, Italy, Germany, Japan, and China were all pale shadows of their former selves, reduced to satellites of the two giants. Not only that, but the two remaining states possessed, if they chose to use it, power that was immense even by the standards of the mid-twentieth century: The Russians had the greatest armed force in the world, and the United States had the atomic bomb.

It is always tempting to think that they need not have confronted each other, that a little more wisdom, honesty, or goodwill among the leaders might have prevented the antagonisms from surfacing, and the Cold War, with all its fear, waste, and worry, from happening, but that is among the might-have-beens of history. For whatever shortcomings of human nature or opposed ideology, the Soviet Union and the United States and their allies or satellites soon stood face to face in an attitude of unwavering hostility.

Korea was but a small part of this, far less important to either than events in Europe or in China, but very much influenced by what was happening elsewhere.

In Europe, the disagreements surfaced even before the end of World War II. For a short time they were papered over, yet by March 1946, Winston Churchill was delivering his famous "Iron Curtain" speech, adding a new phrase to the world's political vocabulary. Three months later the Soviet Union rejected the American proposal for UN control of atomic energy, and in the fall, civil war began in Greece as Communist guerrillas attempted to take over the country. The American government finally responded to these pressures and rebuffs with the Truman Doctrine, which started as aid to Greece and Turkey and gradually expanded into a generalized policy of "containing" the spread of Communism everywhere. Recognizing that they could not police a devastated world, the Americans also tried to rebuild it, and in June 1947 launched the Marshall Plan, offering assistance to everyone, foes as well as friends, to create a more stable world. Again the Russians rejected the proffered olive branch, and when Czechoslovakia, over which their control was a bit tenuous, tried to accept it, they moved overtly and seized control of the government. Most authorities date the definitive beginning of the Cold War from the Prague coup of February 1948, the same month as the proclamation of the People's Republic in North Korea.

In June the famous Berlin Blockade began, countered for nearly a year by the western airlift that kept the beleaguered city alive, until the Communists gave up the siege. But in April 1949 the North Atlantic Treaty Organization was formed. American aid was flowing into western Europe, and the democracies began to get back on their feet. The Federal German Republic, or West Germany, was proclaimed in May. Then in July the Soviets exploded their first atomic bomb, cutting away what the Americans had wishfully thought was several years' lead in technology. They purged the Hungarian government and fastened their control ever tighter on eastern Europe. By the end of the year, there was a dangerous and no more than momentarily stable equilibrium in Europe.

There was even less than that in Asia. Here, the end of World War II meant exhaustion for all the major powers immediately on the scene. The Japanese were completely prostrated by defeat, the Chinese Nationalists by victory, and the former colonial powers by mere struggle for survival. From India all the way around to Korea there was disruption and discord. India wanted the British to get out, and became independent in 1947; Burma became a republic in 1948. There was a Communist-led war against the British in Malaya that lasted for twelve years, from 1948 to 1960. The Indonesians fought first against the Dutch and then against each other. In 1946 in Indochina, the returning French, later replaced by the Americans, got involved in a full-scale war against the nationalist and Communist opposition led by Ho Chi Minh, a conflict not fully resolved until the final triumph of the Communists in 1973.

All of these events were bad enough, but in the late forties the worst was what happened to China. There the Nationalist government of Chiang Kai-shek had waged a long, bitter, and sometimes almost hopeless struggle against the Japanese from 1937 to the end of the war. By 1945, indeed before then, China was virtually exhausted, with millions of people dying of disease or starvation. Victory over Japan did not bring peace, for Chiang Kai-shek's Nationalists faced equally bitter internal opposition, from the Chinese Communists headed by Mao Tse-tung. They had fought hard against the Nationalists during the thirties, then been more or less quiescent during the war with Japan. At the end of that they emerged rejuvenated and ready to fight. The Nationalists, already worn down, riven by corruption and internal dissension, could not stand before the Communists despite American efforts first to mediate and then to help them. By the end of 1947 the Communists held all of Manchuria in the north; by 1948 Chiang was palpably failing. Old and autocratic, he could not or would not initiate reforms, and those few he tried were swamped by increased Communist demands or, worse, military victories. By 1949 it was all over. The Communists controlled China, the Nationalists had withdrawn to the island of Formosa, where they insisted they were still the legitimate government of all of the country. Mao Tse-tung's government immediately signed treaties of friendship and assistance with Soviet Russia, and when the United Nations, at American insistence, refused to oust Nationalist China and replace it with mainland, Communist, China, the Russians indignantly walked out of the Security Council in January 1950.

The Communist victory in China was a bitter blow to the Americans, who for many years had cherished a rather irrational belief that they and China enjoyed some sort of special relationship with each other. The Democratic administration in Washington was lambasted with charges that it had "lost" China, and a demagogic Republican senator named Joseph McCarthy terrorized government and much of American public life with wild, unsupported, but widely believed charges about Communists in high places. To many Americans, it looked as if there were, in the words then current, a "worldwide Communist conspiracy," a "monolith" directed and funded from Moscow. The bright blue skies of 1945 had become covered with dark clouds, showing red; by 1950 the world was an unfriendly place. Americans were wary, and worried, but slowly rousing at last to their role as the leader of the free world.

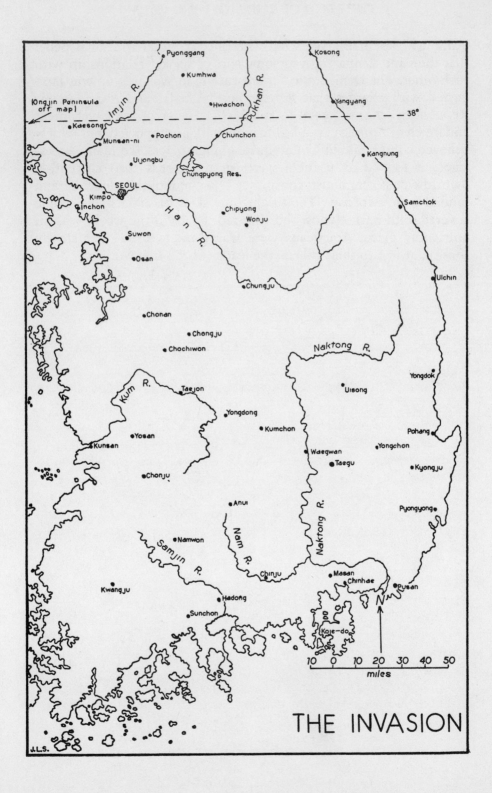

Pyonggang

Kosong

Kumhwa

Hwachon

Yangyang

(Ongjin Peninsula
off map)

38°

Kaesong

Pochon

Munsan-ni

Chunchon

Kangnung

Uijongbu

Chungpyong Res.

SEOUL

Samchok

Kimpo

Chipyong

Inchon

Wonju

Suwon

Ulchin

Osan

Chungju

Chonan

Naktong R.

Chongju

Chochiwon

Yongdok

Uisong

Kum R.

Taejon

Yongdong

Pohang

Kunsan

Yosan

Kumchon

Yongchon

Waegwan

Kyongju

Taegu

Chonju

Pyongyong

Anui

Naktong R.

Nam R.

Namwon

Samjin R.

Chinju

Masan

Kwangju

Hadong

Chinhae

Pusan

Sunchon

Koje-do

10   0   10   20   30   40   50
miles

THE INVASION

J.L.S.

CHAPTER 2
THE INVASION

In the Republic of Korea, as the scope of the Communist attack became apparent, there was dismayed alarm. Politicians issued resounding calls for battle; some units fought desperate little actions before being flanked or overrun, others fled in panic ahead of the lumbering North Korean tanks. The frontier was fully breached, the capital soon threatened; refugees thronged the roads. The American military advisory group was adrift in a sea of Koreans; communications were cut, and men were lost or swamped in the confusion. It was all reminiscent of a scene played over and over in the twentieth century: Belgium in 1914, Poland in 1939, Belgium and the Netherlands and France in 1940. The North Koreans pressed on relentlessly, determined to blanket the entire peninsula and stamp out any vestige of resistance as quickly as possible, to be able to present the world with a *fait accompli,* so that within a week there would be nothing left to fight about.

What was important in this situation was therefore not what the North Koreans intended to do, which was clear enough, or what the South Koreans could do, which was little enough, but rather what the United States could, and would, do. Would the Americans intervene? And if they did, could they do so effectively and in time to reverse the debacle? Those were the first questions that had to be answered.

The answers were not the foregone conclusion that they would later appear. Indeed, since the beginning of the Cold War the United States had been attempting to define, for itself and its allies, exactly what its defense perimeter was. After 1945, the Americans had not realized that by defeating and occupying Germany, they had inherited central Europe's defense problems; and in Asia, by defeating and occupying Japan, they had equally fallen heir to its strategic situation. In the late forties, as mainland Asia went Communist or threatened to, the United States tended to adopt a blue-water defense line. No country in the world could afford to swap manpower with the masses of China. The only reasonable line was offshore: Japan, the Ryukyus, Formosa, the Philippines, the East Indies or Indonesia, perhaps Malaya, whose geography made it particularly susceptible to influence from the sea.

Two places did not fit in this sensible scheme of things: South Korea, a client state of the United States, and Indochina, where the French were resolutely facing backward into the colonial era. Seen in this light, it is no accident at all that America's two biggest conflicts since 1945 have been in those two areas. In getting involved there, the Americans gave hostages to fortune, and paid a dear price for them.

In 1950, all this was ill perceived and undecided. General MacArthur, the American Far East commander, and proconsul of the occupation of Japan, had been invited to the celebrations of Korean independence in 1948. Before the ceremonies began, MacArthur put his arm around President Rhee's shoulder and promised to defend Korea from the Communists "as I would California." In his formal address he referred pointedly to the necessity of unifying Korea, and his remarks, both official and impromptu, caused a degree of heartburn when reported in Washington. For the government at this date did not really know whether it wanted to defend Korea, but it certainly did know that it did not want to encourage Rhee's bellicosity.

Several months later MacArthur seemed to have changed his mind, and he gave an interview to a British journalist, G. Ward Price, in which he said the United States should and would defend the island line off the coast of Asia, though he omitted Formosa from it, and he did not mention Korea at all. In January 1950, President Truman announced his opposition to defending Chiang Kai-shek on Formosa, and in a famous speech to the National Press Club on January 12, Secretary of State Dean Acheson repeated the President's views, and again excluded South Korea from the U.S. defense perimeter, though he hedged this with reservations about acting in concert with the United Nations should Korea or Formosa be attacked. These views were perfectly in accord with the current policy commitment, spelled out in a document known as NSC (National Security Council) 48/2, approved by President Truman on December 30, 1949, so they were merely a public statement of a presumably carefully developed position.

Acheson's speech derived its importance from the fact that authorities on the Korean War have tended to regard it as a green light to North Korea. This probably overemphasizes the impact of the speech, given the already existing hostility of both regimes in Korea, and the fact that each was determined to be rid of the other. Without access to North Korean or Soviet archives, no one can say the speech was a green light, but it may safely be assumed that it was not a red or even a yellow one.

It was one thing to decide rationally that South Korea was not vital to American interests. It was quite a different thing to watch it sink before a tide of Communist invasion. The government that had "lost China" had to do something, and the initial response was diplomatic—an appeal to the United Nations.

But even while that was being prepared, it was obvious that North Korea might not respond positively, and therefore further steps had to be explored. The most important of them came out of a conference held between officials of the State Department and the Army late on the morning of Sunday, June 25. This was a suggestion that if North Korea kept on fighting and if the United Nations called on member countries for assistance, the United States should authorize General MacArthur, in his role as Commander in Chief Far East (CINCFE), to use American forces to stabilize the situation. It should be pointed out that throughout this period, the initiative was taken by the State Department, and the military people rather hesitantly went along; war may be the main reason for

35

the soldier's existence, but he seldom wants it, because he is seldom ready for it.

The suggestion for assistance was soon to come into force, for that afternoon the American deputy ambassador to the UN, Ernest A. Gross, presented a resolution that was passed unanimously after several hours of discussion. The Soviet Union was still boycotting the UN, and Yugoslavia, occupying one of the temporary seats on the Security Council, abstained. The Security Council called upon North Korea to cease its aggressive action and all members of the United Nations to render assistance in achieving that end. This again deserves at least passing comment. Critics of the decision for intervention have charged that in effect, the United States asked the United Nations to ask the United States to do what it wanted to do anyway, and have seen some sort of criminal collusion in the State Department's suggesting to the Army in the morning what it was going to suggest to the UN in the afternoon. Such criticism is patently silly; while the decision actually to intervene may well be open to criticism, given the nature and viability of the Republic of Korea, the process of legitimizing the decision was certainly logical. Even determined critics cannot reasonably suppose that State should tell Army one thing and the UN another, or that, as they apparently would have it, the United States should ask the United Nations to ask the United States to do what it did *not* want to do. The resolution was careful not to name the Soviet Union as a party to aggression or as anything else, though one American official, asked about the relations between the Soviet Union and North Korea, replied caustically that they were the same as the relations between Walt Disney and Donald Duck.

American success in getting South Korea adopted by the United Nations was absolutely vital to the subsequent prosecution of the war, or "police action" as it was officially styled. It also meant enormous frustration, in trying to get member states to go along with the employment of armed force. The British dragged their feet, the French were obstreperous, and it was often difficult to tell which side the Indians were actually on. Later, when the Russians returned to the Security Council, they systematically tried to sabotage the whole effort; they were like Nazi Germany, who had served on the Neutrality Commission while sending troops to fight in the Spanish Civil War. Yet with all the frustrations, it *was* a United Nations action, it *was* a joint attempt to deter aggression, and it provided an apparatus of world support for the American position. Every public figure of the era could vividly and painfully remember the failure of collective security to halt the Germans in the thirties. This might be a small step forward, but it was perceived as a real one.

Far more successful than the actual support of the United Nations was the fact that the Americans then got the UN to agree to let the United States run the war. In effect, the UN designated the United States as its agent. There was to be a unified command, under a United States commander, and the United States was asked to furnish occasional reports as necessary to the UN. Barring the political necessity to consult with and cajole allies, it was a remarkably free hand. On that front at least, the Americans had done very well indeed.

Domestically, President Truman chose not to go to Congress and ask for a declaration of war, largely on the grounds, which he considered valid at the time, that this was not a war. It was, he said, a "bandit incursion," and the powers of the Presidency, coupled with the mandate of the United Nations, were fully adequate to cope with that. From consultation with Congressional leaders, Truman knew he had the support he needed, and he did not wish to lessen impact of American action by a debate that would be pointless anyway. Years later in another war in a different Asian quagmire, the matter might look different.

All of this still leaves unanswered a larger question: Should the United States have intervened at all? Historians of the New Left, or of left-liberal persuasions, have argued that it was the United States that was on the offensive during the 1945–50 period, and that the Soviets were acting only in self-defense to protect their legitimate interests. In the case of Korea, there have been assertions that it was actually President Rhee who caused the war, and that he and General MacArthur plotted to create a crisis, and did so. Korea thus becomes the first success in the move by government, military forces, and big business to start rolling what President Eisenhower in his farewell address called the military-industrial establishment.

As with all such smoke, there has to be a little fire somewhere. President Rhee certainly was repressive and right-wing; there was opposition to him, which he reacted against brutally. He was bellicose. His relations with MacArthur were good, in contrast to his earlier relations with Hodge, who could not stand him. (One observer suggested that MacArthur got along so well with Rhee and with Chiang Kai-shek because they all understood each other—they were all egomaniacs together.) And the war certainly did intensify the buildup of American armed strength, and thereby enrich American capitalism. All of these elements put together make at least a partial, and perhaps plausible, case.

But a historically more valid question than whether the United States should have intervened is whether it could have avoided intervention. And the answer to that is probably no. Rhee was not much, but he was the horse the Americans had chosen to back; the Republic of Korea was perhaps a poor democracy, but it was an American creation, and to argue that it was poor is not to argue, as the New Left would have it, that North Korea automatically was better. Even Kim Il Sung's official biographer admits that a great deal of force and repression was needed to make all North Koreans see and accept the guiding light of Communism. The basic problem is that this is not a perfect, rational world, that decisions are not and can never be totally objective, and that they cannot be made outside of their historical context. The good guys are not all or always good, just as the bad guys are not all or always bad. Therefore the answer must be: In the context of the time, and given the perceptions, preconceptions, and predilections of the men who made the decision, intervention probably could not have been avoided, and probably should not have been avoided. However unpalatable they are, and however many residual doubts they leave, some things just have to be done.

What degree of intervention might be necessary remained the next question. The American government hoped that if it applied naval and air support, the South Koreans on the ground might be able to stop and then drive back the Communists by themselves. That hope shortly proved futile. Events in Korea soon went from bad to disastrous. The North Koreans showed no signs even of slowing down, and the shortcomings of the South Korean military forces were all too evident.

On the day of the invasion, the army of the People's Democratic Republic had an estimated actual strength of 135,000 men. It had eight infantry divisions at a full strength of about 11,000 men each, plus two more at half strength. There were a couple of additional independent infantry units of regimental size, plus five reserve infantry brigades of Border Constabulary, with from 2,600 to 5,000 men each. Most important of all was the 105th Armored Brigade, with about 6,000 men; it had 120 Russian-made T34 tanks, one of the best medium tanks in the world, and there were perhaps thirty more tanks in other formations. Units from battalion to division had their own heavy weapons and artillery, ranging from machine guns and mortars on up to 122mm howitzers. A good third of the personnel of the army were veterans of the Chinese Civil War, or in many cases of World War II; during 1949 and early 1950, Koreans were drafted out of the various Chinese Communist formations and sent home to their own army, and some of them had even been drafted by the Japanese, deserted to the Communists, and then gone on from there. This was not a mob of pajama-clad peasants, but a well-trained, well-equipped, battle-tested, coherent military force. In the summer of 1950, before attrition ground it away, the North Korean People's Army was a first-class outfit.

The South Korean Army was quite a different creation. During their occupation, the Americans had begun the formation of an internal security force; in August 1948 this was transformed into the Republic of Korea Army. By 1949 the ROK Army had 65,000 men, there was a small coast guard, and there were about 45,000 men in the police forces, a paramilitary organization more like the French Gardes Nationales or the Spanish Garda Civil than American police forces. At the time of the invasion, the army had 95,000 men in eight divisions and several cadre formations; the divisions had a strength of about 10,000 men each. There were 6,000 coast guards, a nascent air force of 2,000, and about 48,000 police. These forces were advised and trained by the United States' 500-strong Korean Military Advisory Group (KMAG). The major problem with the army, and as it turned out its major shortcoming when war began, derived from differences between the Americans and the South Korean government. Syngman Rhee had never made any secret of his ambition to use the army offensively to unify the country, and the Americans, in their desire not to let him do so, had structured an army that was not much good for heavy combat. It had no tanks, few antitank weapons, and no heavy artillery; its biggest gun was the 105mm howitzer, of a model that had been used in World War II by the U.S. Army, and there were only ninety of these on inventory in June 1950. As befit an army trained by the Americans, the South Koreans had many vehicles, about 2,100 of them; a lot of them did not work.

One thing the South Koreans had really wanted was an air force, but here too they fell short of their northern neighbors. The North Koreans had about 180 Russian-built planes, including 40 YAK fighters and 70 attack and ground-support aircraft. The South Koreans had twelve unarmed liaison planes, and a training flight of ten North American T6 Texans. The chief of the American advisory mission to the air force, Maj. Dean E. Hess, a famous American World War II ace, had ten Mustangs at his command; the Mustang was arguably the greatest fighter of World War II, but both sides were making do with leftovers in the air as on the ground. Indeed, except for the introduction of the jet aircraft, the war was basically fought with World War II equipment. It was once said of a war between France and Austria that it was a war in 1859 fought between armies of 1809 using tactics of 1759; it might be said of Korea that it was a war of 1950 fought by armies of 1945 using tactics of 1916.

The other element in the equation was the United States, and here if anywhere one might have expected to get to the real thing. Unfortunately that was hardly the case. Much of the history of the war is the history of the American buildup, but in June 1950 the armed forces of the United States were in lamentable, or laughable, condition. In 1945 the United States had spent $50 billion on its army; in 1950 it spent $5 billion. In 1945 there were 8.25 million men on active service; in 1950 there were less than 600,000 and no one had been drafted since March 1947. For defense the United States apparently depended upon its sole possession of the atomic bomb, yet in 1947 it did not have any, and even the Air Force, not noted for its candor, admitted that it was not sure it could deliver one to a target if it had one to deliver. During the height of the Berlin Blockade there was one American division in western Europe. The first two war plans produced by the newly formed Joint Chiefs of Staff admitted that western Europe could not be held, and that if deterrence failed, the United States could rely only on the atomic bomb—the bomb its forces did not have. Finally, in a document labeled NSC 68, the government acknowledged the need to spend money and rebuild the United States armed forces to the point where they presented a credible posture against aggression. But NSC 68 was produced early in 1950, and in its turn sprouted disagreements about what kind of forces the United States should have, and little had been done by the time of the Korean crisis. President Truman remarked that everyone always wanted him to give the Russians hell, but that this was hard to do when they had 260 divisions and he had one and a third, rather recalling Joseph Stalin's contemptuous remark "How many divisions does the Pope have?"

By 1950, in Japan, General MacArthur had four divisions serving on occupation duties. Everything was understrength; the divisions had two regiments instead of the standard three, the regiments had two batallions instead of three, the artillery battalions had two firing batteries instead of three, and so on. And as usual in peacetime, the fighting troops were in shortest supply; there were plenty of drivers, clerks, and cooks, but there were not many riflemen. It was, in numbers and attitudes, a peacetime army. It was in for a terrible surprise.

In the first instance, MacArthur was relying not upon the Army but upon the Air Force to stem the Korean onslaught. But the Far East Air Forces, under the command of Lt. Gen. George E. Stratemeyer, were configured almost completely for the defense of Japan and other American holdings offshore. The U.S. Air Force in 1950 was not in as poor shape as the Army, but it was not equipped up to its authorized strength. Instead of the desired fifty-five wings, there were forty-eight; nine of these, thirty squadrons, were in the Far East. Stratemeyer had a total of 1,172 aircraft under his control, but only 553 were in operational combat units. The rest were in storage or in repair depots, or were training or transport or liaison planes. The Air Force was especially short in the type it needed most, attack and ground-support planes. It had 365 F-80 Shooting Star jet fighters, their pilots among the early, not entirely happy, converts from flying F-51 Mustangs; the Shooting Star had a realistic combat range of only 100 miles. There were only twenty-six B-26 light bombers, and twenty-two B-29 Superfortresses, reclassified since World War II as medium bombers. Base, support, and communication facilities were adequate for peacetime operations, but not for a real war.

The U.S. Navy in the Far East was in better shape, more especially as it was the only real navy around; throughout the entire war there was no challenge to American, or UN, command of the sea, and this fact, which is so easy to mention in passing, was the absolute determinant of the way the war was fought, or indeed the fact that it could be fought at all. Around Japan the Americans had a cruiser, a destroyer division and part of a minesweeping squadron, and a small amphibious force. To the south was the Seventh Fleet, the aircraft carrier *Valley Forge,* a heavy cruiser, and eight destroyers. Before the end of June the British offered a carrier, two cruisers, and destroyers and frigates from their station down at Hong Kong, and the Australians, New Zealanders, and Canadians quickly joined in. All of these units were shaken down into Task Force 77 and were soon operating in Korean waters. Except for its air strikes, the Navy remained something of the "silent service" in the Korean War, but its ubiquitous presence, to bring supplies in, to put soldiers ashore at Inchon or take them off at Hungnam, to provide coastal gunfire support, was a classic demonstration both of the versatility and the vital nature of sea power.

All of these items and forces were still being sorted out in the hectic days of late June. On the peninsula itself, the Republic of Korea Army was beginning to fall apart within two days of the invasion. It launched one strong counterattack against the Communists, but the South Korean soldiers could not hold off the enemy's tank thrusts; units shredded apart, lost control of their flanks and themselves, and what started out as an army began to flee southward as individuals. By the evening of the second day, the government was packing up and moving south to Taejon, then later on to Pusan. The capital city fell on June 27, amid scenes of panic and terror; escape routes to the south ran over the bridges of the Han River, and the bridges were blown up prematurely, when crowded with withdrawing soldiers and fleeing civilians. Several hundred people were killed or wounded, and thousands more were trapped on the north side of the river. A senior engineer officer was subsequently tried and executed, but the order to blow the bridges seems to have been given by a cabinet-rank civilian.

The disaster at the bridges was compounded by the losses of those units still retaining some cohesion north of Seoul. Americans, other foreign nationals, and dependents were being evacuated, first by ship from Inchon, then by air from Kimpo airport. The KMAG people were trying to keep in touch with their assigned Korean units and with each other, but by the end of the first few days, when the South Korean Army reassembled and tried to regroup south of the Han River, it could muster less than a quarter of its original strength of

98,000 men. A mere 22,000 were left, though subsequent return of stragglers and cut-off units brought it up to 54,000. Two out of three men had lost their personal weapons, and almost all the heavy equipment was gone.

By the end of June, U.S. and UN forces were beginning to intervene, though with little effect. During the evacuation of personnel from Kimpo, American fighters shot down six North Korean planes on the 27th; the next day, the Americans were bombing targets in Seoul and flying close-support missions trying to slow the Reds down. Unfortunately, in the confusion of those early days, they often hit South Koreans as well as North. Not until early July and the arrival on the ground of several Tactical Air Control Parties did communications improve to the point where UN air power began to have a real effect on the enemy. Meanwhile, at sea, Task Force 77, under the command of Vice Adm. A. D. Struble, closed up to the coasts of Korea and began shore bombardment, air strikes at North Korean targets, and interdiction of the few small craft, torpedo boats and the like, the enemy was using along the shore. On July 3, British Fireflies and Seafires hit a North Korean airfield at Haeju, while Corsairs, Skyraiders, and Panther jets from the *Valley Forge*—long famous in the Pacific as the "Happy Valley"—worked over the main field at Pyongyang. In the next several days most of the North Korean air force was wiped out, largely caught on the ground.

But though the sky and the water belonged to the UN, the ground still belonged to the Communists. There was as yet nothing in Korea capable of standing up to those T34 tanks, and for a long time there was not going to be. The axis of the advance was fairly straightforward, dictated by the general geography of the peninsula. The main Communist force had crossed the parallel in the west and converged on the capital at Seoul. From there they drove south across the Han to the Kum River, about seventy-five miles. At the Kum, the direction of the advance veered to southeast, heading for Taejon, then Taegu, and finally Pusan, in the southeast corner of the peninsula. Pusan was about 150 miles from the crossing of the Kum. Meanwhile, a part of the main force swept off rightward at the Kum and rolled over the virtually undefended southwest quarter of the country. In addition to this main drive, there were secondary pushes through the mountainous spine of the peninsula, in a generally southerly direction, and there was finally an almost totally independent advance down the narrow east coast.

On June 29, General MacArthur flew over to Korea. The simple fact of MacArthur's presence was a harbinger of active American intervention, for he was virtually the first great proconsul of the new American empire; to many, perhaps most, orientals he *was* the United States. Born in 1880 into the old Indian-fighting Army, naturally he had gone to West Point. By 1918 he was a brigadier general with thirteen decorations and was the youngest divisional commander in France; a year later he was the youngest-ever superintendent of West Point, and from 1930 to 1935 he was America's top-ranking soldier, Chief of Staff of the U.S. Army. He left the Army, and the United States, in 1935 to head a military mission to the Philippines, which was at that time being groomed for eventual independence.

In 1941, as war with Japan loomed, MacArthur was recalled to active duty. He presided skillfully over the disaster in the Philippines, from which he escaped in 1942; for this he was awarded the Medal of Honor by the American government, and earned the undying hatred of those left behind to the Japanese. Years later it became public that he had accepted $500,000, which looked very much like a bribe, from the president of the Philippines. As Allied commander of the Southwest Pacific Area he directed the long, arduous, and brilliant campaign back up the islands into the heart of the Japanese empire, and it was he who accepted the surrender aboard the U.S.S. *Missouri* in September 1945. He then acted as the supreme commander over the occupation of Japan, giving the country a new constitution and many reforms.

He was a man about whom it was impossible to be neutral; people loved or hated, reviled or admired him. He was obsessed with his own view of his mission in life; he was flamboyant, theatrical, brilliant, and utterly self-centered. His reputation, age, and stature had enabled him to bend the entire war in the Pacific to his own conception of it, and now, a man who had not been back in the United States for fifteen years, he would try to do the same thing in Korea.

As MacArthur watched the South Koreans trying to pull themselves together on the south side of the Han River, he quickly realized that these troops were not going to accomplish much, and he reported to Washington that it would be necessary to commit American ground troops. President Truman had already authorized that, for the protection of an enclave around Pusan, but MacArthur needed them as far north and as soon as possible. Permission to use his troops as necessary was soon forthcoming, and the desperate situation of the South Koreans was the genesis of Task Force Smith.

The four American divisions in Japan made up the U.S. Eighth Army, commanded by Lt. Gen. Walton H. Walker, a no-nonsense Texan who had commanded a machine-gun company in France in 1917, served in the old 15th Infantry in China between the wars, and been one of Patton's corps commanders in World War II. MacArthur now ordered Walker to send a division to Korea, and the job went to the 24th Infantry Division, the one that happened to be stationed in southwestern Japan. Its commander, Gen. William F. Dean, in turn designated an advance force, to be known after its commander, Task Force Smith.

So it happened that a rather prosaically named group became the first real American force, setting aside KMAG, some ill-assorted Air Force ground units, and odds and ends, to fight in Korea. Lt. Col. Charles B. Smith was the CO, 1st Battalion, 21st Infantry Regiment, a professional soldier who had also been at Pearl Harbor on December 7, 1941. His command consisted of about 440 men, two under-strength rifle companies, part of a headquarters company, and some infantry heavy weapons platoons. Some officers had to be hastily drafted from other companies in the battalion. Most of them had combat experience, but most of the troops did not, and their average age was about twenty. The bewildered soldiers climbed aboard C-54 transport planes, and they arrived at Pusan airport on the morning of July 1. They were ecstatically greeted, taken to the railroad station, and loaded on a train headed northwest. They reached Taejon early the next morning, and Colonel Smith was briefed by the American KMAG commander, General Church. Church said he needed some men up the road who would not turn and run at the mere sight of a tank. Eighty miles northeast of Taejon was a blocking position at Osan. Smith put his men in trucks and away they went, Leonidas and the Spartans in olive drab.

Colonel Smith reached Osan on the afternoon of July 4. Having studied his position, he brought up his infantry; he had now been joined as well by a battery and a half of 105mm howitzers, a composite force from the 52nd Field Artillery Battalion, which had reached Pusan by LST and rushed forward in support. Just beyond Osan there was a little saddle flanked by low hills. Smith put his two companies straddling the road, with some men out on his right flank as a guard. The artillery went into battery a mile back. The whole front was about a mile wide, and there was nothing much that could be done except dig and wait for the North Koreans to arrive. By a rainy daylight on the 5th, Task Force Smith was as ready as it could be.

The men had a clear view north to their front. At about 0700 they saw the first movement, and an hour later, a column of the enemy was approaching their line, led by eight tanks. At 0816 a 105mm howitzer fired the first round, at 4,000-yard range. A rain of shells quickly fell among the lead tanks, but they plowed steadily along, oblivious to all the noise and smoke. The Americans had 2,000 artillery rounds, but they were high explosive, and were no good against tanks. The gunners had also been given one-third of all the high-explosive antitank (HEAT) ammunition available in the Far East Command; these shells were designed to penetrate a tank's armor and then explode, killing the crew and destroying the tank from inside. Unfortunately, one-third of the available HEAT ammunition consisted of only six rounds, so they had to be be saved to make every one of them count.

When the head of the tank column was within 700 yards, the infantry opened up. In addition to their personal and crew-served weapons, they had 75mm recoilless rifles and 2.36-inch bazookas. The lead tanks were hit repeatedly with bazooka rounds from a range of fifteen yards, but they kept right on, and simply drove through the position until stopped behind it, presumably by the HEAT fire of the sole 105mm using it. The first two tanks slewed off the road, but the remaining six kept going, firing as they passed through the infantry position. To their considerable amazement, the Americans had not scared off the North Koreans by their presence, they had not stopped them by their fire, they had hardly, in fact, even slowed them down. Now what?

The answer soon came: more tanks. A whole column came on now, passed through the infantry again, lumbered by the artillery position, which deluged them with high explosive, and clanked on down the road to Osan. By midmorning the Americans had stopped seven tanks, with major or minor damage, but twenty-seven more were now behind them, and in passing the tanks had shot up and ruined almost all of the U.S. vehicles, parked carefully by the side of the road, destroyed one gun, and inflicted about twenty casualties. A few mines would have stopped the whole tank force, but they were even scarcer than HEAT rounds; there were none of them in Korea at all.

About an hour after the tanks had gone by, North Korean infantry showed up, a truck-borne column about five or six miles long led by three tanks. The Americans let them get within 1,000 yards, then opened up with everything they had. They mortared and machine-gunned the head of the column, which was hard hit and thrown into confusion. But the tanks came on again, and began raking the American ridgeline. Behind them the infantry deployed, and began moving wide around Smith's flanks. They did not make much effort to close, but by afternoon, they were lapping well behind the defense line, and it was clearly time to go. It took a good three hours to disengage, the platoons trying not very successfully to leapfrog back from one spot to the next. They now came under heavy fire, and took most of their casualties at this point. It was the next morning before Task Force Smith regrouped, well below Osan; some stragglers took several days working cross-country before they got back to friendly hands. All told they lost about 150 killed, wounded, or missing. It was not a very auspicious beginning.

Things did not improve over the next several days. As the North Koreans advanced south and then southeast, they met the Americans moving up to block them. Most of the fighting at this time, of course, was done by the remnants of the South Korean Army, who held the vast majority of what front there was. The arriving Americans fell in along the Pusan-Taegu-Taejon-Seoul road, trying to stop the Communists where their drive was most crucial.

By the time Task Force Smith was broken up, General Dean had officially moved his 24th Division to Korea, and was at Taejon. His 34th Infantry Regiment tried to stop the North Koreans at Pyongtaek on the 5th and 6th, and Chonan on the 7th and 8th. The 21st Infantry fought below Chonui on the 9th, and above Chochiwon on the 11th. The 19th Infantry tried, and failed, to hold the Kum River line on the 16th. The Americans got some light tanks into Korea, but they were no match for the T34s.

Time and again the same pattern was repeated. The American forces would come up the roads by truck, offload, and take up a blocking position. The North Koreans would close up to this, develop it, and then move around through the hills to take up their own blocking position in the American rear. Then they would attack, carry the American line, usually wrecking the transport in the process, and break up and destroy the U.S. infantry as it tried to pull back. There were minor variations in this. The attacks were occasionally in daylight, but often at night. Sometimes UN air power hit the North Koreans, sometimes it hit friendly forces, sometimes it was not there at all. In one position there would be South Koreans on the flanks, in another the flanks would be up in the air. And most distressing of all, sometimes the troops would stay to fight, and sometimes they would rush off in panic at the first shot, or simply disappear from their positions, to be discovered later wandering about the rear area.

The North Koreans turned the corner at the Kum River, and on July 20 they reached Taejon. By now there was a new echelon of command in Korea, General Walker having moved across from Japan and established Eighth U.S. Army in Korea (EUSAK), and elements of the 25th and 1st Cavalry Divisions were arriving, both of them infantry in spite of the latter's famous name. The brunt of the battle, however, still fell on Dean's 24th Division, and he was hoping to hold Taejon for at least long enough to provide a breathing spell.

Again it could not be done. Attacked in front and flank by the North Korean 3rd and 4th Divisions, the Americans fell back into and through the city. The Red tanks got past them and roamed around the streets of Taejon. For the first time they ran into trouble, for the new 3.5-inch bazookas had now reached the front, and these at last would stop a T34. As the situation deteriorated, control and communications collapsed, and General Dean himself went off with a bazooka stalking tanks. Late in the afternoon of the 20th, the Americans organized a couple of convoys and tried to get clear of the town, only to run the gauntlet of the inevitable Communist roadblock, where they suffered heavy losses of men and equipment. A count after the battle showed the 24th Division had lost 30 percent of the troops engaged, plus trucks, its few attached tanks, and even guns of 155mm size. It also lost General Dean; he just barely got out of Taejon, then spent the next thirty-six days trying to get back to UN lines before he was led into an ambush and captured, exhausted and starved, and sent to spend the next three years in a North Korean prison camp.

By late July the United Nations forces were staring disaster in the face. The central drive southeast from Taejon toward Taegu showed no signs of losing momentum. To the east, in the mountains, the South Koreans were holding where they could, but slowly being pushed back. On the east coast itself, all the help of naval surface forces and naval and marine air seemed unable to keep the South Koreans from being flanked through the mountains and pushed south. And away around at the bottom of Korea, the North Korean forces who had taken the long southwestern route suddenly appeared as a major threat. There were refugees everywhere; all was confusion and dismay. It was a distinct possibility that the South Koreans, and the United Nations with them, would be pushed into the sea.

CHAPTER 3
THE PUSAN PERIMETER

In the last week of July, United Nations forces were still hard pressed by the North Koreans. From the east coast of the peninsula, the Republic of Korea Army held a broken line running due west almost to the center of the country, around Hamchang. All along this they were in trouble. The road network in the mountains was sparse, and there were few lateral east-west connections. So the Koreans were fighting a series of not quite independent battles, and a defeat along one north-south route usually meant that little assistance could be offered by a neighboring unit, but that that unit had to fall back to protect whatever it could of its flanks. The worst threat was right along the east coast, where there was especially fierce fighting around Yongdok. In this narrow strip, the South Koreans were trying hard to keep the Communists away from the airfield at Pohang, from which the U.S. Air Force was flying vital ground-support missions in Mustang fighters.

From Hamchang the front dropped away almost due south to the Taejon-Taegu road, still the main axis of the North Korean attack and the area where the incoming American units were concentrated.

Then from that road south to the coast, there was the usual story, the North Koreans pressing eastward, and very little in front of them. It was this area that was causing General Walker his most immediate problems, as he frantically shuffled troops about to meet the expanding threat. Every time he tried to pull a unit out of line to create even a minimal reserve, it had to be rushed off to a new road to stop another Communist advance.

Nonetheless, Walker hoped to hold the Reds short of the Naktong River, which was just about the last real natural barrier in front of Taegu, Pusan, and disaster. On August 1, from Hamchang down to the south coast, his units were ten to twenty miles west of the Naktong, and he thought he had a chance to stay there.

At least, he might hold that line *if* the troops would fight. Because he recognized that in many cases they were not doing that; these were the days of the "bug-out," and while there should be no general condemnation, the sad truth was that large numbers of soldiers and officers of the United States Army did not want to fight at all. Repeatedly, companies would go up a hill and dig in for the night, only to find by morning that there were one officer and seventeen men left on the hill; the rest had discovered pressing business elsewhere. Large numbers of soldiers were rounded up and sent back to their holes almost at gunpoint, and there were repeated reliefs of command for officers all the way up the ranks.

General Walker was angry over this, and he made no bones about it. He did not like the performance of the 25th Division or of the 1st Cavalry. As a tanker, he did not like retreating, and he particularly did not like retreating when the troops had not come into contact with the enemy. On July 29 he talked to the 25th Division staff and laid down some home truths, and this talk subsequently became widely known as the "stand or die" order. It was bitterly resented among many of the soldiers; in a fluid situation, where the Communists seemed always to hold the high ground and to have the advantage in infiltration, many soldiers thought voting with their feet was the only sensible thing to do. They could see themselves being cut off and surrounded; they could not see Walker's battle map showing them running out of space. But Walker knew about combat, and he was frustrated and disappointed at his people's performance. He told one senior field officer up at Taegu, "If I see you back here again, it'd better be in a coffin!" As Walker's old commander in Europe, General Patton, had once remarked, "The more you sweat in peace, the less you bleed in war." These troops had just come off occupation duty from soft billets in Japan. They had done little sweating there, and they paid for it with a lot of blood in Korea.

So the 25th Division fought at Sangju, and fell back; and the 1st Cavalry fought at Kumchon, and fell back to Waegwan on the Naktong; and the tired 24th fought at Anui, and fell back to the river line; and elements of the 25th fought on the south coast at Hadong, and fell back. By August 5 the line was on the Naktong. From Yongdok on the east coast it ran due west for seventy miles through the mountains; then it turned a sharp corner and ran due south for eighty miles, mostly along the river; finally it left the Naktong where that river turned eastward, and ran another twenty miles south to the seacoast near Masan. To defend it Walker had five South Korean divisions, holding the northern front and around the corner to Waegwan, a third of the way down the western side; then he had his three American divisions to hold the rest of the front. It looked like a continuous line, but that concept was delusory. U.S. Army tactical doctrine at the time considered 10,000 yards, or five miles, to be a practicable front for a division; in Eighth Army's sector, battalions, officially one-ninth of a division, were holding fronts of 15,000 yards. What that meant was a series of company- or platoon-sized outposts on hills, not a continuous line.

In spite of that, subsequent studies showed that the United Nations forces at the beginning of August were better off than they thought they were. There were actually 141,000 troops inside the perimeter, though only 92,000 of them were combat arms, rather more than half of them South Koreans. Yet the North Koreans had taken far heavier casualties than anyone realized, both in air attacks and from the South Koreans, whose combat skill was generally underrated at the time. MacArthur and Walker and their staffs thought they were still badly outnumbered, but later captured figures revealed that there were only about 70,000 combat troops left to the North Korean Army as it besieged the Pusan perimeter. Though the thinly spread riflemen on the hills above the Naktong would not have appreciated it, the situation recalled Churchill's caustic remark about Anzio: "We must have a great superiority of chauffeurs."

Numbers notwithstanding, the United Nations forces still were on the defensive, and the initiative still lay with the North Koreans. During the first three weeks of August, they attempted a series of attacks around the perimeter in the hope of making the final breakthrough. As these were almost if not quite simultaneous, it will be easier simply to follow them from south to north along the line.

The first of these, along the south coast, turned into a brutal encounter battle. Just as the North Korean 6th Division tried to attack eastward, the Americans launched what was intended as their first, limited, counterattack. Task Force Kean, named after the commander of the 25th Division, consisted of most of that division, plus the newly arrived 5th Regimental Combat Team and the 1st Provisional Marine Brigade, the first U.S. Marine Corps ground troops to reach Korea. It also had the usual attached artillery, and this time some medium tanks, one battalion of Shermans and one of M26 Pershings. The Americans advancing along two roads from Masan toward Chinju ran into Communists moving the other way. The Americans had a common problem of the period: The North Koreans were all over and behind them as well as in front, and they not only had to capture their own line of departure, they had as well to assign units to clear out the rear area of large numbers of infiltrators, including formed units, who were holed up in the mountains.

The result was several days of confused fighting. Along the coast road, Marine Corsairs from the light carrier *Badoeng Strait* tore up a column of Communist trucks and tracked vehicles, and had a regular field day. But along a more northerly road, the North Koreans did on the ground what the Marines did from the air. They closed in on a column consisting mainly of the 555th ("Triple Nickel") Field Artillery Battalion and virtually wiped it out in a pass that earned the ominous name Bloody Gulch. In spite of repeated attempts, the Americans could not pry the Communists out of a range of hills called Sobuk-san, just to the west of Masan, and until they could do that, they were not going anywhere significant along the south coast. After five days, General Walker dissolved Task Force Kean; the whole perimeter was in trouble, and it was too early to think of counterattacks yet.

Twenty miles above the coast, the Naktong takes a great turn to the east after running generally south. Just north of this turn is a twenty-five-mile stretch of large, lazy loops whose effect is to carry the river slightly to the westward of its regular course. The biggest of the loops, in front of the town of Yongsan, came to be known as the Naktong bulge. On August 5, the bulge was held by elements of the 34th Infantry Regiment of the 24th Division. The divisional front was thirty-four miles along the river, so the rifle companies were spread pretty thinly. On the night of August 5–6, troops of the North Korean 4th Division made an easy crossing in the gaps between the Americans, quickly bypassed the company perimeters on the hills, and ended up on the dominant feature of the whole bulge, a long north-south ridge called Obong-ni, shortly christened No Name Ridge by the Americans.

The Communists now threatened to compromise the whole southern part of the perimeter, and it was absolutely necessary to drive them back across the river. As they tried to reinforce and to push forward to Yongsan, the Americans pushed back. The Marines were brought up from Task Force Kean and committed against the ridge; two more infantry regiments, the 9th and the 19th, were put in; for two weeks the battle flared up, died down, and burst out again as one side or the other took the initiative. The same hills were taken, lost to counterattacks, taken, and lost again. And taken again. The Americans were punch-drunk, but the North Koreans were slowly being ground down, their supplies interdicted, and their numbers thinned by the constant attrition. Finally they could stand no more, and they went off the ridge, then back over the hills to the river, setting up blocking positions and having to be pushed all the way. By the 19th the bulge had been cleared and the river line reconstituted; the North Korean 4th Division was virtually destroyed, incapable of action for the immediate future.

They had better luck in the mountains north of Taegu. Here, in the middle two weeks of August, they launched major drives that pushed the South Korean divisions facing them nearly forty miles. This was very bad country to fight in—high, sharp, tumbled hills, poor communications, and no river front to help establish a major position. The South Koreans were very nearly fought out, their ranks thinned by earlier heavy losses, their replacements hardly trained at all. The North Koreans were at last contained a mere ten miles from Taegu; at a nice straight stretch of road, with hills on either side, American infantry and artillery set up a blocking position with the South Koreans. This earned the nickname "the bowling alley," as on the next several nights the Reds sent their tanks straight down the road to be knocked out by direct fire. The U.S. 27th Infantry, the Wolfhounds, watched the Communists use a system of flares to signal their attacks, got some flares of its own, and drew them into ambushes, a highly satisfying experience for

Americans who had themselves been subjected to repeated ambushes by their enemy.

Other episodes stood out in the confused fighting before Taegu. There had already been repeated instances of atrocities committed on prisoners of war. Substantial numbers of Americans had been found dead, their hands wired behind their backs, shot through the head. Several had obviously been tortured and in some cases burned alive. On August 15, troops of the North Korean 105th Armored Division forced a crossing of the Naktong around Waegwan, in the process cutting off and then capturing a platoon of mortarmen of H Company, 5th Cavalry Regiment, on Hill 303. The captured soldiers had been shuttled about for a day among various captors, then herded into a gully and machine-gunned. A few were wounded and escaped by feigning death, but twenty-six were killed. This prompted General MacArthur to send a message to the North Koreans, dropp⸺ by leaflet and widely circulated, threatening to hold the enemy command responsible for atrocities and war crimes. The North Koreans seem to have been acting independently at the lower levels, rather than as a matter of policy, but the United Nations would later be appalled at the small number of prisoners the Communists admitted they actually held.

Just north of Waegwan the Communists pressed hard, held back by the excellent effort of General Paik Sun Yup's ROK 1st Division. By mid-August it looked as if they might well break through to Taegu, and President Rhee moved his government from there to Pusan, which set off a panic among the swarms of refugees already overcrowding the city. To relieve the pressure, General MacArthur himself ordered a carpet bombing of the area across the Naktong where he believed there was a strong concentration of North Korean troops. The Air Force was somewhat skeptical of this whole idea—it had had rather mixed results in World War II—but laid on a strike by nearly 100 B-29s on the morning of August 16. The area to be bombed was a rectangle of twenty-seven square miles, and it was hit by five bomber groups in succession. There was no specific target marking, as there were no specific targets. Each group simply took a portion of the rectangle and plastered it. It was either an impressive display of strength or an equally impressive waste of effort, and the general opinion was that it was the latter. Maj. Gen. Emmett O'Donnell, who led the Far East Air Forces Bomber Command, flew his own reconnaissance the afternoon of the strike, and reported he could see no sign of enemy life at all, but that may well have been because there was none there in the first place. MacArthur wanted to do it again a couple of days later, but the Air Force people talked him out of it. The B-29s simply lacked the flexibility to be of much service in a close tactical situation, and they were far better employed elsewhere.

Even more than the fighting around Taegu, the Communist advance along the east coast looked as if it might reach paydirt. On August 5 the South Koreans were still holding their own north of Yongdok, where their 3rd Division faced the North Korean 5th. But while this went on, two other Communist divisions and a separate regiment-sized unit were filtering through the mountains behind the coast. On August 10 they suddenly appeared around Pohang-dong, twenty-five miles south of Yongdok, cutting off the 3rd Division and threatening the American airfield at Yonil. On the 11th the Mustangs based there had to fly out to safer strips, and their ground equipment was taken off the nearby beaches by LSTs. Shortly after, the Navy lifted the 3rd Division off the beaches where they were trapped below Yongdok, while the U.S.S. *Helena* and a destroyer division laid down covering fire. Carried south and then off-loaded, the division was soon back in action. There was bitter fighting around Pohang-dong for the next several days, with American and South Korean forces all mixed up, occasionally surrounded, and trying desperately to keep their lines open. But the Communists were out on a very thin limb, with their supply lines back through the mountains unable to sustain them, and after about a week, they could go no farther. They were out of ammunition, their men had no rations, there were no replacements for casualties; they were simply fought out. They were soon pushed north again, at least far enough to provide some breathing room, and the planes came back to Yonil to add even more pressure.

Throughout this period of perimeter fighting, the United Nations control of the sky was of vital importance. In the tactical sense, it was probably Marine air support that was most visible. Lightly equipped and organized for amphibious assaults, the Marines lacked the heavy artillery of the Army, and had therefore made a specialty of close air support of troops on the ground. The Air Force was quite differently configured, and its tactical air support was more of an improvisation, using planes such as the Texan and the Mustang, which had just been relegated to second-line duties. Both the Navy and some of the first non-American United Nations forces on the scene, the Royal Australian Air Force, also joined in the tactical battle. Less visibly, the Air Force and Navy went after the supply lines of the Communists, and ranged over the whole peninsula, hitting truck convoys, rail lines, marshaling yards, bridges, and any concentrations they could find. The Communists did much of their moving by night, and the Americans then went after them with B-26 light bombers, an updated version of what in World War II would have been a "night intruder." Unfortunately, this was a type of operation that had been largely neglected in the years since 1945, and although the night operations were useful, they were not in sufficient number for much more than nuisance value. Throughout the period, the air forces made a major contribution to blunting the strength of the Communist drive, but they were far from able to halt it by themselves.

If the troops along the Naktong were not always conscious of the assistance they received from UN command of the air, they were even less aware of the value of command of the sea, for the horizon of an infantryman huddling in a hole while someone shoots at him is necessarily and understandably limited. Yet the naval presence was the *sine qua non* of the entire operation. That could be demonstrated simply by recounting the buildup of the opposing forces around the perimeter, and it would shortly have an even more graphic illustration.

Ever since the invasion began, both sides had been racing against the clock. The North Koreans had to finish off the job before the United Nations could muster sufficient force to prevent it, while the United Nations, principally the Americans, had to stiffen up the South Koreans long enough for outside intervention to take effect. It was about mid-August that some sort of equilibrium was reached; at that point the lines on the graph crossed, with UN strength and resources surpassing those of the North Koreans.

Part of the problem was distance, but distance is not simply miles on a map; it is also a question of how difficult those miles are to traverse. It is 5,500 miles from Seattle to Korea by the great-circle route, or 6,800 from San Francisco via Pearl Harbor. In July the U.S.S. *Boxer,* going flat out all the way, delivered 145 F-51s to Korea from the West Coast in eight days and seven hours. That was of course an exceptional run; the norm was about twice that for the Navy's regular cargo ships or amphibious transports. Then within the theater itself, there was, in addition to the seaborne capacity, an enormous amount of cargo handled by the Air Force, whose planes ran a regular shuttle service from Japan to Korea and carried a prodigious amount both of cargo and personnel. Indeed, the Air Force's Logistics Force and Combat Cargo Command functioned so efficiently that they eventually were able to reduce their flights from peak periods, because they were in fact overproducing.

On the other side, the Communists were faced with far shorter distances; it was just over 400 miles direct from Sinuiju, at the mouth of the Yalu, or about 600 from Russian territory down the east coast, to Pusan. But these were much more difficult miles to get over, traveling by train, truck, or foot, and hunted all the way by UN air power. The situation was similar to the Peninsular War of 1809–14, where it took the French six weeks to march across the Pyrenees and Spain, harried by guerrillas all the way, while the British reached the theater after a leisurely three-week sail from England.

Another part of the problem was the availability of assets, not in terms of the total either side possessed, but in terms of what could actually be deployed in Korea. The North Koreans could, and did, give it all they had. The United States, the only UN member whose assistance was in sufficient numbers to be really significant, had all sorts of commitments, and at the moment very little with which to meet them. Sending units or equipment to Korea meant letting the buildup in Europe wait, and the government, and particularly the Joint Chiefs of Staff, went through a perpetual juggling act trying to satisfy three or four demands with the same item or outfit. Equipment inventories had been allowed to run down since 1945, and the ammunition shortage, especially in certain types of artillery shells, became quite critical, because the United States had not only not replenished stocks, it had actually dismantled the entire ammunition industry after the end of the war. What company wanted to make 105mm shells that no one wanted to buy, when the consumer market was clamoring for baby carriages?

The troop shortage was much the same. Activating units of the Reserve or the National Guard was a move fraught with political consequences, but in some cases it had to be done. Veterans who had just nicely reestablished their lives after 1945 now found themselves back in uniform again, and most were not happy about it. Distribution remained critical. In Japan, MacArthur was constantly being called on for troops for Korea, but at the same time he was extremely conscious that defense of Japan was his prime consideration. That worry now appears excessive, but at the time U.S. planners were afraid that Korea might be merely the prelude to a generalized Communist assault, on Japan and on Europe as well. There was little in the entire range of the American arsenal to stop them if they indeed chose to move.

Still, in July and August 1950, Korea was where the action was, and it had to have priority. One answer was to build up the Republic of Korea Army, and that process was a constant subplot to the war. In August the ROK Army had a strength of 85,000 men. During the fall, General Walker planned to add an additional five divisions, one a month starting in September. This proved to be too ambitious, but there was nonetheless a constant growth of the force throughout the entire war. Increasing the size of the American forces was equally difficult. One answer was "Operation Flush-out" in Japan, designed to fill the depleted ranks of the rifle companies with superfluous personnel from occupation billets. The problem here, which seems to cause armies perpetual surprise, is that casualties are always higher among riflemen than they are among truck drivers and clerks; therefore any army that engages in combat for even a short period of time soon runs low on riflemen. Operation Flush-out was a Korean repeat of what had happened in northwestern Europe in 1944, when the Army found itself in the same situation. Needless to say, it was accompanied by vast amounts of annoyance and griping.

Another, less successful attempt to grapple with the manpower shortage was the KATUSA, an acronym for Korean Augmentation to United States Army. This had happened casually when Korean stragglers joined in with American units, just for rations and a home. In August the Army made it official, and planned to take 30,000 to 40,000 Korean army recruits and integrate them with American combat units, at the rate of about 100 per company or battery. Each Korean would be paired with an American, who would theoretically teach him the rudiments of the trade of fighting. It was a desperate expedient, designed particularly to flesh out formations that had already been either worn down by battle or cannibalized to help other units; the 7th Infantry Division in Japan, for example, was a mere skeleton, having contributed successive drafts to the other divisions already in Korea. Unfortunately, the KATUSA program proved to be far better in theory than in practice. The language barrier was totally insurmountable, and that was only the first of many. A U.S. Army that had not yet integrated American blacks with any success was not going to do well with a Korean buddy system, and most of the KATUSAs were eventually used as laborers and porters.

Yet in spite of shortages and occasionally unsuccessful expedients, the United Nations buildup inside the perimeter went on. It was actually more impressive than it looked on paper, for there were fewer new units than there was an increase up to authorized strength of the forces already there. Regiments got their third battalions back, and divisions their third regiment; artillery battalions regained their third firing batteries. Some new units did arrive, such as the 38th Infantry, famous in the Army as the Rock of the Marne, to join the tired 19th with its even older nickname, the Rock of Chickamauga. On August 29 the first ground forces from other members of the United Nations arrived, the British 27th Brigade from Hong Kong. This consisted of the 1st Battalion of the Middlesex Regiment and the 1st Battalion of the Argyll and Sutherland Highlanders, to become universally known in Korea as the Agile and Suffering Highlanders. By September 1 the UN forces in the perimeter had a strength of 180,000 men.

On that date the North Koreans launched their last do-or-die offensives. They had lost the race against time, but were not quite prepared to admit it. They too had attempted to rebuild and reequip, but had been far less successful, if more ruthless, in doing so. Most of their replacements were actually conscripted South Koreans, gathered up from the territory they had overrun, in accord with the idea that the whole country was theirs anyway. These young men had minimal training and often no equipment at all; in many cases they were told to pick up rifles from the dead as they went into combat, and they were kept to their work at gunpoint. They were lucky to get handfuls of rice to live on. Until they got to the front they were hunted by UN airpower, and when they arrived they were thrown into combat of which they were totally ignorant. By September 1 the estimated strength of the North Korean Army was about 98,000 men; on average their thirteen infantry divisions had about 7,000 men in them. They had only about 100 tanks left, while the UN now had 500 in the area. Their logistics and communications were a shambles. The wonder of the period is not that they collapsed so quickly, but that they did as well as they did before the collapse came.

Their last offensive was basically a repeat of their earlier one, intense attacks all around the perimeter. Authorities have commented that these dispersed attacks were strategically poorly done, and that the Communists would have done better to concentrate on one vital spot, perhaps Taegu, for example. But given the fact that the UN command possessed the interior lines, command of the air, and better transportation facilities for moving reserves about, it is difficult to see that the North Koreans could have done things much differently.

In the south they drove again toward Masan, and were turned back. They occupied the Naktong bulge once more, and again had to be pushed off Obong-ni or No-Name Ridge by the Marines. North of Taegu they hit hard, and there was heavy fighting around Hill 902, a 3,000 foot-high mountain known as the Walled City, from an ancient perimeter wall that crowned it. One battalion of the 8th Cavalry was overrun, and it took a major effort by scratch forces to contain the drive.

East of that, against the South Koreans, the Reds made even better progress. They drove the ROK I and II Corps back as much as twenty miles and threatened the main road between Taegu and the coast at Pohang. For a while the situation looked pretty grim, but General Walker now had some reserves to maneuver; the 24th Division came up from the south and restored the northern front after some hard fighting.

By September 10 the perimeter began to settle down once again. On its western face the Americans had taken back all the North Koreans had gained, and a little more. In the north, once the Taegu-Pohang road was free of immediate danger, Walker was content to leave things alone. Ten or fifteen miles of mountains did not offer the Reds that much. They had used up their offensive clout, and had, in fact, gone as far as they were going to go. General Walker could now look forward with some confidence not simply to maintaining his position, but to an actual counteroffensive. Even better than that, the United Nations Command was on the verge of springing one of the great strategic surprises of the century.

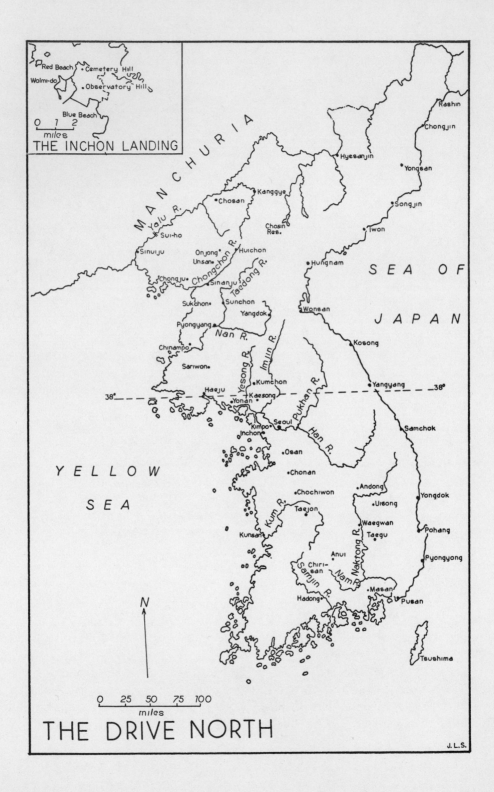

Red Beach
Cemetery Hill
Wolmi-do
Observatory Hill
Blue Beach

0 1 2
miles

MANCHURIA

Yalu R.

Rashin

Chongjin

Hyesanjin

Yongsan

Kanggye

Chosan

Songjin

Chosin
Res.

Iwon

Sui-ho

Sinuiju

Onjong
Unsan
Huichon

Chongju
Sinanju

Chongchon R.

Taedong R.

Hungnam

SEA OF

Sukchon
Sunchon

Yangdok

Wonsan

JAPAN

Pyongyang

Nan R.

Chinampo

Kosong

Sariwon

Yesong R.

Imjin R.

Haeju

Kumchon

Yangyang

38°

Kaesong

Yonan

Pukhan R.

38°

Seoul

Kimpo
Inchon

Han R.

Samchok

Osan

YELLOW

Chonan

SEA

Chochiwon

Andong

Yongdok

Uisong

Kum R.

Taejon

Waegwan
Taegu

Pohang

Kunsan

Naktong R.

Pyongyong

Anui

Chiri-
san

Nam R.

Samjin R.

Masan

Hadong

Pusan

N

Tsushima

0 25 50 75 100
miles

THE DRIVE NORTH

J.L.S.

CHAPTER 4
INCHON

The situation in Korea at the end of August 1950 had all the makings of military disaster for someone. It was not apparent to observers that any definitive change had taken place, and newspapers were still reporting that the UN forces were heavily outnumbered, perhaps by as much as four to one, and that the troops were literally fighting with their backs to the sea. The North Korean high command was still exhorting its soldiers to one last ultimate effort, an effort that would bring well-deserved victory and end the hated regime of the criminal Rhee and his imperialist masters. Therefore the stroke being prepared by General MacArthur and his staff, when it actually came, was a bolt from the blue. It was not perhaps one of history's decisive battles, but it certainly was a classic military operation, the kind of move that warms the hearts of professional soldiers and amateur historians alike.

As the Communists drove south, the geography of the peninsula imposed special logistical constraints on them. The east-coast roads were capable of sustaining no more than the troops moving along them, and not even of doing that very well. The roads south through the mountains were even worse. The main Communist supply artery therefore had to run from western North Korea, down through a bottleneck at Seoul, and on from there. Even the east-coast port of Wonsan was connected not to Pusan by rail, but rather to Seoul in the west, and from there the rail line ran back southeast to Pusan. Then from the South Korean capital the road and rail network fanned out to the south once more, connecting with the whole lower part of the peninsula. The vast majority of the support for the Communist offensive, therefore, funneled through the fairly narrow corridor in and around the capital city. To overrun South Korea, the Communists had to go out on a long limb, and the farther out they got, the thinner the limb became. As the perimeter firmed up in the south and the lines stabilized, that supply limb was increasingly battered by United Nations air power, but it was not broken. The Communists might have to move by night, hide their trains in tunnels, conscript huge numbers of local peasants for road and rail repair, but they kept doing it. Air power had slowed them, but it had not stopped them.

The Seoul area, though it was a target that automatically caught the eye of a commander, presented major difficulties for an operation. Seoul itself is some twenty-odd miles inland from the Yellow Sea, on the Han River, broad, shallow, and not a useful stream for major shipping operations. The actual port for the capital city is Inchon, which lies almost due west and is connected with Seoul by road and rail rather than by water. American and other foreign dependents in the capital had been evacuated from Inchon by ship during the opening days of the invasion, and the port was the natural focus of military attention.

Unfortunately, Inchon presents difficulties bordering on the bizarre for military purposes. It happens that the highest tides in the world rush into two similarly shaped bodies, the Bay of Fundy on Canada's east coast, and the Yellow Sea between China and Korea. The seaward approaches to the port of Inchon are covered by numerous islands, the channel is narrow and treacherous, and shallow for major vessels, and worst of all, the tidal range is a whopping thirty-three feet at spring tides. To make it worse, if possible, that much water running in and out creates a current of five or six knots. In short, Inchon is a navigator's nightmare. And these were only the problems of getting to Inchon; taking it might be even worse.

Yet an attack aimed at Inchon and Seoul immediately came to

General MacArthur's mind. From start to finish it was his idea; he made it work, and probably only he could have done so. He later said that he developed the idea from his first visit to the front in Korea; as he stood on the hills below the Han and watched Seoul falling to the enemy, he decided that they would first have to be contained, then defeated by an amphibious operation at Inchon. That was on June 29.

If this seems highly prescient, it flowed naturally from MacArthur's background and accomplishments during World War II. In New Guinea and the Philippines he ran the most successful series of amphibious operations in history, a string of hard-won battles that carried Allied forces more than 2,500 miles into the heart of the Japanese empire. The landing at Leyte was the most famous of them, in October 1944, but a year earlier around the Huon peninsula of New Guinea, MacArthur had achieved the greatest of military victories, the destruction of a field army without fighting it, by cutting off its supplies and leaving it isolated and starving. In these great battles, MacArthur's relations with the U.S. Navy had not always been entirely harmonious, but they had always been effective. As he said when he was pushing the Inchon idea, "The Navy has never turned me down yet."

Aside from its military achievement, MacArthur's Inchon scheme might be judged by the quality of the opposition it aroused, for almost everyone was opposed to it. Gen. Omar Bradley, Chairman of the Joint Chiefs of Staff, was rather inclined to think that the day of the big amphibious operation was past. Gen. J. Lawton Collins, "Lightning Joe" of World War II fame, now Chief of Staff of the U.S. Army, thought the proposed operation was too deep in the North Korean rear and might well leave the invaders stranded and contained. The Navy's objections were largely couched in terms of the technical difficulties; the same was true of the Marines, who were the amphibious assault forces, but who were not keen to land over a seawall and charge directly into a city. That was not quite in keeping with their experience. Most of these other commanders agreed with the idea of a landing, but wanted it in some other, less difficult place, such as perhaps Kunsan, the smaller west-coast port 100 miles south of Seoul.

MacArthur was adamant, and he had a reply for everyone. He quoted the old military adages about the nearer the front the more immediate, the farther back the more profound, the effect of an incursion; he pointed out the immense psychological benefits of retaking the South Korean capital in one great counterstroke. He whispered in the Marines' ear that an operation such as this would guarantee their continued independence, an alluring song to a service then under heavy attack as redundant.

Yet when MacArthur definitively opted for a landing at Inchon, the Joint Chiefs still dragged their feet. Finally, they sent General Collins and the Chief of Naval Operations, Adm. Forrest P. Sherman, over to Tokyo to have the whole matter threshed out. MacArthur and his officers, especially his own chief of staff, Maj. Gen. Edward M. Almond, designated as commander of the invading force, and the naval commanders from the Far East, met with the visitors from Washington on July 23. Much of the meeting was dominated by the naval briefing presented by Rear Adm. James H. Doyle, who was to command the naval assault force; the best the Navy would say was "It is not impossible."

At that point MacArthur began to speak, almost conversationally, more as if telling a story than giving a briefing. He ranged over all the pluses and minuses, and he ended up by stealing the show. Collins and Sherman went home, if not wholeheartedly in support, at least accepting his view of the matter, and the Joint Chiefs, though they still tried to hedge their bets a little, essentially gave MacArthur free rein to do it his way.

The biggest hurdle was where to find the troops to do the job. MacArthur's planners, known as the Joint Strategic Plans and Operations Group, or JSPOG, found that every time they designated a unit for the invasion force, it was stolen from them by events in Korea itself; successive divisions slated for Inchon went off instead to hold the lines along the Naktong. Eventually, however, X Corps was established, to consist of the 1st Marine Division and the 7th Infantry Division, with General Almond as the corps commander. The 7th had repeatedly lost drafts for the formations already in Korea, and it was 9,000 men understrength when ordered to prepare for the operation, and many of its missing personnel were made up by hastily drafted Korean civilians. It required legerdemain of the first order to produce a whole Marine division, including among other things the transfer of Marines from the Mediterranean via Suez. The Marines fighting in the Pusan perimeter were repeatedly held back by one crisis after another, until finally released in the nick of time to take part in the operation. They were not available until the beginning of the second week in September, and it was not until then that Washington finally gave in to MacArthur's importunities and cabled its approval of the Inchon site. Of all the various elements involved in Inchon, the Navy was the best prepared and equipped. It set up Joint Task Force 7 with Admiral Struble in overall command, and it provided air cover, shore bombardment, blockade, minesweeping, and logistics support for Admiral Doyle's attack force. Altogether some 230 vessels were involved in one stage or another of the invasion.

Amphibious operations have a long and somewhat mixed history and are among the most complex of all military undertakings. At the end of World War I, after their unhappy experience at Gallipoli and elsewhere, the British had concluded that an opposed amphibious landing under modern conditions was impossible for practical purposes. Yet by the end of World War II, after Sicily, Salerno, Anzio, Normandy, and southern France, and even more after the American experience in the Pacific, authorities had reached the opposite conclusion: A well-prepared and adequately supported landing, under proper conditions, would inevitably succeed.

Inchon, however, stretched those proper conditions to their farthest limits. To the hazards of tide and current had to be added the peculiar configuration of the target area. Not only was Inchon surrounded by a whole mess of small islands, but the actual port was split in two. There was an outer harbor, and then an inner one created by the small island of Wolmi-do, which was connected to the mainland by a long causeway. Wolmi-do, if held by a determined garrison, might lay down such heavy flanking fire as to make the landings impossible; therefore it must be neutralized and taken first. Tide ranges were such, though, that all this meant Wolmi-do and Inchon had to be first bombarded, then the island taken on a high tide, and then the main landing made on the *next* high tide. A pre-invasion bombardment was going to forfeit the element of surprise, and then the troops taking and holding Wolmi-do were going to be isolated for at least twelve hours, before the next phase of the landing could be carried out. No one planning an operation would do it this way by choice, and the only thing to recommend it was that there was no other way to go about it. The planners decided the Marines would hit Wolmi-do at high tide on the morning of September 15, at 0630; the main landing at Inchon would come eleven hours later, at the afternoon high tide. For the two weeks before the invasion, the Navy put Lt. E. F. Clark on one of the offshore islands, where he spent his time gathering tide and current information and carrying out a small war against Communist sampans and coastal craft; his contribution to the invasion won him a well-deserved Navy Cross.

The big thing the planners did not know, and could not accurately discover, was how much opposition they might face. If the Communists were there in major force, Inchon was going to be a very tough job, with heavy opposition added to all the natural hazards. But they thought that the area was not too strongly garrisoned, that most of the North Korean strength was fully occupied in the south at the perimeter.

The preliminary bombardment began on September 10 with strikes by Marine aircraft. For two days they worked over Wolmi-do with napalm, until the island looked like a burned husk. On the morning of the 13th, surface ships joined in. Two American cruisers, *Toledo* and *Rochester,* and two Royal Navy cruisers, *Kenya* and *Jamaica,* steamed up Flying Fish Channel, anchored offshore, and began firing measured salvos at the island. The two British ships were light cruisers with 6-inch guns, and the Americans carried 8-inch main batteries—not battleship ordnance perhaps, but huge weapons by land or army standards. With them came a destroyer division of six ships, which proceeded steadily up the channel and anchored within 1,000 yards of the island. The American ships calmly opened fire. For more than an hour they pounded Wolmi with their 5-inch guns at what was virtually point-blank range. Return fire wounded several sailors and killed one officer. When the destroyers left, the naval and marine aircraft resumed their attack as well.

The Navy came back and did the same thing again on the 14th, but this time all was silent on the battered island; it was difficult to tell how much damage had actually been done and how strong the enemy remained.

The next morning saw the main event. Again under an intense naval bombardment, the 3rd Battalion of the 5th Marines went ashore in the early morning. There was little resistance; the surviving North Koreans were dazed after the last three days, and the island was under Marine control within forty-five minutes, though it took several more hours to root the last of the defenders out of their holes, which the Americans did at a cost of twenty wounded. About 120 North Koreans were killed, with almost 200 captured.

The Marines now had a day-long wait on their island for the next round, but the hours passed quietly, if busily, as they dug in and prepared their positions. The main landing had peculiar difficulties of its own. The Marines would have to get up a stone seawall and attack directly into a built-up area, with night coming on. They also had to be supported by immediate landings of LSTs, which would then be grounded overnight on the mud flats as the tide receded; the Navy was so worried about leaving its ships high and dry and possibly losing them to enemy fire, that it used for the landing eight old LSTs that had previously been decommissioned, and had been kicking around Japanese waters slowly rusting for the last five years. One of them actually had to be towed to Inchon.

Once more, however, fortune favored boldness. Late in the afternoon the Marines hit Red and Blue Beaches, the former right in the city, the latter south of it. The troops went up and over the walls with scaling ladders and grappling lines, as if they were in John Paul Jones's navy, and the LSTs banged into the seawall, in some cases breaking right through it or riding up onto it. Unloading of bulldozers, tanks, and heavy equipment began under fire. It was pretty chaotic for a while, with heavy fire coming in, and the sailors from the gun tubs on the LSTs hosing down everything in sight—including some Marines—with 20mm and 40mm cannon. But the Marines filtered through to the buildings fronting the seawall and began cleaning up snipers and machine-gun positions. Within an hour and a half they had secured Cemetery Hill overlooking Red Beach. By the next morning the two beaches were linked up, and that day the Marines rapidly advanced inland, so that at day's end the city and beachhead area were under their control.

All in all, the Inchon operation was a remarkable demonstration of the Navy's and Marines' ability to do an excellent job under highly adverse conditions. Inchon was taken with fewer than 200 casualties, including 20 killed. Yet the major contributors to the victory were surprise and the weakness of the enemy in the area. The intelligence estimates had said there were probably only about 6,500 North Koreans around, perhaps 5,000 in Seoul, 500 around Kimpo airport, and 1,000 in Inchon. This seems to have been about correct, and not only did the Marines outnumber the defenders, but the Navy far outclassed them in firepower. Yet it need not have gone this way;

at Gallipoli a mere handful of Turkish machine gunners wiped out whole battalions of British soldiers. To say that the North Koreans were few and their strategic dispositions amateurish is only to point up the obvious truism that that is what war is all about. The fact that Inchon succeeded so well at such relatively small cost is a measure of how great a gamble it was; its success was well deserved.

Immediately ahead lay Kimpo airfield, which the Marines soon reached. Again it was ill defended, and its garrison soon scattered, leaving the invaluable hard-surface strip, one of the few such in the country, to the invaders. The Marines pressed on to the Han River, and as the 7th Division came ashore and moved up, X Corps got ready for the taking of Seoul. General MacArthur came in to look over his handiwork, and was immensely pleased with the results so far. He also very nearly got in trouble, as he and some of his staff officers went up to see the fighting. At one point they stopped at the scene of a tank and infantry firefight; the area was littered with six knocked-out T34s and North Korean bodies. A few minutes after they left, half a dozen Communists came out of a culvert and surrendered.

The landing of Almond's X Corps at Inchon was designed to be an anvil. Walker's Eighth Army was to play the hammer. It was to launch an all-out assault on the Communists around the Pusan perimeter, to coincide with the Inchon landing, and then to drive the North Koreans back against X Corps. The concept worked almost exactly the way it was intended, but it proved far harder to do than might have been expected.

Even with the siphoning off of units for Inchon, the growth of Eighth Army had continued. By September 16, the day the offensive began, there were slightly more than 150,000 UN troops in the area. There were four United States divisions, the 2nd, 24th, and 25th Infantry and the 1st Cavalry, with an average strength of 15,000 men; these were still organized as I Corps, but a second corps, IX, was soon to be activated. The South Korean Army had six divisions, with an average strength of 10,000 men; the only other United Nations ground combat contingent was still the British 27th Brigade, less than 2,000 strong. In spite of the impressive total, the number of riflemen remained low, proportionately, and some companies in the line were at less than 50 percent strength. There was a vast superiority of armor and artillery, but even during the offensive, the firing batteries were on ammunition rations, because of the shortage of shells. Nonetheless, when all the limitations are taken into account, the UN forces still should have had a very comfortable margin of strength.

The North Korean Army was in a peculiar condition. It had only about 70,000 effectives remaining, and just how effective they were was a subject for speculation. The Americans estimated that the enemy divisions had no more than 30 percent of their original members left, and that replacements were almost entirely South Korean conscripts. Most of these, naturally, did not want to fight. Yet few deserted; the officers and NCOs shot out of hand anyone who refused to obey orders instantly or who was caught trying to desert, and it was widely believed in the North Korean Army that the Americans and South Koreans were shooting anyone who tried to surrender to them. There had been heavy losses in equipment as well as men, and Eighth Army thought that the Red divisions were down to about 75 percent, though in actual fact they were even lower than that. No one on the UN side was sure quite what would happen; the pessimists thought a breakout would not even be possible, the optimists thought the North Koreans would simply collapse.

Neither were wholly correct. The big attack began on September 16, a day after the Inchon landing. This was calculated to fix North Korean forces in place and prevent their rushing north to attack X Corps; it was also believed that news of Inchon would further demoralize the North Korean troops. The demoralization did not take immediate effect, however, for the simple reason that the North Korean commanders did not tell their troops about Inchon, an interesting example of the differences between an open and a controlled society, and the kind of misassessments one tends to make of the other. In fact, in many places along the perimeter it was the North Koreans, not the UN troops, who did the attacking on the 16th.

Yet weight soon began to tell. In the old area of the Naktong bulge, the 2nd Infantry Division repulsed North Korean attacks on the morning of the 16th, then launched its own, scheduled, assault. By midafternoon it was clear that something was beginning to happen. The Communists were pulling out of their positions and heading for the river. At that point they really started to suffer. Air Force F-51s were after them, strafing and dropping napalm tanks, and the 2nd Division's attached armor started to move forward, intending to cut off numbers of North Koreans. The next day they were pounded as they tried to get across the Naktong, and on the 18th, the Americans themselves were across and taking the hills, largely undefended, on the western side of the river. They were two days ahead of their timetable, and they were beginning to bag prisoners, not only infantry but rear-echelon people as well, and to overrun supply dumps.

The heady feeling of being on the offensive, of actually making some progress, was soon shared all along the line. North of the 2nd Division, the 5th Regimental Combat Team, attached to 1st Cavalry, took the town of Waegwan after a hard fight, and thus flanked the entire North Korean position on the main line of advance or retreat. With Waegwan taken, the 24th Division passed by the 5th RCT and took up the attack. Meanwhile the 1st Cavalry drove up the road toward Taejon, running into very heavy opposition west of Waegwan. Once the crust was broken, however, things again began to move. The three regiments of the division managed major encirclement drives, breaking up the North Korean division in front of them.

Air observers reported groups of fleeing Communists all over the place, and the Air Force, presented with a sudden plethora of targets, practically went crazy. Planes had been grounded on the 16th because of bad weather, but it began to break up on the afternoon of the 17th. The next day the F-51s and F-80s were out in force, strafing, bombing, and napalming. In some cases, where the Communists tried to hold on, fighter planes made attacks less than fifty yards in front of their own ground troops. In one extreme instance, the pilot of a T-6 spotter plane dropped a note on a group of Communists, ordering them to surrender, and then directed a couple of American ground patrols over to take them into custody.

Around the corner on the northern side of the perimeter, the South Korean and North Korean divisions were both in states of near-exhaustion, but the North Koreans again were closer to it. Each side virtually fought the other into the ground, and slowly the Communists went back and began to break up. Right on the coast itself, it took first gunfire support from the U.S.S. *Missouri*, firing its 16-inch guns, and then virtual suicide attacks by South Korean infantry to lever the North Koreans out of Pohang-dong.

By the beginning of the fourth week in September, the 22nd, the front was opening up at last. From then until the end of the month, UN forces spread over South Korea in a mirror image of the retreats and defeats they had suffered earlier. Everywhere before them the

North Korean Army fled, broke up, or went into the hills to fight as guerrillas. Action became increasingly confused, but highly satisfying, to the United Nations troops and commanders. In the south, the 25th Division finally broke the impasse along the coast and got past the terrible mountains of Sobuk-san with their memories of Bloody Gulch, the Notch, and other defeats of a few weeks ago. Driving in columns of trucks led by armor, they headed west along the coast and then northwest to Kunsan. The 2nd Division kept pace inland of them, and on its right, the 24th went up the road to Taejon. The troops went by truck as much as possible, with tanks leading the way and fighter-bombers and Tactical Air Control Parties keeping them company, and spotting and scouting on their flanks. When the North Koreans stopped to fight, the troops would detruck, deploy, and clear the block, with tank or aircraft support, then climb into their trucks and go on to the next block.

There were strange incidents along the route. In Namwon a lone American tank drove into town, liberated nearly 100 American POWs, and then realized it was surrounded by a mass of North Koreans; the rest of the column arrived just in time, before the Communists recovered from their shock. More often than that, however, the UN forces found that the Communists had executed prisoners, military or civilian, as they retreated. Several thousand people—soldiers, government officials, landowners, teachers, priests—had been shot in batches of 100 around Taejon. In other towns they had been locked inside buildings and burned alive. It was the old technique of wiping out anyone who might form a core of disagreement; it had happened before in Poland, and it would happen again in Cambodia.

The excitement of linking up with the forces at Inchon fell to a composite unit of the 1st Cavalry Division. Designated Task Force 777, as the infantry, artillery, and armor in it all had the number 7 in their designations, this unit moved out on the morning of September 22. Its lead element was called Task Force Lynch after its commander, Lt. Col. James H. Lynch. They crossed the Naktong on the night of the 22nd and 23rd and began overrunning fleeing North Koreans. By the 23rd they were traveling along in column, with Communists scattering before them or throwing up their hands in panic and amazement. They reached Poun on the 24th, and halted for resupply and on orders not to go any farther because of the general confusion of the situation. However, the 1st Cavalry commander, Gen. Hobart Gay, finally got them sprung, and on the 26th they were off again. At suppertime, sixty miles up the road, the tanks ran out of gas. Refueled from their own spare cans in trucks, and in three North Korean trucks that blundered into them, they kept on once more. After dark they reached Chonan and found it full of Communist soldiers. Here they connected with the main highway to Seoul, and the commander of the lead tank asked a surprised North Korean soldier for directions. Put on the right road, they barreled on up the highway, getting progressively more strung out, with a trail of astonished, fearful, or bemused North Koreans in their wake. South of Osan the Americans passed through a force of Communist T34 tanks, and above it through the front lines of the enemy facing northward against the advance of X Corps. The two American forces met at 2226 on the night of September 26; Task Force Lynch had traveled 100 miles since leaving in the morning, most of it through North Koreans. The two American forces met at almost exactly the same spot where Task Force Smith had tried unsuccessfully to stop the North Koreans for the first time on July 5.

The meeting between the Inchon forces and the Pusan-perimeter breakout was important but not definitive. It meant the North Koreans were finished as an army, but not as soldiers. All over the country, units headed northward. The UN dominated the skies and the roads, but thousands of Communist soldiers took to the hills; they had throughout the war so far shown an amazing ability to move across country, and almost invariably it had been they who had held the high ground, that old axiom of infantry fighting. Group after group might be caught in the open or on the roads or around towns, and most of these went into POW camps. But a large number either made it back north or stayed to fight on as guerrillas in the south. These were to cause the United Nations, and South Korea, endless trouble in succeeding months.

For the moment, however, everything was going well, and ahead of schedule. The buildup of X Corps through Inchon continued. The Marines moved toward Seoul; the 7th Division swung wider, guarding the southern flank and then moving around to approach the capital from the south and southeast. The 187th Airborne Regimental Combat Team flew into Kimpo airport and was soon employed on the left flank of the Marines, as were units of Korean marines.

Seoul was not to be had for nothing, however, for the North Koreans had still some reinforcement capacity, and they brought in elements of their 9th Division to hold the city. The Americans produced a two-pronged drive, with the Marines crossing the Han River below the capital and fighting their way in from the west, while the 7th Division, with Korean infantry units attached, crossed the river right into the heart of the city. In both cases, the North Koreans tried to block the advance by holding defensive positions on hills; the Marines faced a range of hills running north from the river on the western edge of the city, while the Army infantrymen had to take a hill known as South Mountain that dominated the river crossing and the southern part of Seoul.

The fighting was especially desperate on the Marines' front, and all the effort of tanks, flamethrowers, and air support from Corsairs was just barely enough to take the successive heights one by one. On September 24, for example, D Company of the 5th Marines started the day with 206 effectives; it suffered 176 casualties, and it took the key to the ridgeline, Hill 66, with a bayonet charge by its last thirty-three men. Another day's fighting cleared the remainder of the ridge, and the Marines moved on into the city.

To the south, General Almond, dissatisfied with the Marines' being held in the west, committed the 7th Division to its attack. It got across the river and secured South Mountain, aided by a providential ground fog, with little trouble. It then fanned out eastward to take commanding heights a couple of miles outside the capital, in a neat operation that netted a surprised enemy column, caught unawares along a road and nearly wiped out.

By the 25th the North Koreans were beginning to pull out, but they left roadblocks behind. Though General Almond announced the liberation of Seoul on the 25th and MacArthur on the 26th, they were a bit premature. The Marines were still fighting their way through the northern part of the city two days later, clearing out snipers and machine-gun nests.

The United Nations commander was anxious to present the world his victory as quickly as possible. He, his staff, President Rhee and his wife, and assorted dignitaries flew into Kimpo on the 29th, and from there made a ceremonial entry into Seoul. The signs of battle were still everywhere, with troops on the alert, and tanks standing by while bulldozers tried to clear away blocks in the road and rubble from destroyed buildings. During the ceremony, which began at noon in the National Assembly, vibration from nearby artillery brought down several panes of glass, sniper fire could be clearly heard, and those in the group who had helmets put them on. Mac-Arthur spoke for only five minutes; his tone, as usual on such occasions, was somewhat grandiose. He led the largely non-Christian audience in the Lord's Prayer. President Rhee in his response referred to General MacArthur as "the savior of our race." By early afternoon, MacArthur was on his way back to Tokyo, where a flood of congratulatory official messages awaited him. That was fair enough; the whole Inchon conception was his, and he deserved to enjoy it. This may not have been quite the high point of his career, but it was just about his last best moment.

While their commander flew back to Japan, the troops of X Corps and Eighth Army and the United Nations and the Republic of Korea took up their pursuit of a now thoroughly beaten and demoralized enemy. The war had lasted just over three months. The time it should take to finish it off might be measured in weeks, or even days. About the only remaining question was how far they should go.

CHAPTER 5
TO THE YALU

At the beginning of October, with the United Nations forces and their commander both in triumphant full cry, it was time again for some serious diplomatic and political decisions. The question now facing them was how far to go into North Korea. There were basically three options, with possible variations on each.

The first one was that pursuit should simply stop at the old boundary between the two Koreas, the 38th parallel. To do this would be to accept a return to the status quo at the start of the action, and to argue that the "incursion" had been turned back and the enemy's forces destroyed, and that that was sufficient punishment. In retrospect, as this was the final resolution to the matter nearly three years later, this would undoubtedly have been the most sensible alternative.

A second possibility was to continue the advance past the North Korean capital of Pyongyang, taking it, and then halting at the waist of the peninsula, roughly on a line from Sinanju on the west coast to either Wonsan or Hungnam on the east coast. This would have left such a truncated North Korea that it would have possessed little

79

war-making capacity for the foreseeable future, but it would still have provided a buffer zone between an American-sponsored South Korea and a deeply hostile Red China and Manchuria, and the Soviet Union, and if this alternative had been chosen, it might still have been possible to win the war without intervention by North Korea's friends and neighbors.

Finally, the third option was to go all the way to the Yalu River, to destroy the North Korean regime and unite the whole of the peninsula. This would thoroughly punish aggression; it would carry out, by force, all the earlier UN resolutions about uniting Korea, and it would remove the festering sore of the partition. But it carried with it the risk of massive reaction by either China or the Soviet Union, or both.

Debate was necessarily short-lived, for the pace of events meant that decisions had to be reached quickly. At one end of the spectrum of opinion, President Rhee of South Korea was of course most adamant that the advance be continued right to the Yalu, and that his long-standing aim of the unification of the entire peninsula under a democratic government, by which he meant himself, be completed.

Official American attitudes were slightly less aggressive. MacArthur and Generals Collins of the Army and Vandenberg of the Air Force had discussed the matter in July, largely from the point of view of operations, and concentrating on the necessity of destroying North Korea's military capability. The United Nations directive was vague on this point, enjoining its agents "to restore international peace and security in the area," a mission that was obviously subject to wide interpretation. In August the government in Washington began looking toward unification and adopted a more aggressive line in public. Ambassador Austin spoke in the United Nations of a democratic and a "reunited" Korea. Containment was, after all, a policy of reaction that left the initiative largely in the hands of the opposition. Here in Korea, where that opposition had now so patently overreached itself, there was an opportunity to do more than simply "contain" Communism; here was a chance to reverse what the Marxists saw as the inevitable tide of history. Secretary of State Dean Acheson pushed for this, and American policy was finally laid down in NSC 81/1, a document of September 11 which was passed on in modified form as a Joint Chiefs of Staff directive to MacArthur on September 27. Though the document was full of caveats about Chinese or Soviet intervention, its basic point was to permit operations across the parallel into North Korea, and it even contained a longer-range provision for contingency planning on the occupation of the country. In his response to this directive, MacArthur asked for removal of some restrictions and made it clear that he was intending to operate in, and eventually to occupy, all of North Korea; the government in Washington accepted this, and the troops in the field had, in effect, a green light.

The support from and in the United Nations was a bit more tenuous, as might be expected from the nature of the organization, but not unduly so. For one thing, the Russians had returned to the Security Council on August 1, when Soviet Ambassador Jacob Malik not only took up his seat again but also inherited the revolving presidency of the council. From then until mid-September this body fruitlessly debated one motion after another, without accomplishing anything more substantial than the frustration of all the participants.

The General Assembly met on September 19, but it did not discuss Korea in detail until September 30. Meanwhile, Secretary Acheson addressed the Assembly, leaving Korea largely untouched; British Foreign Secretary Ernest Bevin, a Labour statesman of impeccable liberal credentials, called for the unification of Korea; and in a report early in the month, a UN commission on Korea, headed by an Indian, also said unification was the only possible solution for the country. UN Secretary General Trygve Lie's military observer in Korea cautioned against any artificial pause at the 38th parallel. The resolution introduced on September 30 was partially drafted by the Americans, but brought in by Great Britain and jointly sponsored by seven other countries; its wording was unfortunately a bit imprecise, but it called essentially for unification, elections, democratic government, and then the ultimate withdrawal of UN forces. In a week-long debate the Soviets of course opposed it, as did the Yugoslavs. More worrisome was the opposition of India, on the grounds that this motion exceeded the original UN mandate and constituted, in effect, an invasion of North Korea. On October 7 the resolution passed the General Assembly by a vote of forty-seven to five, with seven abstentions. South Korean forces had already crossed the parallel on October 1, but UN forces did not cross until the 9th.

The problem with the UN resolution was that it was based on a false premise: the assumption that the war was all but over, and that all that remained was to round up the residual enemy forces, establish order, hold the elections, and go home. The aim of war, in the famous Clausewitzian phrase, is to destroy the enemy's will to resist. That may or may not entail destroying the enemy. In the case of North Korea, its army was all but destroyed, yet Premier Kim Il Sung kept insisting that his forces had suffered but a temporary setback, and that they would soon be ready to resume the offensive. As far as North Korea itself was concerned, that was so much nonsense. But if the "enemy" should be defined as North Korea plus Communist China and/or Soviet Russia, then it was patently a different equation, and in that case the United Nations' view of the matter, as expressed in its "the war is over and this is how we shall put the pieces back together" resolution, was sadly out of touch with reality.

What, then, was the other side planning or intending to do? No one knew, and assessing Soviet or Chinese intentions was the great guessing game of the moment. American reconnaissance aircraft along the Yalu had several times strayed over into Communist airspace, and there were a couple of serious incidents; in late August two American fighters had strafed a Chinese airfield near Antung in Manchuria; on September 4 a foreign aircraft strayed into an American naval combat air patrol over the Yellow Sea, opened fire, and was shot down. A Navy destroyer recovered the body of one of the crew, a Russian officer. Then on October 8 the Russians complained that two American aircraft had strafed a field a good sixty miles inside Siberia; investigation showed them to be correct, and the United States government formally apologized before the Security Council and offered to pay damages.

Far more ominous than a possible Communist reaction to what were after all accidents of war was the steady movement northward of Chinese Communist troops into Manchuria. A major problem for the Americans was that they were never sure who was pulling whose strings, and whether the Russians or the Chinese represented the greater threat. In the opening months of the war, the Chinese had seemingly paid it little attention, and been much more interested in the ongoing matter of Chiang Kai-shek and the Nationalist presence on Taiwan, a distraction from Korea that confused, complicated, and bothered everyone involved in the Far East. But increasingly from August on, as equilibrium was reached in Korea and the balance tilted toward the United Nations, the Chinese took an interest. In July, American intelligence estimated that the Chinese had 115,000 regular troops in Manchuria and 176,000 in northern China; by late August they thought there were 246,000 in Manchuria, and three weeks later 450,000. Since the United States government had not recognized Communist China, it asked India to pass on messages to soothe Chinese ears. Indian Ambassador to China K. M. Pannikar did so, and reported back that intervention in Korea was highly unlikely. President Truman in a radio broadcast on September 1 disclaimed any desire for Asian territory and specifically sought to reassure, and at the same time warn off, the Chinese.

Unfortunately, at about the same time, General MacArthur and various other American public figures were talking very tough, so that thoroughly confusing signals were emanating from what China might see as official Washington. At the end of September, Chinese Premier Chou En-lai called in Ambassador Pannikar and flatly told him China would intervene if United States troops crossed the 38th parallel, though not if just South Korean ones did. The Indians immediately passed this on to the British, who sent it to the Americans. Almost everyone concerned gave this far less credence than it deserved; the Central Intelligence Agency discounted it, and both President Truman and Secretary Acheson thought it part of a bluff to scare off the United Nations, then debating its Korean resolution. Though government communications to MacArthur grew increasingly cautionary, they did not effectively rein him in.

Within the combat area itself, further decisions at this time were creating difficulties. At first sight they seemed to be of an esoteric military nature, but they subsequently had a bearing on the situation at the time of the Chinese intervention.

When General Almond's X Corps landed at Inchon and carried out the liberation of Seoul, it was under General MacArthur's direct command, independent of Walker's Eighth Army in the Pusan perimeter. However, when Eighth Army broke out, advanced up to Seoul, and linked up with X Corps, it was to be expected that Almond would come under Walker, forming a third corps in his army. This at least was what Walker expected, and he queried MacArthur about it late in September. MacArthur replied, however, that he was going to move X Corps into General Headquarters Reserve, and keep it under his own control. MacArthur had decided that he would use the corps on the east coast, for a landing at Wonsan.

The official explanation for this was that the east and west coasts were so substantially split by the Taebaek Mountains that it was not feasible for Walker on the west to command Almond on the east; but most authorities have thought that there were a number of other, less tangible, reasons, and that the split was a mistake. Every field commander wants to be as nearly independent as possible—the idea is simply built into the military system. Almond certainly did, and it was obvious that he would have far more freedom of action under the distant command of MacArthur in Japan than under the close control of Walker in Korea. Almond was also MacArthur's protégé and loyal follower, and the two enjoyed a closer relationship than either did with Walker. MacArthur also seems to have wanted to keep command, as much as possible, of a field force, another element inherent in the military framework. So for all these reasons, geographical ones which may have been valid and personal ones which probably were not, MacArthur split his forces, not against the advice—no one gave MacArthur advice when he had not asked for it—but certainly against the instincts of most of his senior people.

The idea of a landing on Wonsan had been current since the dark days of the perimeter fighting, but it had on the whole relatively little to recommend it. Taking Wonsan, or the Wonsan-Hungnam area, would interdict east-coast movement, but that point in its favor was rapidly being made irrelevant by events. The ROK I Corps had crossed the 38th parallel on October 1; a week later, against relatively light resistance, it was already more than halfway to Wonsan, and in the event, it reached the port long before X Corps made its landing there. But even more thorny than all this was the logistics and movement question involved.

There were three possible ways to get X Corps from Seoul and Inchon on the west coast to Wonsan on the east coast. Each had its drawbacks. The first was by sea around the peninsula; unfortunately, outloading the corps through Inchon would tie up both naval shipping and port facilities, both already strained by bringing supplies in through Inchon for the fighting there. The second alternative was to take the corps back by road and rail to Pusan, down the roads that Eighth Army had just come up. Here again the traffic snarls and the strain on a marginal and war-damaged transportation system would be enormous. The third alternative would be to use X Corps as part of the advance northward on Pyongyang; from there either it could be shifted over to Wonsan, or Eighth Army could line up in the central part of the peninsula east of it. This had the advantage of keeping the pressure on the North Koreans and being administratively simple; Walker favored it, and for obvious reasons so did the naval commanders, who were rapidly reaching the conclusion that the Wonsan landing was going to be entirely superfluous. It offered, however, no excuse for Almond to retain his independence under MacArthur.

At the first of October, MacArthur decided to move X Corps around to the east coast. The 1st Marine Division was to go by ship from Inchon to Wonsan; the 7th Division went by road and rail all the way back to Pusan, loaded aboard ship, and went up the east coast from there. Neither division had to make an opposed landing, which was of course fortunate for them. But the advance was slowed, and communications and transport facilities were strained; and the whole question left commanders with an unhappy sense that matters had gone slightly adrift, and decisions been made for reasons that would not quite hold water. The shuffle also landed the Navy in trouble for the first time in the war.

In any military service, as in any other human institution, there are high-profile elements and poor relations. In the United States Navy, during the post–World War II years, emphasis was placed very much on the aircraft carrier and what it could do, especially while the Navy battled the nascent U.S. Air Force for pride of place and primacy of mission. Until Inchon, amphibious forces, for example, received little consideration. But the poorest relation of all was the mine forces. No one really likes mines. Since their first use in the mid-nineteenth century, when they were called torpedoes—when Admiral Farragut at Mobile Bay shouted "Damn the torpedoes; full speed ahead!" he was really damning mines—they have always been a weapon of the inferior naval power. The Russians had used them effectively, and actually had a viable tradition of mine warfare; the Germans temporarily scared the Royal Navy out of the North Sea with them in 1914. But they are basically a passive weapon; they just lie there, secretly, waiting to blow the bottom out of honest, unsuspecting ships, so they are generally regarded with something close to loathing by most sailors. Another reason for mine warfare's poor status is that the work is done by small vessels, commanded by relatively junior officers; few commanders get promoted to admiral in the mine business, and, of course, it is admirals who make policy decisions about navies and naval construction. After World War II, the United States almost totally dismantled its mine warfare forces. There had been 550 minesweepers in the Pacific Fleet in World War II; in July 1950 there were one operational sweeper and six wooden-hulled auxiliaries available for Korea. There were a few more scattered around the Pacific, where for five years they had been engaged in the grueling drudgery of removing mines left over from the war.

But the Russians, and therefore the North Koreans, were adept at mine warfare, and the Navy found itself engaged in a full-scale battle of little ships to clear the approaches to Wonsan harbor. The sweepers did not arrive until October 10, and the landing was scheduled for the 20th. Fortunately they did not realize that the Communists had mined 400 square miles with more than 3,000 mines, both contact and magnetic, covered, until the drive up the coast of the ROK Army, by shore batteries.

The sweepers were soon in trouble, and it took some novel efforts, most of them not very successful, to get the job done. Aircraft carriers supplied bombing strikes on the minefields, trying to blast a path through them. Long-range patrol planes, and some early helicopter patrols, were used to try to spot the mines below the surface; underwater demolition teams, "frogmen," were brought in by small boat to help as well. But most of the work was done by the little steel- or wooden-hulled sweepers, with paravanes and cables, and tried-and-true, but tedious and dangerous, methods of World War II. On October 12, a mine blew up under U.S.S. *Pirate*, breaking the ship's back; the sweeper capsized in four minutes. Soon after, *Pledge* was mined and sunk; there were ninety-two casualties between the two ships. Two more were subsequently lost, one of them a South Korean wooden sweeper that was literally blown to bits. It was October 25 before the Navy had pushed a safe channel through the minefield, so for a small investment the Communists inflicted both delay and casualties—and made the U.S. Navy rethink some of its priorities.

Meanwhile, Eighth Army continued its pursuit of the North Koreans. From Seoul to the 38th parallel was about thirty miles, from there to Pyongyang another sixty. Walker ordered U.S. I Corps to advance north from the capital toward Kaesong, then to fan out to the western bulge of the peninsula. In the central mountains, the South Korean II Corps was to push ahead, while the ROK I Corps continued its drive up the east coast. Walker's second American corps, IX, was still busy clearing up bypassed units and stragglers in central South Korea. It was to move up behind U.S. I Corps. The leading elements of the 1st Cavalry moved out of Seoul on October

5 and reached Kaesong, and the 38th parallel, on the 7th. By the evening of the 8th, the rest of the division was concentrated around Kaesong. They were ready to cross the parallel the next morning.

Numbers were still growing. The South Koreans had added a new division to their forces. In late September the first unit from the Philippines arrived, the 10th Infantry Battalion Combat Team, with a strength of 1,200 men, and on October 3 the 3rd Battalion of the Royal Australian Regiment joined the British Brigade, which now became the British Commonwealth Brigade. This force, all volunteers or long-service professional soldiers, became something of the wonder of the war, and American accounts, both official and personal, speak with near awe of both the military conduct and combat ferocity of the Commonwealth troops.

For the drive into North Korea, the United Nations had available just about 350,000 troops, of whom 230,000 were in combat units. They thought there might be 100,000 remnants and untrained replacements still left in the North Korean Army, and in his operation order of October 2, MacArthur had been more concerned with terrain features than with possible enemy opposition. The Air Force, for example, had all but run out of worthwhile targets for B-29s by the time the ground forces closed up to the parallel. On October 1, and again on the 7th, MacArthur broadcast messages prepared in Washington, calling on North Korea to surrender, but, as expected, neither got any positive response from Kim Il Sung; what the first one did elicit was Chou En-lai's conversation with Ambassador Pannikar, but no one was disposed to credit it. So on the morning of the 9th, the UN forces started up the road to Pyongyang.

In the first stages of this move, it did not seem at all as if the enemy was finished. The 7th Cavalry Regiment had to fight its way across the Yesong River, and the 8th and 5th Cavalry got involved in a very nasty fight with parts of two North Korean infantry divisions as they moved north of Kaesong. This battle became known as the Kumchon pocket, and it took four or five days before the Communists finally were broken up. To the right of the Americans the ROK 1st Division moved steadily northward through remnants of the North Korean 17th Armored. And away over on the east coast, the South Koreans got to Wonsan on the 10th, the same day the minesweepers arrived, and moved from there fifty miles north to Hungnam by the 17th. Of the units of X Corps, the 1st Marines landed administratively, or unopposed, at Wonsan on the 26th. For seven days they had steamed back and forth off the port, waiting for the mines to be cleared, a week that was disgustedly christened Operation Yo-Yo. The 7th Infantry Division, after having traveled overland back to Pusan, sat aboard ship for ten days, then steamed up the coast to land north of Wonsan, at Iwon, again behind the advancing South Koreans. The off-loading here was not completed until November 9.

Once the thin North Korean crust was cracked below Pyongyang, there was not much resistance left. The Communists mined the roads and did their best to demolish what the Air Force had not already destroyed for them. They blocked the advance where they could, often with single artillery pieces or machine-gun nests, but by October 15, UN troops were less than thirty miles from Pyongyang, and its fall was assured. The war did look as if it was indeed all but over, and it was against this backdrop that General MacArthur and President Truman met at the celebrated Wake Island Conference.

Wake Island is a small flyspeck in the middle of the Pacific Ocean. Its chief claim to fame was its spirited defense by a little garrison of U.S. Marines who resisted the Japanese in December 1941. President Truman decided early in October that it was high time he and MacArthur met face to face, and he suggested the meeting to Gen. George C. Marshall, the new Secretary of Defense, on the 9th. Truman actually suggested Pearl Harbor on the 14th or 16th as the site for the meeting, and when MacArthur opted for Wake on the 15th, that was agreeable to everyone, even though Wake is about 1,500 miles farther west from Pearl Harbor.

The meeting was indeed overdue. The President and his Far East commander had never met, MacArthur had been many years out of the United States, and though there was at this point no real antagonism between the two men, there was a certain creeping sense that the government in Washington and its general were operating on slightly divergent wavelengths. Truman, who thought of himself as an essentially simple, straightforward man—though few who think of themselves that way actually are—just wanted a meeting and a discussion, and quite possibly a little political capital. MacArthur's attitude was rather more complex, but he was neither the initiator nor the senior at the meeting; he seems to have treated it as a bit of an intrusion at what was a very busy time for him, and perhaps to have disliked a reminder, however pleasant Truman was, that MacArthur was not as independent as he would have liked to be.

The actual conference has been incredibly overdramatized, to the point where some narrators have the two principals glaring out of airplane windows, each determined that the other shall be the first to land, a twentieth-century version of Napoleon's meeting with Czar Alexander on the raft at Tilsit. In fact, MacArthur arrived on the evening of the 14th, and was waiting to greet the President when his plane touched down early the next morning. They had a private meeting, lasting nearly an hour, which seems to have been of an exploratory, getting-to-know-you nature; the only touchy issue was perhaps a comment on a message MacArthur had sent in August to the Veterans of Foreign Wars over American policy toward the Chinese Nationalists, but this now appeared to be a dead issue.

In the general conference which followed, lasting about an hour and a half, there was no agenda and no formal minutes were kept, though several people took notes, which subsequently formed the basis for a memorandum on the discussion. Much of the conference was devoted to what should be done with Korea, after the war was successfully concluded. When asked, MacArthur completely discounted the possibility of Chinese or Soviet intervention, saying that if the Chinese came in, "there would be the greatest slaughter." Though this has been regarded by MacArthur's detractors as almost criminal complacence or stupidity, it coincided with the views of just about everyone else in the U.S. government at the time, and therefore did not elicit the more searching examination that it warranted.

By midmorning the conference was over; there then followed some conversations between individual participants on various items, some political, some technical, and a final short meeting between Truman and MacArthur in which they issued a statement, previously prepared by the White House staff, to the crowd of accompanying newsmen. Before noon, the President was on his way back to Washington and MacArthur was flying toward Tokyo. The whole conference was really very superficial, and its effect was but to place a temporary, and ultimately misleading, patch over what were actually profound differences of both personality and philosophy between the general and the President.

Against steadily lessening opposition, the advance into North Korea continued. As the drive opened up, it turned into a race to be the first into Pyongyang, with units leapfrogging and bypassing each other on the roads going north. There was a great deal of confusion; the 27th British Commonwealth Brigade, for example, reached the town of Sariwon on one road before large numbers of North Koreans, fleeing before the U.S. 24th Division, on another road. On the night of the 17th and 18th, the North Koreans passed through the town, ran into roadblocks north of it, passed back through the town a second time, and were finally broken up and captured in the morning. Throughout the night, isolated British or Australians pretended they were Russians, while isolated North Koreans pretended they were South Koreans.

In the more mountainous regions southeast of Pyongyang, the Republic of Korea forces were making even better progress, as the enemy faded away before them. And yet farther east of that, over on the other coast, they were fanning out to the north and west; indeed, one of the units from Wonsan, the ROK 6th Division, was actually coming west on the roads from that port, and was part of the race for Pyongyang.

The city was entered almost simultaneously by the troops of the 1st Cavalry Division from the south and of the ROK 1st Division from the east. The defenders held a couple of ridgelines and blew up bridges in front of the cavalrymen, and they held even harder against the South Koreans during their approach, but there were not enough Communists left to delay the fall of the city for any appreciable time. The survivors, following their government, fled northward.

The next useful marking point was the Chongchon River; halfway from Pyongyang to the Yalu, it was indeed the last major terrain feature in western Korea before the border. In an attempt to cut off the North Korean retreat, to capture government officials, and to rescue American prisoners who were being evacuated northward, MacArthur decided to employ his only airborne unit in a blocking position. This was the 187th Regimental Combat Team, and it dropped successfully on October 20. One battalion jumped over Sukchon and the other over Sunchon, thus seizing the two main roads leading north from the capital. MacArthur observed the operation, the first in which heavy equipment was parachuted in with the troops, and pronounced it a great success. Technically it was, but it did little to the North Koreans; their government had long fled, and there were few troops south of the blocking position, most of them having already crossed the Chongchon. The rear guards that were caught between the airborne forces and the advancing ground troops were destroyed or broken up in some nasty little firefights over the next few days.

The hope of rescuing prisoners was equally, and even more tragically, disappointed. Regularly during the advance, the UN forces found escaped prisoners wandering around the hills; local peasants also frequently led them to new graves, where prisoners had been executed and hastily buried. There was constant rumor of trains full of POWs, who were always just a little bit ahead, or hidden in a tunnel, or off on another spur line, like the El Dorado of the conquistadores. On October 21, north of Sunchon, just past a railroad tunnel, the Americans found a mass grave; several survivors staggered out of the brush, where they had been hiding after playing dead. The North Koreans had stopped a train at that point, removed about 100 American prisoners from it, ostensibly for the evening meal, and then shot them as they sat in circles waiting their turns to be fed. Some seventy-three bodies were found, plus about twenty survivors, most wounded, who had escaped the massacre. Two days later the South Korean 6th Division found another twenty-eight bodies, and a few more survivors, a little farther north.

The war was now virtually over. The North Korean government had moved first to Sinuiju, on the south bank at the mouth of the Yalu, and then had gone upstream to Kanggye in the mountains; this might have been considered ominous, for this was old-time guerrilla country, back from the days of fighting the Japanese. But there was really nothing much left for the North Koreans to fight with. In September MacArthur had proposed to hold his non–South Korean forces at a line running roughly from the mouth of the Chongchon across to Hamhung; in mid-October he extended this limit north to a gentle arc which allowed a buffer zone of about twenty miles in the west and sixty or more in the east. This still seemed to satisfy everyone, and the South Korean troops kept on advancing against increasingly light, and disintegrating, opposition.

Then on October 24, MacArthur changed his mind yet again; he lifted all restrictions on the movement of his forces and urged an all-out pursuit right to the Yalu. On both east and west coasts the ground forces took off on what they thought and hoped was the mopping-up phase of the war. In Washington there was some consternation, and the Joint Chiefs immediately asked MacArthur why he had seized the bit in this way. He replied that it was necessary militarily, and that he considered it within the spirit of his general mandate, though in fact it was far from it. The Joint Chiefs might well have balked at this; after all, they were MacArthur's boss.

Instead they swallowed both their misgivings and their pride and let him have his way. MacArthur's stock was high after the success of Inchon, and General Collins, the Army Chief of Staff and MacArthur's ostensible superior, had been a captain and instructor at West Point when MacArthur was superintendent. Setting all those intangibles aside, the tradition in the United States Army is that the man on the spot is left to do his job, and this was one of those decisions which just might, by stretching things a little, still be construed as a military one.

On the 25th the UN forces went off again. The U.S. 24th Infantry and 1st Cavalry divisions, with the British Commonwealth Brigade attached, crossed the Chongchon and fanned out to the north and west. To their right the ROK 1st Division moved northward, and to the right again the ROK II Corps also pushed north in the mountains. One element of this corps, a reinforced reconnaissance platoon of the 7th Regiment, ROK 6th Division, was away out on a limb, a good thirty miles ahead of everyone else, and actually reached the Yalu on the 26th. There was a great gap to the east, through the mountains, but over on the other coast the 1st Marines were landing at Wonsan, to be followed by the 3rd Division, and the 7th Division was about to land at Iwon. The ROK I Corps was already moving up into the mountains, where it would shortly be followed by the Americans.

Back in Pusan, new troops were arriving to share the task of the United Nations. A battalion was en route from Thailand, and a Turkish brigade arrived; so did a Netherlands battalion, and the advance party of the 29th British Brigade. Ten thousand Canadians had volunteered for service in Korea, and their advance group reached Pusan early in November; most were held back in Canada. They were all going to be too late; the Americans were expecting to eat turkey back in Japan for Thanksgiving dinner.

Yet someone had missed something. For ahead of the South Koreans and the United Nations forces, or squatting silently in the hills as they went by, were thousands of Chinese soldiers. In the mountains above the east coast sat the Chinese 42nd Army, and facing the troops on the west coast were the Chinese 38th Army, the Chinese 39th Army, the Chinese 40th Army, the Chinese 50th Army, and the Chinese 66th Army. The terms are a little misleading, for what in the Chinese forces was called an army would be called a corps in western military parlance. Nonetheless, there were still elements of six corps-sized formations facing the UN command, and at that moment, nobody knew they were there.

Even when the Chinese first attacked, the Americans were so convinced they were on the edge of victory they refused to believe the evidence. Starting on the 25th, the Chinese hit the ROK 6th Infantry Division; in the space of a few hours, the division was virtually destroyed, several of its separate regiments dissolving before the Chinese attack; those individuals who survived did so by taking to the hills, and a few formations fought their way back to the Chong-chon with the help of tactical air support that intervened during the daylight hours. All of a sudden, the ROK II Corps was on the point of total collapse.

At the same time, a few miles farther to the west, South Koreans and Americans were cut off and surrounded at the little town of Unsan. Eighth Army headquarters could not believe the reports it was getting, and was still pushing on the "pursuit" of the "remnants" while some of its units were being overrun. Unsan turned into a full-scale ordeal. For some time it had to be supplied by air, then the Americans pushed the 8th Cavalry through to open up the road, then the Chinese cut it again, and ambushed the Americans and Koreans trying to fight their way out. The ROK 15th Infantry Regiment was destroyed, and the 8th Cavalry was nearly so, losing about 600 men in the battle.

Faced with an intervention they could no longer ignore, the UN forces, even those who had not been directly attacked, pulled back to the Chongchon and held a bridgehead over the river. While they thought this new development over, X Corps on the east coast was continuing its advance. The ROK Capital Division, which had led all the way up the coast, continued on to the northeast. The 1st Marines were on the road into the mountains, heading for some reservoirs upcountry, and troops of the 7th Infantry Division, moving out of Iwon, got all the way to the border; the 17th Infantry reached Hyesanjin on the morning of November 21, and General Almond came up to stand on the banks of the Yalu, looking across into Manchuria.

The Chinese, meanwhile, after their startling and disturbing appearance, faded back into the countryside, leaving Eighth Army, MacArthur, and everyone else to wonder what on earth was going on. Was this the precursor to a full-scale invasion? Was it a scratch force of mixed Koreans and Chinese? Did they mean business or not?

Gradually the alarm subsided, as the early November days went by and the Chinese did not resume their attacks. The intelligence estimates became more optimistic, and the Chinese seemed less threatening. The Americans were in fact suffering from the victory disease, and from their own preconceptions, which made them discount the tangible but spotty evidence before them. They would admit that there might be as many as 50,000 Chinese in North Korea; the pessimists went as high as 70,000. They would have been utterly appalled to know that there were now six Chinese armies, eighteen divisions, between them and the Yalu River and the end of the war.

November 23 was Thanksgiving; the Americans had not made it back to Japan for turkey, though most of them managed to get it in Korea. The next morning they started north again. Maybe they'd be home for Christmas.

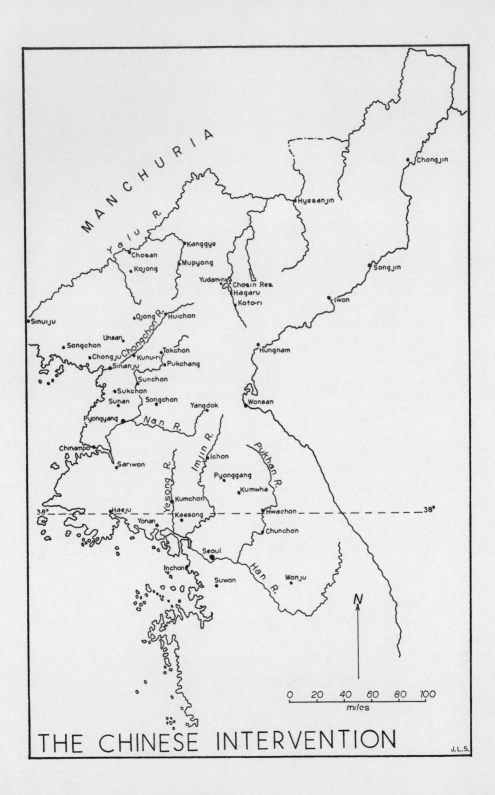

MANCHURIA

Chongjin

Hyesanjin

Kanggye
Chosan   Songjin
Kojong   Mupyong
              Yudam-ni
              Chosin Res.
              Hagaru   Iwon
              Koto-ri
Sinuiju   Ojong R. Huichon
        Unsan   Hungnam
    Songchon
    Chongju Kunu-ri Tokchon
        Sinanju Pukchang
              Sunchon
    Sukchon
Sunan Songchon Yangdok
Pyongyang   Wonsan
            Nan R.
Chinampo
        Sariwon   Ichon
                        Pyonggang
                    Kumwha
              Kumchon
38°   Haeju   Kaesong   Hwachon   38°
        Yonan   Chunchon
              Seoul
        Inchon   Wonju
            Suwon

N

0   20   40   60   80   100
        miles

THE CHINESE INTERVENTION

J.L.S.

CHAPTER 6
THE CHINESE INTERVENTION

When the United Nations forces resumed their offensive on November 24, no one was quite sure what was going on. General MacArthur's view of the campaign was one of classic simplicity. Eighth Army would drive to the border; X Corps would move northwest, also toward the border; the enemy would be caught in the pincer between the two, and his residual forces destroyed. Intelligence estimates were that there might be as many as 80,000 North Koreans, in more or less reconstituted formations, supported by something between 40,000 and 80,000 Chinese. Even taking the upper estimates, a possible 160,000 Communists, battered by the events of the last months, should not pose an insurmountable problem.

General Walker, at least, proposed a fairly cautious advance. He had three corps in line now, U.S. I and IX, and ROK II on his eastern flank. He developed a series of phase lines for the drive, and did not want any one outfit strung out on a limb. Over on the X Corps front, General Almond had a peculiar situation, for the center of his position was already on the border. To his extreme right the ROK Capital Division was away up at Chongjin on the coast, the farthest north of any UN formation. The U.S. 7th Division was in the center, touching the Manchurian border. The major advance was to be made by the 1st Marine Division, around the Changjin or Chosin Reservoir. Behind it, security was provided by the 3rd Infantry Division, which was also, with great difficulty, patrolling into the western gap between X Corps and Eighth Army. That gap was still a good fifty miles wide, and only once in the whole period had X Corps units actually linked up for a short moment with patrols from Eighth Army, an effort that had taken several days and borne no fruit. Both commanders were very conscious of the gap and the danger it represented, but there was little they could do about it. Intensified aerial reconnaissance before and during the offensive failed to reveal anything; there might be some enemy soldiers there somewhere, but if they were, the Air Force could not find them.

The low estimate of enemy resources seemed initially to be correct. Things went well on the 24th; on the left flank, the 24th Infantry Division led off the attack and made good progress against light opposition. The rest of I Corps, and IX Corps to its right, also went ahead. The South Koreans met a bit stiffer opposition inland, but still they too made some gains. The second day looked like being a repeat of the first. Assessments from MacArthur's staff were mildly optimistic.

Then on the evening of the 25th the Chinese Communists slammed into Eighth Army's inland flank. The front was suddenly alive with enemy soldiers, in a repetition on an even larger scale of the late-October surprise. By design or good luck the Chinese hit the weakest elements of Walker's army. First they struck against the ROK II Corps; they hit the 8th Division, on the inland flank, and within hours they had broken it up. Then their attack spread to the 7th and 6th divisions, and these in their turn were sent streaming off in defeat. It was the same old tactics as before: infiltration, roadblocks, and then massive frontal assaults that swamped the ROK positions and threw their soldiers back against the blocks to be destroyed. The U.S. 2nd Infantry Division, the righthand element of IX Corps, hitherto in the middle of the advance, suddenly found itself with an open right flank, an invitation to disaster. Farther west the Chinese struck against the ROK 1st Division, in the middle of the U.S. I Corps line. This was a good division, and it held after being pushed back a couple of miles. But then the attack spread all along the line, in such numbers that the UN offensive simply stopped cold. Only the 24th

Division on the seaward flank was left momentarily alone, and it could do no good by a further advance. It too stopped, and was soon caught up in what was undeniably a retreat. By daylight of the 26th, the war, at least in western Korea, had assumed a whole new complexion.

The advance of Almond's X Corps was not even sheduled to begin until the 27th. Some formations of the corps were in fact countermarching before that date, for the ROK troops above Chongjin on the coast were being brought back, as were the 7th Infantry Division troops from Hyesanjin on the Manchurian border. The brunt of the advance was to be borne by the 1st Marines, supported by other units of the 7th Infantry. General Almond had not been especially happy with the Marines' advance toward the Changjin Reservoir, and they had not been happy with it either. Almond wanted them to move faster than they did, and the divisional commander, Maj. Gen. Oliver Smith, having very little confidence in his mission, had instead moved with caution not usually associated with the Marines. It was extremely fortunate that he had done so. On the eve of the offensive, Smith had his division more or less concentrated at three points along the winding, narrow road that ran from the coast at Hungnam eighty miles up to the reservoir. Fifty-three miles from the coast was Koto-ri; here Col. Lewis Puller, the legendary "Chesty" Puller, the most highly decorated man in the history of the Marine Corps, had his own 1st Marine Regiment, some Army infantry, and some Royal Marine Commandos from the British, about 4,200 men in all. Smith himself had his headquarters another twelve miles north, at Hakawoo-ri; there were about 3,000 men here, and they were building an airstrip at the south end of the reservoir. The point of the division was fourteen miles up the western side of the reservoir, and here were the 5th and 7th Marine regiments, at Yudam-ni, slated to lead the advance to the northwest. Finally, on the eastern side of the reservoir were two flanking units, a battalion each of the 31st and 32nd Infantry of the 7th Division, and a supporting battalion, the 57th Field Artillery, another 2,500 men.

Thus with the ROK II Corps already collapsing, the two prongs of the United Nations pincer were represented by the Americans around the Changjin Reservoir on the east, and the 2nd Infantry Division at Kunu-ri on the west. Between them, they now knew, there were a great many Chinese; they did not know much more than that. Intelligence analysts at X Corps, at Eighth Army, at Far East Command in Tokyo, and in Washington itself were desperately trying to figure out how many Chinese there actually were, where they had come from and how they got there, and what they were now going to do.

It was indeed difficult to figure out how strong the enemy was, or what formations were present. Captured Chinese troops constantly, but inconsistently, referred to their parent organizations as "units," but where the Americans interpreted that term as meaning "battalion," it often meant "division" instead. There was thus a repeated underrating of the Chinese numbers, deriving not only from this simple failure, but more generally from the American refusal to believe the Chinese were present in the force that they actually were. In fact, by the end of November, the Chinese strength had grown even greater than it had been in October. Only slowly were the UN commands able to put names on their opponents and fit them into a coherent organization. They looked something like this.

The overall commander of the People's Liberation Army, as they called themselves, or the Chinese Communist Forces, as the United Nations called them, was Gen. Chu Teh; in his mid-sixties, he had been on the Long March and was one of the leading figures in the Communist victory in the Chinese Civil War. His deputy commander was Peng Teh-huai, another veteran of the Long March and the war for control of China. Under these men were two formations, the 4th and 3rd field armies. The 4th Field Army, commanded by Gen. Lin Piao, had crossed into Korea in October, and it was this body that had struck the Eighth Army and caused its retreat to the Chongchon, in the campaign which the Communists called their "first phase intervention." The 3rd Field Army was commanded by Gen. Chen Yi, and it crossed the Yalu and moved into Korea in the interval between the October battles and the opening of the major offensive in November. Once in Korea, units from these two field armies were subordinated to different commands, so that most, but not all, of the 4th Field Army divisions were controlled by XIII Army Group, and most, but again not all, of 3rd Field Army's divisions were controlled by IX Army Group. Though this scheme is somewhat simplified, XIII Army Group generally opposed Eighth Army, while IX Army Group stood against X Corps. Again, just as a Chinese army is about the size of a western or American corps, a Chinese army group is about the size of an American army. The dozen or so remaining North Korean divisions retained a largely fictional independence; from the time of their intervention, the Chinese took over the running of the war.

Interpolating back from the way it worked to what it must have been originally, the plan of the Chinese was that they should use their cross-country mobility to filter into the fatal gap between the United Nations forces on the two coasts, and then attack them more or less simultaneously on their open flanks. Pushing down through the mountains, they would cut them off from the south, drive them back to the seacoasts, and either destroy them in the field or force them into the sea. It was an ambitious program, but it had begun well—the Chinese were in place, and the victims were ignorant of the trap. MacArthur might well have echoed Wellington's complaint of Napoleon before Waterloo, ". . . humbugged me, by God!"

How had it happened? How had the Chinese slipped a force that now numbered thirty divisions and 300,000 fighting men into Korea under the noses of the United Nations and their commander? The answer to that must be twofold. Psychologically, people tend to see what they want to see. Even though American intelligence analysts knew of major troop movements northward through China to Manchuria, they chose not to see in that imminent intervention. Just as in December 1941 they were convinced that Japan would not attack them, and therefore disregarded subtle signs that it was about to do so, in the fall of 1950 they ignored whatever signs there were that the Chinese were about to move into Korea, including, in this case, Chou En-lai's statement to the Indians that they would do just that. The distinguished British authority on the Korean War, Davis Rees, said that Inchon was imagination and intuition over sound military logic; the intelligence failure two months later was that too.

On a much more practical level, the Chinese had done their work extraordinarily well. There was an enormous amount of after-the-fact complaint about intelligence failures, but the simple point was that the Chinese armies successfully evaded UN reconnaissance efforts. They were not picked up by air, and ground reconnaissance did not penetrate the huge gap between the two UN forces. A couple of truck convoys were spotted by aircraft, but nothing to give away the presence of thirty divisions; peasants reported "lots of soldiers" in the hills, but to the untrained eye of a scared peasant, lots of soldiers might be anything from a squad out foraging to a regiment on the march. What was really more striking than the United Nations' failure was the supreme march discipline of the Chinese forces. These were no amateurs. They were instead well-trained, battle-hardened troops, and they were something quite unusual in the last century of Chinese history—they were winners. They had fought against the Japanese, and against the Chinese Nationalists; they were a lean army, strong on infantry, short on logistics. They could, and did, march twenty miles a day for days on end, and when they got within the range of UN reconnaissance, they could march twenty miles a night for nights on end. An entire battalion would freeze at the first sound of an aircraft, and stay frozen until the sound was gone; officers could and did shoot anyone who moved, for whatever reason. At first light they faded into the hills and gullies, and their camouflage was as good as their marching discipline. They were in many ways more like the armies of World War I than the motorized and mechanized western armies of World War II, or of the UN in Korea, but as Kipling said, often "the odds are on the cheaper man." These were the people who were now going to try conclusions with the United Nations.

By the morning of November 26, the storm which had blown away ROK II Corps was beating against General Walker's open right flank. Large numbers of Chinese were bypassing Eighth Army and moving almost unhindered to the south, and the envelopment of the UN force was in full swing. Walker tried to use Gen. Laurence Keiser's 2nd Infantry Division as the shoulder to shore up his flank, and he committed his reserves on Keiser's right. It was like trying to stop a flood by holding out one's hand.

The first to go were the newly arrived Turkish Brigade; 5,000 strong, they were told to march up from Kunu-ri to the north and stem the Chinese assault. The Turks were widely hailed as fierce and enduring fighters, which indeed they were, but with the normal confusions of war, and the added difficulties of language in this new war, and the overwhelming strength of the Chinese, they got almost nowhere. In fact, they got about seven miles, to a little village called Wawon, and there the Chinese ground them to shreds. Prisoners they reported having taken turned out to be a few hundred forlorn South Koreans, trying to find someone to shelter them in the disaster. After a day's hard fighting, sometimes with bayonets, what was left of the Turks was lucky to reach 2nd Division's lines. Walker then tried putting his general reserve, the 1st Cavalry, into the gap, then the British Commonwealth Brigade, but there simply was not enough strength to push the Chinese back, or even to deflect them much in their march south. Walker ordered a general retreat.

Meanwhile the 2nd Division had been holding that shoulder position for Eighth Army; now, when the reserve commitment had failed to rebuild a flank, it began to come back. They got across the Chongchon all right, but around Kunu-ri they ran into an ambush. It was a giant repeat of what had happened in the early days of the campaign. About 7,000 men of the division were aboard trucks for the run south, a long unwieldy column interspread with ambulances, towed guns, service trucks, and all other kinds of vehicles that a modern army drags behind it to give it mobility. After the heavy fighting and anxiety of the last week as rear guard, the soldiers were blissfully happy to hunker down in the trucks and relax, to look forward to a hot meal and a change of clothes.

But an entire Chinese division had gotten ahead of them, and now lined a five-mile-long stretch south of Kunu-ri. This narrow defile was corked at its southern end by an even narrower piece of road simply called "the pass." The Communists had machine guns, mortars, rifles, and even heavy weapons; in some cases they were dug in a mere 100 yards from the road. When the head of the American column reached the pass, they opened up all along the line. The road was too narrow to deploy or maneuver; all the Chinese had to do was knock out the lead vehicle and the last one, and they had a shooting gallery. Within seconds the entire column was a shambles, trucks burning, slewed off the road, crashing into each other, overturning. The soldiers were lashed by machine guns and pounded by mortars. Nothing is harder for tired troops than to have to bring themselves back up to battle awareness again after they have relaxed and begun to rest. The column just fell apart. Dead and wounded were everywhere, and most of the soldiers sat in the ditches, scrambled under trucks, or simply milled about aimlessly in the road while the Chinese raked them. An appalled Keiser worked his way forward through the wreckage. Here and there he saw a man shooting back; one was calmly firing a mortar; some were helping wounded; most were useless. He finally got to the head of column at the pass. He stumbled over what he took to be a corpse lying in the road, whereupon it sat up and called him a son of a bitch; Keiser was so surprised all he could think of to do was apologize.

Slowly, painfully, the soldiers began to react. It was the Air Force that saved those who were saved. The fliers responded unstintingly to the division's calls for help. Fighter-bombers flew sortie after sortie, up and down the line, strafing and dropping napalm on the Chinese position. In some cases they came so close that napalm spattered onto the road, and cartridge cases from the planes' machine guns virtually rained down on the soldiers.

Help came too from the British, who attacked north along the road to reach the embattled column and open the southern block at the pass. Finally the Americans began to shake loose; by the end of the action about 4,000 of the original 7,000 got through the ambush. They lost all their vehicles and heavy equipment. Withdrawn south to Sunchong, the division was no longer battleworthy after its ordeal.

Fortunately the Chinese gave the UN forces a bit of respite. Walker would have liked to hold before Pyongyang, but he could not stop there. A retreat gathers momentum just as an advance does, and on December 5 the Eighth Army gave up the North Korean capital and moved on south, to draw up in a long semicircular arc just south of the city. Walker hoped he might be able to rebuild his line.

Eighth Army's ordeal was matched by that of X Corps. In northeastern Korea it was already winter, and up in the mountains around the reservoirs, the temperature had fallen to thirty or forty degrees below zero, with forty-to-fifty-mile-an-hour winds dropping it even further. Engine oil froze, gun breeches froze, morphine froze, blood plasma froze, hands and feet froze. The ground, what was not already rock, was frozen like rock; no one could dig a hole. It was under these conditions that seven Chinese divisions hit the Marines and soldiers around the reservoirs.

General Almond still expected the 1st Marines to advance on November 27, and General Smith was still reluctant to push farther out into the void. That day the tip of his advance, the 5th and 7th Marines, made a couple of tentative probes west from Yudam-ni. The Chinese had been there three days and more, waiting for them, and soon after making contact the Marines pulled back and began organizing Yudam-ni for all-around defense. General Almond might want an advance, but he was not up in the hills overlooking the reservoir. The rest of X Corps was already contracting back into the original beachheads around Iwon, Hungnam, and Wonsan. This left the 1st Marines, and the 7th Division soldiers east of the reservoir, the most exposed of all the UN units of the corps. As they tried to dig in, it was pretty easy to see that they were in for trouble.

The area was wildly picturesque, high, snow-clad hills, tumbling gullies where streams flowed in warmer weather. The reservoirs were up on a high plateau. There is some confusion over names, for modern Korean usage calls the two major bodies of the region the Changjin and Pujon reservoirs, but the troops in 1950 were using Japanese maps, and these had the names from the occupation days, when the Japanese had called them the Chosin and Fusen reservoirs. To the troops who fought there, the rhyme of "Frozen Chosin" was irresistible. What road there was snaked south toward the coast and Hungnam, narrow, curving, easily cut or interdicted, dominated by the hills to either side. There were power stations along the way, a railroad partway into the hills, but not a great deal to sustain life and combat.

After dark on the night of November 28 the Chinese, six of their seven divisions, took the offensive against the 1st Marines. They launched heavy attacks, both frontal and flanking, on the perimeter at Yudam-ni, with three divisions up. There were also lesser attacks against the Hakawoo-ri base, and on the soldiers of 7th Division east of the reservoir. The Americans held these until December 1, but by then it was obvious that there was going to be no more United Nations offensive, and General Almond was instructed to pull his corps out and evacuate.

This meant a fighting retreat for the Changjin Reservoir forces, and General Smith was now fully justified in his foresight and caution. He had to pull his extended units back, like a contracting telescope, and keep his road line to the south open. Since the Chinese were attacking both the head of his advance and at least thirty-five miles of his supply line, it was a tall order. Three actions made up the first phase of the withdrawal: the Yudam-ni extrication, and the ordeals of Task Force Faith and Task Force Drysdale.

On December 1 the 5th and 7th Marines pulled out of Yudam-ni, with their wounded and dead on trucks, and headed south. Heavy air support from the Marine Air Wing, flying off the carriers in the Sea of Japan, kept the Chinese at a distance as much as they could, but the Marines still faced a brutal passage. The temperature was well below zero, and progress was minimal, with every commanding hill requiring an assault up the frozen slopes. It took them three days to reach Hakawoo-ri; the key position on the route was the Toktong Pass, held in a literal death grip by one Marine company on Fox Hill until the column linked up with them and got through. On the afternoon of December 4 the two regiments marched into Hakawoo-ri, bone-tired and with 1,500 casualties from the move, still cohesive and ready to fight.

But disaster overtook the soldiers on the other side of the reservoir. The two infantry battalions, 1st Battalion of the 32nd Regiment and 3rd Battalion of the 31st Regiment, were designated as Task Force Faith after Lt. Col. D. C. Faith, Jr., who commanded the 1st Battalion. He had recently been awarded the Silver Star by General Almond, and had reportedly torn it off his jacket and thrown it away in his disgust at the casual way operations were being conducted. On December 1 the battalions loaded up their casualties, already about 600 of their 2,500 men, and moved out, heading for Hakawoo-ri. They destroyed their field artillery pieces and took only enough trucks to carry wounded. The column came under harassing fire immediately, and then was tragically hit by planes flying close support, which strafed and dropped napalm on the two lead companies, which had to scatter to avoid the attack. Meanwhile the Chinese were coalescing in front of them. Colonel Faith was mortally wounded leading a counterattack on a blocking position—he was posthumously awarded the Medal of Honor—and the column began to fray out. Trucks stalled or overturned, and Faith's successor eventually could not carry his wounded and began to leave them behind. At nightfall the troops were only halfway to Hakawoo-ri when they reached the village of Hudang-ni, only to find it full of Chinese and the road totally blocked. The remaining trucks tried to race through the town, but could not make it; lashed by fire from three sides, the force disintegrated. Soldiers took to the hills, or the ice of the reservoir, in the hope of slipping by individually. General Smith had tried to send a small task force up from Hakawoo-ri, but this too ran into roadblocks and could not get through. Of the 2,500 men in Task Force Faith, only about 1,000 filtered through to the friendly lines at last; of them, only 400 were fit to be formed into a provisional formation and sent back into the firing line.

Meanwhile, on November 29, a Royal Marine Commando force under Lt. Col. Douglas Drysdale had tried to fight its way north from Koto-ri to Hakawoo-ri, to keep the original line open. This was about 1,000 strong, with 150 trucks and 30 tanks; it too was ambushed, and the column cut to pieces. Two-thirds of the Royal Marines were lost, and most of the vehicles. About 350 men, a few trucks, and a dozen tanks got through to Hakawoo-ri, where all were warmly welcomed and desperately needed.

All these actions were in fact merely preliminaries; General Smith now had his people concentrated at Hakawoo-ri, at the south end of the reservoir, but he was faced with the prospect of fighting his way south to friendly lines. The fact that the Marines were completely surrounded was the genesis of Smith's widely misquoted remark; what he said, to some correspondents, was: "Gentlemen, we are not retreating. We are merely attacking in another direction." It turned up in the papers as: "Retreat, hell—we're just attacking in another direction," which comported more with the public view of the Marine Corps.

While the troops on the ground floundered, froze, and fought, seismic shocks were occurring in Tokyo and Washington. General MacArthur and his staff, unduly optimistic before their last offensive began, were now plunged into the depths of despair. MacArthur himself did a complete reversal from the flamboyant confidence he had radiated but a few weeks before, and it is obvious from his reports, with their plaintive, querulous, and offended tone, that his equilibrium was seriously, perhaps fatally, shaken. On November 28 he radioed to the Joint Chiefs of Staff: "All hope of localization of the Korean conflict to enemy forces composed of North Korean troops with alien token elements can now be completely abandoned. . . . We face an entirely new war. . . . Our present strength of force is not sufficient to meet this undeclared war by the Chinese. . . . This command had done everything humanly possible within its capabilities but now is faced with conditions beyond its control and its strength." MacArthur was therefore going over to the defensive, and would hold out as long as possible.

In Washington the National Security Council met on the 28th and held a lengthy and somber session. Basically its members acknowledged that they had proceeded so far on the assumption that all would turn out for the best, and they now had to recognize that they had been wrong. They were as always worried that this was but a prelude to bigger things, to a full-scale Chinese assault, to air intervention, to Soviet participation. But there was in the end not much they could do. They were unwilling to go deeper into what was now becoming a morass; they had few disposable troops; they might ask the UN for help, but knew they would not get a great deal. In the end they concurred with MacArthur's move to the defensive, told him to be careful, and waited upon events.

There was frustration and irritation in Washington, and anger and heartburn in Tokyo, but there was fighting and death in Korea. Eighth Army was below Pyongyang, and on December 6, General Smith began moving south out of Hakawoo-ri. The airstrip had been a blessing; 4,300 wounded had been evacuated, and supplies and ammunition flown in. Indeed, the close air support the Marines received was the more dramatic element, but given a choice between it and the more mundane services of Far East Cargo Command, Smith would have had to choose the latter; without its help, not a Marine would have made it back to Hungnam. The Air Force had in fact offered to evacuate the entire command, but as that would have meant sacrificing all his equipment, and might have meant a debacle in the last stage, Smith chose, for better or worse, to fight his way out.

It took the Marines two days to travel the twelve miles down to Koto-ri, but by the evening of December 7, General Smith had his division concentrated there. He had about 14,000 men, of whom something less than 12,000 were Marines; most of the rest were Army, and there were a few Royal Marines and ROKs. They had to reach Chinhung-ni, some fifteen miles south, at which point they would come down off the plateau into more livable country, and more important, within friendly lines. Fifteen miles does not sound like a great deal; your average backpacker can do that in a very comfortable day. But these were men who had not been out of their clothes for weeks, who had slept only in snatches in subzero temperatures, who wolfed down candy bars for a quick burst of energy, but were lucky to have had two hot meals in ten days, and who were faced at every turn and every hill by a skillful and courageous enemy, determined to wipe them out. They were down to that hard core where the world divided into things that give cover and things that do not, and where all that matters is survival, friendship, and a man's sense of himself, in whichever order one chooses.

There were two major obstacles along the way, in addition to the by now usual hazards. First was a complete break in the road just south of Koto-ri. An apron bridge that had spanned a 1,500-feet deep gorge had been blown, and unless that was replaced, no one was going anywhere. Then, beyond that, was a stretch of road known as the Funchilin Pass. This was dominated by a mass called simply the Big Hill; as the gorge had to be bridged, the hill had to be taken and held if the Marines were to get out.

The bridging operation was a marvel of ingenuity under fire. The material was dropped by air, eight spans of treadway bridge, each weighing two tons. No one was sure it could be done, as it had never been tried before; each span weighed as much as the bomb load of a World War II Flying Fortress, and the only test drop the Air Force had had time to try was a failure. Nonetheless, the spans were each loaded aboard a C-119 Flying Boxcar, attached to the largest parachutes available, and released from 800 feet. One was damaged in the drop, one landed on the Chinese; the Marines got six, and four would be enough to do the job. While the column inched toward the gorge, the troops at the head fought savagely to clear the heights around it. Climbing among the jagged ridges, they drove the Chinese from one height after another. Often they found Chinese frozen to death in their positions, but those still alive fought desperately. Companies withered away, and at the end of the action, whole battalions could muster no more than a platoon of effectives, but somehow the road was cleared, and then the bridge laid, and the Marines moved on across and into the pass.

General Smith had ordered Lt. Col. Donald Schmuck to attack north from Chinhung-ni and take the Big Hill, clearing the Funchilin Pass. His battalion moved out on the 8th in the middle of a below-zero blizzard, and attacked the hills on the 9th. Again the Chinese held hard; again they were driven off, and the road to the south was open. The Marines' thirteen days of isolation were ended; they came out with their dead and wounded, their weapons and equipment, having survived one of the small but epic ordeals of this or any war.

It was now the Navy's turn. As the ground forces fell back in the east and in the west, there had to be evacuations. The UN naval units went into high gear again, pulling people off places where they had a few months earlier fought to put them ashore. On the west coast, at the port of Chinnampo thirty miles from Pyongyang, a Commonwealth task force of three Canadian, two Australian, and one American destroyers successfully lifted nearly 8,000 ROKs, naval shore parties, Army port personnel, and civilians out of the hands of the advancing Chinese. Destroyers are not meant to carry passengers, especially in numbers such as that, but the approaches to the port were so shallow and twisting, and so dangerous, that they were the best ships to send in. A little farther south, the Navy began pulling rear-echelon units out of Inchon. In just under a month, from December 7 to January 5, the Navy took off almost 70,000 personnel and more than 60,000 tons of supplies, as well as 1,400 vehicles.

The real activity came on the east coast, however, for the whole of X Corps was going out by sea in a Dunkirk-style operation. The Navy began loading at Wonsan on December 3, taking military people, supplies, vehicles, and all the impedimenta that an army carries with it. In addition to military items, the Navy was soon embarrassed by a horde of civilians. There had been estimates that perhaps 1,000 North Koreans would want to leave; when 7,000 had been packed aboard ships, three times that many were still imploring refuge. There was no more space available, and they were simply left behind.

The main operation was at Hungnam. The order of evacuation was 1st Marines, ROKs, 7th Infanty, and then 3rd Infantry, so that as soon as the Marines had fought their way out into the perimeter, they were trucked to the harbor and loaded aboard the attack transports, LSTs, and even some chartered commercial vessels. By the morning of the 15th, the division sailed from Hungnam. No one was sorry to see the coastline recede. Three days later the South Koreans followed, and the last of the soldiers went out on Christmas Eve. While this went on, the cruisers, destroyers, and aircraft carriers provided first gunfire and air support, then destructive fire against the town and installations as the perimeter contracted. The Chinese launched repeated probes against the defense line, but did not make a concerted effort to interfere with the extraction. One of the biggest problems was refugees once again. Many North Koreans were seizing a last opportunity to vote with their feet, and the Navy actually took off 91,000 of them, almost as many civilians as troops. Admiral Doyle, who directed the operation, thought that if the shipping and time had been available, all of eastern North Korea would have been depopulated, for as at Wonsan, thousands were left behind; they were still trudging into the city as the last demolitions were going off in the port area.

The blows continued to fall. Walker could not put a defensible line together just below Pyongyang. The Chinese pushed past Eighth Army in the mountains and flanked its new positions yet again. The tired troops went back farther. By the end of the year, they were on the 38th parallel, and it did not look as though they would be able to stop there, either. They now had a new commander. General Walker, the tough cavalryman who had presided over defeat, triumph, and defeat again, was killed, ironically, in an automobile accident when his jeep collided with a ROK truck that pulled out in front of it on an icy road. Walker died almost instantly. He was replaced by Gen. Matthew Ridgway, who had expected to spend Christmas in Washington with his family, and found himself instead in Japan, pulling together the threads of his new command. There were a lot of loose threads lying around.

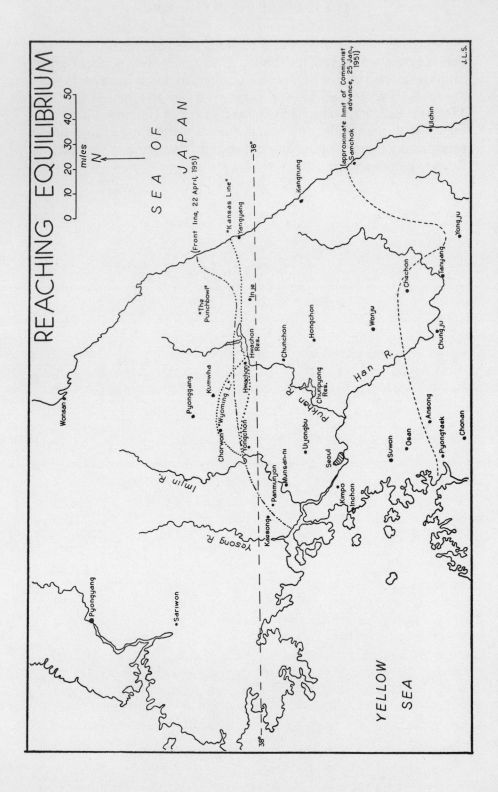

REACHING EQUILIBRIUM

SEA OF JAPAN

miles
0 10 20 30 40 50

N

(Front line, 22 April, 1951)
"Kansas Line"

38°

approximate limit of Communist
advance, 25 Jan., 1951)

Samchok

Uichin

Kangnung

Yangyang

Wonsan

"The
Punchbowl"

In je

Yong-ju

Pyonggang

Kumwha

Hwachon
Res.

Chunchon

Hongchon

Chechon

Wonju

Tanyang

"Wyoming L."

Hwachon

Chorwon

Yongchon

Pukhan R.

Chunpyong
Res.

Han R.

Chungju

Imjin R.

Uijongbu

Seoul

Suwon

Osan

Ansong

Pyongyang

Panmunjon

Munsan-ni

Kimpo

Inchon

Pyongtaek

Chonan

Sariwon

Kaesong

Yesong R.

38°

38°

YELLOW
SEA

J.L.S.

CHAPTER 7
THE DISMISSAL OF MACARTHUR

When he took over command of Eighth Army, Lt. Gen. Matthew B. Ridgway already had a brilliant career behind him, and he was subsequently destined for the office of Chief of Staff of the Army. He was himself somewhat of the MacArthur mold, for he was a dynamic leader with a well-developed sense of the drama of war. In World War II he had commanded the 82nd Airborne Division, and then XVIII Airborne Corps; at the time of his appointment, he was at the Pentagon, as Deputy Chief of Staff for Army Administration. As such, he was aware of, but not responsible for, MacArthur's and the government's divergence of view on how the war ought to be fought. He was thus in a more or less unique position, for personally he could understand MacArthur, but he also was fully aware of the new attitudes toward war in general, and this war in particular, that were current in the United States government. His period of actual field command was short, less than four months, but it included the most dramatic individual event of the war, MacArthur's relief of command by President Truman.

As a military policymaker, Ridgway understood the need to limit the war in Korea; as commander of the Eighth Army, he naturally wanted to win it. Like Bonaparte in Italy, however, he found that his first task was not to defeat the enemy, but to win over his own troops. The American forces in Korea were unhappy, and justifiably so. In Washington this was seen as a "police action," to be kept within ill-defined but narrow limits; but up along the Chongchon or around "frozen Chosin" it had not seemed like a limited war, and from the vantage point of a slit trench or the cockpit of an F-80, it was hard to see why the enemy, who was so busily trying to kill you, should be given all the advantages of the rules.

From his arrival in the theater and his first interview with MacArthur, Ridgway began to discover that all was not well. MacArthur told him the army was roadbound, wasteful of supplies, and careless in the winter weather. As soon as he reached Korea, Ridgway recovered an old trick learned during the Battle of the Bulge, to carry with him in his jeep a spare supply of gloves for the infantrymen who lost theirs while fighting or just living on the country. He interviewed his corps and divisional commanders, and he went out to look for himself at the troops, and he found them unhappy. Servicemen always complain, of course; the worst outfit in the service is always the one a man happens to be in at the moment. So it was not the fact of griping but rather the manner of it that had to be assessed.

Ridgway was a quietly theatrical man. He always wore a hand grenade strapped to his harness; he once knelt down to tie the laces of a loaded and tired Marine. Yet he seemed to do this not for effect, but simply because he was that sort of man. He told President Rhee that he was glad to be in Korea, and he meant to stay there. He told his own troops that the answers to why they were there and what they were fighting for were straightforward: "We are here because of the decisions of the properly constituted authorities of our respective governments"; and ". . . the issue now joined here in Korea is whether Communism or individual freedom shall prevail." It was as simple as that, and he told his army, "You will have my utmost. I shall expect yours."

Given his choice, Ridgway would have opened an immediate counteroffensive, but Eighth Army was not up to that, and X Corps, from the east-coast evacuation, was still putting itself back together after the passage south. The 2nd Division was being rebuilt. The pressure had slackened off over Christmas, but as the New Year came, it was much more likely to be the Chinese who would attack than the

United Nations. As usual in this intelligence-starved war, it was a bit of a guessing game as to who possessed what.

Ridgway now had about 365,000 men under his command. With the evacuation of eastern North Korea the fiction of X Corps independence was no longer maintained, and it became part of Eighth Army at last. His three American corps, I, IX, and X, had both American and South Korean divisions in them, as well as the smaller units from the United Nations contributors; several of these were hospital or support units, and the most notable combat contributions were still the Commonwealth and the Turkish brigades. He had two South Korean corps, III and I, on the east, so he did have, on the map, a continuous line across the peninsula. On the ground it was fairly thin, or, as one young British subaltern expressed it, "a bit drafty up here," meaning that his unit was, as far as he could see, totally alone.

The United Nations command still did not know how many Communists were facing them. Ridgway complained that the first intelligence picture he got was a big goose egg scrawled across the map of North Korea with the figure "174,000" in the middle of it. It was this sort of thing that made him order his troops to get out of their trucks and onto their boots, and his commanders to lead from the front. Actually, at the turn of the year, there were just about half a million Communists facing across the parallel, including something more than 400,000 Chinese and the rest North Koreans who were now back in the battle line, rebuilt and reequipped.

By year's end, it was possible to form some assessment of the Chinese fighting qualities, just as they had formed their own of those of the UN troops, especially of the Americans. The Chinese fought almost as swarms of guerrillas, or as light infantry. They were hardy and persevering, and they specialized in cross-country movement, living cheaply, infiltrating, surrounding and ambushing their opponents. They lacked a great deal of armor, and their artillery was relatively weak, compared to that of the Americans, though as the war stabilized it would increase immensely. Most of their equipment in the early stages of their intervention had not been Russian, but American, captured from the Chinese Nationalists. Their weakest point was in their logistics and support systems, especially when these had been subjected to attack by Air Force or naval air interdiction. They could build up enough stocks to launch an offensive, and carry them for up to a week; they could not create the ammunition or supply reserves to sustain a drive for much longer than that, particularly not under the kind of pounding their support system received from air power once an attack was committed.

Their view of the Americans was that they were in many ways the antithesis of the Chinese Communists. They had an absolute over-abundance of almost everything—food, ammunition, transport. They had incredible technical competence, and American engineers and transport and communications personnel performed unsung marvels of keeping the combat soldiers mobile and supplied. Their artillery and their firepower were awesome. But in the Chinese view, the Americans were overly dependent upon this kind of technical war. They were weakest in what the Chinese were strongest in, infantry. An often-quoted Chinese assessment stated, "Their infan-trymen are weak, afraid to die, and haven't the courage to attack or defend. They depend on their planes, tanks, and artillery." To which, of course, the American response would be that if you've got it, use it, and that only a damned fool is *not* afraid to die.

The two armies invite interesting comparisons, one strong on tech-nology, the other on manpower, both trying to fight a war as cheaply as possible, but each having different concepts of what is expensive. They were like the sophisticated and technically superior Byzantines faced with swarms of Bulgars or Turks; like Napoleon's fast-moving divisions facing the manpower of Russia, Prussia, and Austria; or like Germany's technically superior armies facing a sea of Czarist or Soviet Russians.

For the United Nations forces, the South Koreans remained a weak link. Their army had been built so fast, and expanded so rapidly, and also hammered so hard, that its fighting quality was always a bit of a question mark. The Americans desperately wanted the war fought as much as possible by ROK manpower, but they had to recognize that building the army while fighting the war was extremely difficult. The best South Korean soldiers and officers became very good, but there were not enough of them for an ever-growing army in a costly war. The tradition of political or family appointment to command was strong, and production of battle-tested and dependable leaders, from noncommissioned officers on up, simply could not keep up with the demand. Ridgway took immediate steps to encourage the growth and maturity of the ROK Army, but it was an uphill job. The Chinese knew whom to hit.

* * *

On New Year's Eve the Chinese attacked again, and Ridgway's rapidly diminishing hope for an early offensive went skittering down the drain. The UN forces were poorly disposed to receive a new assault, and the Chinese soon gathered momentum; initially they hit the ROK 1st Division, attached to the U.S. I Corps, and the ROK 6th Division in IX Corps. The latter broke, and when Ridgway went up to the line on New Year's Day he found himself in the midst of an army fleeing in panic, trucks jammed with South Korean soldiers and their officers, with not a weapon per truck among them. It was like the June days all over again. Unable to stop the rout, all the general could do was set up collection posts in the rear to gather in stragglers. This was actually successful, and the panic was not as widespread, as demoralizing, or as long-lasting as in the early days. The troops were soon reequipped and put back in the line.

But the breakage meant that Seoul must go. There was not enough space north of the Han River to hold on to, and that meant Eighth Army had to fall back south of it, and Seoul had to change hands once more. One by one, the divisions came back across the Han bridges, pontoon bridges now, which threatened to sink under the weight of tanks and heavy traffic. At least this time they were not blown prematurely as a result of panic, but again as before, thousands of refugees were left stranded on the north side.

In the center of the peninsula the situation looked even worse. Here X Corps came into the line on January 2, just in time to witness and feel the effects of the collapse of the newly formed ROK III Corps on its right, attacked by two North Korean corps. The result of that was another ordeal for the 2nd Infantry Division, which had just barely recovered from its smashing defeat at Kunu-ri. The 2nd was again in the position of holding a shoulder and an open flank, but could not hold on. The weather was so bad there was no close air support for four crucial days, and eventually the division was pushed south out of Wonju. The 1st Marines then came up, into the gap on the 2nd's right, and the North Koreans slowed and halted.

Faced with these pressures, Ridgway fell back below the Han to a position called the D Line, running roughly from the west coast at Pyongtaek to the east coast at Samchok. This was about as far back as he dared go, for the peninsula broadened out again south of that, and a further retreat would put the army in the same predicament as in July and August; in fact, in some quarters there was talk of another "perimeter," of possible Soviet intervention, and of the abandonment of Korea altogether, talk that Ridgway was concerned might have an extremely adverse effect upon the South Koreans.

Fortunately, events on the battlefield soon made it apparent that these ideas were alarmist. The evacuation of Seoul was mostly a geographic necessity, and the pressure on the center eased after a week or so. The rest of the withdrawal to the new line was made in comparative peace as the Communists let up, and it became apparent that UN assessments were correct: The Chinese could put on a major drive, but their logistics were such that they could not sustain it for much more than a few days. And of course, the farther south they got, the more trouble they had with communications.

For one thing, and it was perhaps the most important thing, the longer the supply lines were, the more there was for the Air Force to hit. The weather was good from New Year's Day to the 6th, then bad until the 11th, and then cleared again. During the two clear periods, the Fifth Air Force, counterpart to Eighth Army, pounded the Communists with everything it had. There were, for example, 564 sorties on New Year's Day, and 531, 556, 498, and 447 on the next four. These figures dropped a bit when the air bases around Seoul had to be given up and the fighter-bombers were forced to fly from fields farther south, but all along the front, nothing that moved was immune. Thousands of Chinese and North Koreans were strafed and bombed, driven into hiding or out of ruined buildings. At night a much smaller number of B-26 night intruders carried on the same task; in fact the B-26s, only one bombardment wing, called themselves "the other half" of Fifth Air Force. Meanwhile the medium bombers, the B-29s, hit Pyongyang on the 3rd and again on the 5th of January. Naval and Marine air from the *Valley Forge* and the *Philippine Sea* carried the close-support burden in the central part of the peninsula, repeating what they had done for X Corps up in the north. Then as soon as Wonju was lost, it was hit by B-29s, so that even if the Communists had it, they could get little use out of it.

Throughout this period the Air Force commanders expected either a major intervention from the Chinese Air Force, which was building up units in Manchuria, or on the outside, entry by the Soviets into the combat. Yet it did not come; there were occasional forays by North Korean aircraft, but they did not accomplish anything, and the Americans ruled the skies virtually unchallenged. This became a subject of bitter recrimination in the Chinese high command, with Gen. Lin Piao complaining that he had been totally left in the lurch by the Chinese Air Force and that if it had done its part, he would have driven the United Nations forces into the sea. The claim was patently exaggerated, but it was true that of the estimated 38,000 Communist casualties in the January offensive, more than half of them had been inflicted by the air forces; and though ground forces usually think air forces overstate their case, this was one time when the people on the ground actually thought the air force had done more than it claimed.

The January attack was called by the Chinese Communists their "third phase offensive," and its results were paradoxical. On the ground and the map it appeared they had won another victory; they had advanced the front line fifty to sixty miles across the whole breadth of the peninsula, and they had captured, for the second time, the South Korean capital. They had inflicted about 13,000 casualties on the UN troops, they had caused dismay in high quarters in the United States and among the UN, where it finally began to dawn that this was likely to be a long, hard war, and not a quick little police action. But to do that they had lost three men to the United Nations' one, they had exhausted their offensive capacity for the immediate future, and instead of sharing the laurels of victory, their commanders were squabbling over whose fault the lack of success was. Even more important, they now faced an enemy who for the first time seemed prepared to settle down and fight a careful, thorough, professional war. For Eighth Army, far from being cast down by its further retreat, now began to snap back, to utilize its extensive advantages of firepower and mobility, and to wage a war that it was actually, to everyone's surprise and delight, pretty good at.

The turnaround began on January 15, in a modest effort named Operation Wolfhound, after the 27th Infantry Regiment that carried it out. Once on the D Line, Eighth Army found itself losing contact with the Communists. This was something that Ridgway had inveighed against; he did not like the idea of his troops falling back when not under pressure, or not knowing what was in front of them. So on the 15th a task force moved out from the I Corps line, and found to its relief that there was nothing in front of it. The troops went several miles up the road to Osan before they found any Chinese at all, and then they exchanged fire with some Communists who immediately disengaged and pulled out. So the soldiers went a little farther, and they got all the way to Suwon before they actually developed a Communist position in strength. This was almost halfway back to Seoul; clearly something was up. The air support for the reconnaissance reported that the enemy soldiers they spotted were all going north instead of south. At about the same time, the pressure on the central front below Wonju began to ease off; it was curiouser and curiouser. Ridgway was delighted; Generals Collins and Vandenberg, over to have a look for the Joint Chiefs of Staff, were delighted too; in fact, everyone in the entire Far East Command appeared delighted. Another reconnaissance by IX Corps produced the same evidence; the Communists were going back.

That being the case, they might as well be speeded on their way. On January 25, Eighth Army launched Operation Thunderbolt, designed to push all the way back to the Han River. This was to be a two-corps drive, with one division and one ROK regiment from each of the corps, I and IX, leading the way. There was some hard fighting around Suwon, but eventually the Communists gave it up and went back to the Han, abandoning Inchon without a struggle and letting the Air Force once again return to Kimpo airport, just south of the river and west of Seoul. By the second week of February, the drive finally ran down.

Ridgway's approach was quite different from Walker's and MacArthur's before him; Walker had had little freedom to act, and MacArthur had been wedded firmly to the flamboyant gesture. When Ridgway took over, however, he had been given a clear hand by MacArthur, and his battlefield style was quite different. One of the great temptations of command is to occupy territory, because it looks so good on a map; it takes a Napoleon to say, "Never mind towns, bring me prisoners!" Ridgway conceived his mission as less the liberation of Seoul or the regaining of the 38th parallel, and more the destruction of the forces opposing him. His advances therefore were carefully constructed and kept limited; they were designed to take full advantage of UN firepower, of artillery, armor, and air strength. Casualties were to be kept to a minimum; if the UN was going to fight China, it could never have enough manpower to waste it. Ground itself was unimportant; destroying the Chinese armies, and leaving nothing behind as guerrillas, was important. Within the army in Korea, the idea was known as the "meatgrinder." The Chinese masses were to be driven out in the open, where they could be pummeled by artillery and air support. It was not as dramatic as the dash north of Task Force Lynch, but it kept the battlefield tidy and the UN casualties relatively low. It had a single overriding virtue: It worked.

The next drive was in the center. The Communists had given up Wonju, which they had fought so hard to get, so Ridgway launched another two-corps attack, by X and ROK III Corps, aimed at bringing up the previously sagging center line as far as the west. This one was called Roundup, and it had tougher going than Thunderbolt, for the Communists fought hard against it. They did more than that—they launched a counterattack around Chipyong-ni that surrounded the 23rd Infantry Regiment and its attached French Battalion. The Communist attack, both Chinese and North Korean, had hit the ROK III Corps and driven its three weak divisions to the south. Chipyong-ni was X Corps' right flank, another of those shoulder-blocking positions, and it had to be held. The infantrymen of the 23rd, and the French, held on grimly; the latter were commanded by a general who had taken a demotion to lieutenant colonel to get a combat command. For several days they were surrounded, but constantly supplied and supported by the Air Force, until a task force from the 1st Cavalry fought through to them. The battle of Chipyong-ni turned out to be the major effort of the Communists' "fourth phase offensive," and it blunted their strength for the immediate future. Once again it was the UN that retained the initiative.

Eighth Army was off again on February 21. This time it was Operation Killer, aimed at cutting off and destroying the Communist forces that had come down the eastern part of the peninsula. The name elicited some protest from Washington, where there was distress over its unpleasant connotations and their possible effect upon the public. But the name stood, and Ridgway later tartly remarked in his memoirs that it would not hurt civilians to be reminded that war was about killing people; maybe if they remembered that they would be more reluctant to get involved in it.

Killer gained more ground, and it did have the effect again of destroying large numbers of enemy troops. The Chinese were palpably weakened now. Their soldiers were undersupplied and undernourished; thousands were caught by artillery or close air-support, and they were taking a terrible beating. Some of their units were racked by disease, especially typhus, that age-old killer that has destroyed more armies than other armies have. The offensive lasted only eight days; it took its ground objectives, but in spite of the mute evidence of enemy dead as the soldiers advanced, Killer did not destroy as many Chinese as originally intended. The rain and the beginning of the spring thaw slowed the advance, and the Communists would not stay to be killed; they were going back.

The next of Eighth Army's advances in this series was Operation Ripper, launched on March 7. It was opened by IX and X Corps, designed to bring the line in central Korea almost up to the 38th parallel. That would have the effect of uncovering Seoul from the east, and that was what it did. For three days the 25th Division had a hard fight to secure a bridgehead across the Han River, to the east of the capital, but once it did that, the Communists had to go back again. The ROK 1st Division also fought its way past Seoul on the west, and the city was liberated for the second time on March 15.

On this occasion there was no celebration; the capital was a shambles. MacArthur had been in Korea for the opening of Ripper, but he did not come back again for a ceremonial liberation. There was more a sense of business as usual this time, and the fighting just went on to the northward.

Ridgway now decided to push on to the parallel, and he enlarged Ripper's objectives accordingly. Eighth Army tried another airborne drop, of the 187th Regimental Combat Team at Munsan-ni, twenty miles up the road from Seoul. But as before, it failed to trap large numbers of enemy forces or government leaders and turned out to be just a part of the overall advance. At the end of March, the UN forces were closed up to the parallel for almost the entire breadth of the peninsula.

There was even less discussion about it this time than there had been before. It was now recognized, by most leaders, that North Korea was not going to be liberated/conquered, but also that the war was not going to be over until the other side said it was. Ridgway was simply instructed to be guided by the military situation, and to disregard the parallel as insignificant. On April 3 he met with MacArthur, who flew over from Tokyo for a conference. The former had decided that the best option for him was to advance into North Korea, on a series of phase lines; these were named Idaho, Kansas, Utah, and Wyoming. Kansas was a few miles north of the parallel, for most of its length, and ran across the peninsula roughly from Munsan-ni to Yangyang on the east coast. It was the best defensive position Ridgway could find in the area. Utah was a minor extension of Kansas, and Wyoming a larger, later extension, a hump in the line. This brought the UN forces north as far as a complex in central Korea known as the Iron Triangle.

Ridgway was thinking defensively, in spite of his impressive advances over the last several weeks, for there was intelligence evidence that the Communists were building up for a new major offensive in the spring. The UN field commander wanted to move north to a good position, Kansas, foray out of that to destroy enemy preparations to Utah and ultimately Wyoming, and then be prepared to fall back as necessary, on phased withdrawals to established positions. The end result of this was that both coming and going the UN forces should inflict heavy casualties and damage on the enemy, and make them pay dearly for everything they got. It was a sensible program for fighting what might be a long war.

On April 5, the troops set off yet again, and four days' fighting, some of it very nasty around the Hwachon Reservoir, carried them to the Kansas line; this drive was known as Operation Rugged. On April 9, they began to head toward Line Utah. Two days later, President Truman suddenly fired General MacArthur.

The famous Truman-MacArthur controversy is really misnamed. It was not so much a matter between the general and the President, though in the course of it they managed to work up a substantial dislike for each other; nor was it, in its essentials, too much of a controversy, even if it seemed to be a matter of great import at the time. The issue was not, for example, civilian control of the military, which was never seriously questioned. Such a problem would have been clear-cut black and white. MacArthur's relief, like almost everything else in the Korean War, or the whole era, was a matter of grays, of blurred nuances and shadowy distinctions.

The feeling had long been growing in Washington, among the Joint Chiefs of Staff, the State Department, and the President and his advisers, that General MacArthur neither was in sympathy with nor entirely understood the evolution of national policy toward the rest of the world. Part of the difficulty arose, certainly, from the fact that the government was not sure itself exactly what its policy was. The United States had decided to rebuild the free world and to resist the spread of Communism, but by what means and to what extent were uncertain. There were a few hard points: Europe was more important than Asia; the United States did not want to fight a third world war; the United States, under present circumstances, *could* not fight a third world war. But beyond these, it was a matter of responding to crises as they arose, trying to deal with urgent matters on a day-to-day basis, and often trying to make one resource answer two or three different needs.

For example, the war in Korea impeded the military buildup of United States forces in Europe; enlarging the Republic of Korea Army meant slowing the rearmament not only of America's European allies but even of the United States Army itself. So it went; the government, no matter how hard it tried to juggle resources, was still robbing Peter to pay Paul.

Korea was therefore seen as a very limited commitment, but the trouble with it was that it refused to stay within the limits Washington would have preferred. Indeed, Korea was a classic example of Clausewitz's dictum about force generating more force. North Korea's aggression led to the United Nations's intervention; the United Nations' intervention led in turn to Communist China's intervention; and, theoretically, so on and so on. The United States, however, did not now wish to pursue the "and so on"; it wished to end the war, not to fight World War III over a piece of Asian real estate that in itself was of only slight interest to the rest of the world.

As a result of these considerations, which of course are presented here in a vastly simplified form, the government sent General MacArthur, in his role as Commander in Chief Far East, a new directive on December 29. This new statement changed his primary mission in Korea; from the earlier "restore international peace and security" to "defend in successive positions . . . inflicting such damage to hostile forces in Korea as is possible, subject to the primary consideration of the safety of your troops." The directive then continued on to talk of the possibility of withdrawal from the peninsula. MacArthur responded to this by suggesting that since Red China had now entered the war, it ought to be carried to the Chinese mainland, possibly by blockade of the coast, air and naval bombardment, or the use of Chinese Nationalist forces, either in Korea or on the mainland itself. He concluded by challenging the whole policy of the government to avoid major Asian commitments while building up strength in Europe.

This was all old stuff, for MacArthur had suggested use of the Chinese Nationalists, and direct action against China, before, and been rejected; but that was before Red China had intervened in Korea. Now he was trying it again. It must be noted here, parenthetically, that the issue of Chiang Kai-shek and the Nationalists kept intruding on the Korean problem. The Truman administration consistently tried to soft-pedal the Nationalist question, while General MacArthur, and the more aggressive elements in Washington, and the Republican opposition, equally often demanded or threatened Nationalist action against Communist China; there was a desire, in the phrase of the day, to "unleash the Nationalists." As a policy alternative, this would have been roughly equivalent to urging a mouse to attack a tiger, but it was a matter that bedeviled the whole period.

The real problem, of course, was not the Chinese Nationalists; it was rather the almost unique position occupied by MacArthur on the American scene. Officially he was but the military commander in the Far East; in fact he was far more than that. As an active soldier for close to half a century, he was far senior to his ostensible superiors in the Pentagon, and they treated him with a deference he really should not have had. This was especially true in the aftermath of Inchon, when he had been right and everyone else was wrong. But he also typified—and this was what the "controversy" was actually all about—the dilemma, indeed the impossibility, of drawing a clear line between what was "military" and what was "political" in the modern world, and what kind of advice, loyalty, acquiescence, obedience, or opposition the soldier owes to his political masters.

Two days after MacArthur received his new directive, the Chinese attacked across the 38th parallel, then Seoul fell, and prospects in Korea looked dim indeed. But Eighth Army and the ROK forces rallied, the situation stabilized, and the United Nations recovered the initiative. President Truman thought the time had come for a negotiated settlement. China had shown that it would not permit the Democratic People's Republic of (North) Korea to be destroyed, and the United States and the United Nations had now shown, twice, that they would not permit the Republic of (South) Korea to be destroyed. The short-lived myth of Chinese battlefield invincibility was being shattered by Ridgway's advances, and as the UN forces got back to the parallel, an obvious equilibrium was reached. Truman therefore prepared an announcement that the United Nations would welcome negotiations. Earlier UN attempts to move in this direction had been spurned by China, but that was before the battlefield defeats of February. While Truman's announcement was being cleared with the other governments supporting the Korean action, and MacArthur informed of its imminent release, the general took matters into his own hands.

On March 24 he issued a public statement. In it he pointed out that Red China was vastly overrated as a military power, and that if the United Nations chose to extend the war to their homeland, the Chinese would precipitately collapse. Then he offered to open negotiations to end the war. His statement totally eclipsed any Truman might have made, and was couched in an arrogant tone that made a positive response to it unthinkable.

President Truman was furious. He had already, on December 6, ordered that any such public pronouncements had to be cleared with Washington, and now here was the Great Pooh-Bah undercutting the government's carefully constructed plans. MacArthur blithely responded to Washington's complaints that he thought he was acting within the bounds of his authority.

He was, however, already on the way out. For on March 20, four days before his famous public statement, he had written a letter to Congressman Joseph W. Martin, Jr. Mr. Martin happened to be the Republican minority leader in the House of Representatives, and he happened to be one of the advocates of "unleashing" Nationalist China. In his letter, MacArthur agreed fully with Mr. Martin's ideas, deplored the priority accorded Europe, announced that "we must win" in Asia, and concluded, "There is no substitute for victory." On April 5, Mr. Martin stood up on the floor of the House of Representatives and read General MacArthur's letter into the Congressional Record.

That did it. It took a few days for the Joint Chiefs, the Secretaries of State and Defense, and assorted other advisers to meet with the President and round it all off, but there was no question after April 5; MacArthur had to go.

The manner of his going was singularly unfortunate. He was to be relieved of command April 12, and since Secretary of the Army Frank Pace was touring the Far East Command at that time, the government's intention was to have Pace relieve him in a personal interview. But Pace was isolated by a communications breakdown in Korea, and the news of the impending blow got out to the reporters. Washington therefore decided to wire direct to Far East Command in Tokyo. The commercial wire services beat the Army's communications network. On April 11 the MacArthurs were hosting a luncheon at the U.S. Embassy when the General's aide, Col. Sidney Huff, heard the news on a Japanese radio station. He interrupted the meal to whisper to Mrs. MacArthur, who then whispered to her husband.

MacArthur took it in his stride, finished hosting the meal, and immediately began making preparations to give up his command and return to the United States.

His successor was General Ridgway, at the moment up on the front lines in Korea showing Secretary Pace around. Neither of them knew anything about it for some time, but Ridgway was soon ensconced in Tokyo, and Gen. James A. Van Fleet took over Eighth Army.

MacArthur returned home to a hero's welcome in the States. His relief was a *cause célèbre*. He was lionized, but so was Truman; he was vilified, but so was Truman; some unions were for him, some were for Truman. State legislatures and universities debated the pros and cons, commending or condemning one side or the other. There was a parade in Honolulu, another in San Francisco, one in Washington, one in New York. In his most famous appearance, MacArthur spoke before Congress, defending his ideas, in fact repeating many of them, and he closed with the lines of the old army ballad, "Old soldiers never die; they just fade away."

He of course did not quite fade away, at least not for a while. There were books, there were public appearances, there were meetings. MacArthur was the man of the hour. There were several records released of the old soldier ballad, which at least had the virtue of being a pretty good song. Of MacArthur's speech before Congress, one listener, a congressman, thought it was the "voice of God." Truman, privately, fortunately not publicly, thought it was "a bunch of bullshit." In fact it was a terrific speech, though like many such, it did not say a great deal.

There was inevitably a Congressional hearing, in the Senate, and it went on interminably, from early May until August. By then almost everyone had had his innings—the transcript ran to 2 million words—and this had the effect such proceedings regularly do; it confused and obfuscated the issues, and eventually bored everyone. After that, MacArthur could truly fade away.

The war went on.

CHAPTER 8
APPROACHING A STALEMATE

By the time General Ridgway took over Far East Command from General MacArthur, Washington had at last decided just what it wanted to achieve in Korea and how far it was willing to go to do it. This position was embodied in the policy document known as NSC 48/4, which replaced the older NSC 48/2. The government sought a unified, independent Korea, but this was to be attained by "political, as distinguished from military, means," a major clarification over the earlier document, and one which had, in effect, been forced on the government by China, and by MacArthur. Militarily, the United States now sought an armistice, security for South Korea on a defensible line north of the 38th parallel, withdrawal of all non-Korean forces, and a buildup of the ROK armed services to the point where they could defend themselves. What the United States explicitly wanted to avoid was "war with the Soviet Union," and also "the extension beyond Korea of hostilities with Communist China, particularly without the support of our major allies." To get these things, Washington was unwilling to sacrifice its position with respect to the Soviet Union, Formosa, or seating Communist China in the United Nations. In other words, the idea of rolling Communism back having failed, the United States government was willing to keep fighting until its enemies accepted the status quo at the beginning of the conflict. What General MacArthur professed to see as supineness in the face of aggression, and what the opposition saw as concessions to the creeping menace of worldwide Communism, the administration now believed was the only sane middle-of-the-road course. It was a necessary but unpalatable recognition that the world of the 1950s was going to be a different one from the past, and to a country which saw its last two wars as total struggles of good versus evil, the idea of fighting a war to achieve nothing more at the end than you had at the beginning was hard to accept.

But General Ridgway had already, implicitly, accepted it, and one of the major differences between his tenure and that of his predecessor was that Ridgway was fully conversant, and in agreement, with the ideas that now dominated the U.S. government. In his own directive to his new field commander, Gen. James A. Van Fleet, he instructed that there be no advance deep into North Korea without prior consultation and approval, and in amplification of these orders, he sent Van Fleet a memorandum with the title "Prevention of War with the Soviet Union." Eighth Army's mission was no longer to "liberate" or "unify" Korea, but rather, more mundanely, to "repel aggression against so much of the territory (and the people therein) of the Republic of Korea as you now occupy." To achieve this Van Fleet was permitted to advance, a little bit, and encouraged to inflict as much damage and as many casualties as possible on the Chinese and North Koreans. In effect, the United Nations were to build a wall, then let the Communists bang their heads against it until they finally decided they had had enough. It was not much of a policy to ask men to risk their lives for, and its only virtues were that it recognized reality, and it at least avoided the flamboyant ambiguities of the MacArthur period.

The new commander of the Eighth Army had to adjust to the rules. General Van Fleet arrived on April 16, having been named to the post two days earlier, and he remained there until he returned to the United States to retire in February 1953. A West Pointer of the class of 1915, legendary as "the class the stars fell on," those men who were exactly the right age to achieve general's rank in World War II, he had commanded a corps in France and Germany. He might have gone even higher, but unfortunately he had gotten confused in George

Marshall's mind with another officer of similar name of whom Marshall disapproved. He was therefore only a colonel on D-Day, and he jumped from a regimental to a corps command in the space of less than a year. After the war ended he had led the American military assistance advisory group that went to Greece to help stop the Communists trying to take over that country, and he had earned high marks there.

As someone who had already fought Communism in Greece, Van Fleet might have been expected to be a bit of a crusader; he was not. Nor did he provide very good copy for hungry newsmen. Asked what his goal was in Korea, he replied, "I don't know, the answer must come from higher authority." If he didn't know what the goal was, how would he know when it was achieved? "Somebody higher up will have to tell us." If that sounded pedestrian, Van Fleet was thoroughly professional; he occasionally chafed under the restrictions put on his operations, but he had a well-developed sense of the importance of fighting as cheap a war as possible. "Cheap" to him meant using what the United States was rich in, material, and conserving what it was poor in, manpower; he demanded and got enormously increased ammunition allowances, so that five times the normal ration became known as "the Van Fleet load," and his reply to complaints was that the United States must "expend fire and steel, not men." His kind of leadership and attitude managed to maintain Eighth Army's morale under increasingly stagnant conditions.

In mid-April when Van Fleet arrived, Eighth Army was still moving forward. The United Nations forces were on the Kansas line, and in spite of growing evidence that the Communists were about to launch another major offensive, Van Fleet wanted to go on a little farther to clear his front, inflict more casualties, and slow the Communists down. By April 19, both I and IX Corps had the Utah line, an intermediate position in the middle of the peninsula threatening the city of Chorwon. This was the southwestern anchor of the area known as the Iron Triangle, and this was as far as Van Fleet's troopers got when the Chinese began to move once more. On April 22 they opened the first part of their "fifth phase offensive."

The United Nations forces now pretty well understood the rhythm of the Communist war machine. The Communists had been going back for almost a month now, constructing defensive positions and retreating to them as they were forced to do so; their casualties were heavier than their opponents', but they were not squandering men in wasteful attacks or last-man defenses. The manpower profligacy of Chinese tactics was largely a fiction of the newspaper reporters in Korea at the time. Now that they had gone back to what for them was a secure base, they began to look to the offensive once more.

A number of portents telegraphed the Communists' intentions. Most of these derived from UN control of the air, and the ability of aerial reconnaissance to pick up the signs, for now, as had not been the case in October and November, the Chinese were fully committed, and the reconnaissance people knew what they were looking for. The most ominous sign was that the Chinese were building airfields in northern Korea, and this looked to Fifth Air Force as if they intended at last to launch a major contest for the air over the battlefield. There were also larger numbers of tanks spotted than had been seen for some time, so Eighth Army was ready for an armored battle once more. Intelligence estimates now put the number of Communist troops in North Korea as high as 700,000, so it was obvious to everyone that the next blow, when it came, would be a hard one.

Ridgway, in his advance north of the parallel, and Van Fleet after him, moved carefully, keeping unit flanks secure and leaving behind them defensive positions to which the troops could retreat on order. Eighth Army's advance in early 1951 was a far cry from the confident pursuit of the previous autumn.

But when the Communist attack opened on April 22, it still hit hard. The expected armor did not materialize, nor did a major enemy air effort, largely because the UN air power had gone after the new airstrips as fast as the Chinese tried to build them. The attack was therefore in the old style—lots of artillery, more in fact than in earlier battles, and heavy infantry assaults. The Chinese preferred to come at night, in masses of infantry, hard on the heels of their own artillery barrages. They came with bugles and drums and flares and whistles, and at first the UN soldiers thought this was all false courage, trying to scare them, until they realized the Chinese used these noisemakers and lights for tactical signals. Then the UN troops got their own noisemakers and lights, and played games trying to confuse the attackers. The games were deadly, for the Chinese meant business, and they would lap around, and then into, and then over, the company perimeters if they could manage to do it. They did not employ the "human wave," with its implications of careless spending of bodies, but they did have, and they used, heavy formations of troops, and they pushed hard.

Against most of the UN formations, these tactics and assaults resulted only in heavy losses for the Communists. However, in two places they succeeded in breaking the line. Their main attempts were in the very center of the peninsula, just east of the Hwachon Reservoir, and over near the west coast, along the Imjin River, where they opened a drive toward Seoul. Both of these hit South Korean units. The central drive landed on the ROK 6th Division, holding the line between the U.S. 24th Infantry of I Corps on its left, and the 1st Marines of its own IX Corps on the right. The division broke, and started the usual fraying out, with individuals and then companies heading for points south. The Chinese immediately put fresh forces into the gap now existing between the 24th Division and the Marines, and they too headed south. The Chinese were more concerned to push on than they were to widen their breach, but both the infantrymen and the Marines were hard pressed and could not move to close the line back up. Van Fleet brought up elements of the 1st Cavalry, then the British 27th Brigade, but the Chinese still kept coming, and he therefore finally gave the order for both I and IX Corps to fall back. They came back slowly, to and past the Kansas line, covered by heavy artillery barrages and a blanket of tactical air support. It took a week before the Communists ran out of supplies and men, and they paid a terrible price in casualties for some real estate that did not offer much advantage.

The attack on the west, against I Corps' left, also hit a ROK formation, the 1st Division. This was levered off the Kansas line, and as it retreated, it uncovered the left flank of the British 29th Brigade. This brigade consisted of about 6,000 men, made up of artillery, some tanks from the 8th Hussars, and three infantry battalions from the Northumberland Fusiliers, the Royal Ulster Rifles, and the Gloucestershire Regiment. They also had an attached Belgian Battalion. For three days they held up the Communist drive and anchored I Corps' left flank, and then they were ordered out. The Gloucesters, covering the brigade's withdrawal, were surrounded and cut off at a hill called Point 235. Under Lt. Col. J. P. Carnes, the battalion held on to its hill for another three days, while I Corps made frantic but unsuccessful efforts to break through to it. Men, and supplies, dwindled away, and at last the Gloucesters were out of ammunition, and the position was on the verge of being overrun. At that point the surviving effectives gathered themselves together and charged north straight into the Chinese lines in the general direction of Manchuria. It was a desperate, brilliant gamble, and it deserved the little success it had. The British broke through the Chinese lines and made it, some of them, into open country. Of the entire battalion, about forty got back through the Chinese to friendly lines. General Van Fleet later, with no exaggeration, called it "the most outstanding example of unit bravery in modern warfare." The Gloucesters happen to wear a cap badge on the back of their headdress, to commemorate the occasion at the Battle of Alexandria, on March 21, 1801, when they were attacked from both front and rear by the French, and the rear rank simply faced about and fought off the new attack. So the fight on Point 235 in Korea renewed a long-standing regimental tradition.

The crisis of the offensive came on the 27th, when the Chinese were still pushing hard for Seoul, but though they came close, they could not stand the costs Eighth Army and Fifth Air Force were inflicting on them. They had advanced about twenty-five miles, and the UN forces were well below the parallel and had lost some important lateral roads. But by the 29th they were fought out, and the front settled down again. It now ran from the seacoast just above Seoul roughly east to the center of the peninsula, and then it angled northeast all the way to the seacoast about ten miles above the parallel. This was not a planned phase line, so Van Fleet called it the "no-name line." Neither side thought to stay there long.

With the turn of the month, the UN forces began probing attacks from their new positions. They found, as in the past, that there was not much in front of them. Having pushed south to a firm line, the Communists had now paused to regroup once again. They had to build up their supplies, bring in reinforcements and new ammunition, and catch their breath before starting off again. While they did this, they withdrew ten or more miles, to keep themselves out of Eighth Army's artillery range and to seek relief from the unending attacks by UN air power.

Van Fleet desired if possible to expand these probes into a major offensive, and there were substantial gains by the UN forces. The approaches to Seoul were cleared, with nasty fighting around Uijongbu, the town that controlled the northern road to and from the capital. Communist forces were also driven off the Kimpo peninsula west of Seoul, the body of land formed by the northern trend of the

Han River. In the center of the peninsula the Marines had another heavy battle, coming to bayonets, around Chunchon. For the first week of May, there was a steady grinding northward.

Then the Chinese began to hold even harder, and it became obvious in the next week that they had paused only to regroup, that their offensive had not been definitively halted. Aerial reconnaissance, as well as intelligence gathered in North Korea, revealed two things. One was that the Communists were resupplying frantically, in spite of all the efforts of Fifth Air Force and the Navy and Marines to interdict them. The roads and rail lines running south were full of truck convoys, trains, and columns of marching men. No matter how many the fliers hit, there were always more, and no matter how many times rail lines were bombed or culverts blown up, masses of peasant workers were out repairing them. It was rather like trying to stop army ants with a sledgehammer. The second thing was that the Communists were shifting the axis of their strength. Their first push had been generally aimed at Seoul and enveloping it from the west and center. In response to that, Van Fleet had shuffled his units about so that most of the American and UN forces were in the west, while the comparatively quiet east was manned largely by ROK divisions. Now the Communists were moving units from west to east across the peninsula, and were obviously intending to attack the South Korean forces on the eastern side. The country there was worse, and though that impeded mobility, it generally impeded the motorized and road-bound UN forces more than it did the Communists. The "second impulse" of this "fifth phase offensive" was going to land once again on the Koreans.

The seacoast was held by the ROK I Corps, and inland of it was ROK III Corps. Next came U.S. X Corps, but its right-flank division was the ROK 7th, and next to it was the ROK 5th Division. These formations were all weaker than American ones, with less artillery and heavy weapons, and fewer experienced junior and middle-grade officers. This was still in part a residue of the Korean penchant for basing promotions and commands on influence and family, but it was also due to the pounding the South Koreans had been taking ever since the war began and the unnaturally forced pace of their military expansion. They had just been catapulted prematurely into the big leagues.

Van Fleet was aware of this, and he prepared to move his American units eastward as the need should arise. By May 12 he was slowing down, conscious of the thickening Chinese in front of him, and Eighth Army was battening down the hatches, getting ready for the next storm to hit. The interlude between April 29 and May 15 was similar to the eye of a hurricane.

In spite of the beating they had taken in the last few weeks, the Communist forces in North Korea, and available for reinforcement from Manchuria, vastly outnumbered the United Nations and ROK forces. There were very nearly three-quarters of a million Chinese or North Koreans in the peninsula, and there were about the same number more in Manchuria. Against them were pitted about 270,000 American and allied soldiers and marines, and some 235,000 South Korean soldiers. So the Communists had approximately a three-to-two manpower superiority on the battlefield, and a potential three-to-one superiority if they chose to use it. The "second impulse" of their spring offensive they saw as the final act; they would either destroy the enemy or drive them off the peninsula altogether. This was going to end the war. On the night of May 15–16, they attacked with twenty-one Chinese and nine North Korean divisions.

The assault hit the right side of U.S. X Corps, and all along the front of ROK III Corps. The two right-hand divisions of Almond's corps, both South Korean, broke before the drive and went off to the rear. This left X Corps' flank held by none other than 2nd Division, which for the third time in the war found itself holding the open door. Now commanded by Maj. Gen. Clark L. Ruffner, the division felt that it knew pretty much all there was to know about this sort of situation. Facing north, they shifted their attention eastward, then southward. Divisional artillery pounded the onrushing Chinese with "the Van Fleet load"; the 38th Field Artillery Battalion fired off more than 12,000 rounds of 105mm ammunition in one twenty-four-hour period. The infantrymen of the 2nd Division's regiments, plus the French and Dutch battalions attached to them, took an enormous toll of enemy soldiers, and when the division pulled out of the line on the 18th, they had inflicted 35,000 casualties on the Communists at a cost of 900 of their own.

If the western shoulder of the break held firm, though, the same was not true to the east. The Communist attack also spread along the front of ROK III Corps, and under that pressure, plus the enemy's lapping around behind them from the X Corps break, III Corps simply collapsed and disappeared. The Chinese gained twenty miles,

ROK I Corps on the seacoast had to pull back too in order to avoid being isolated, and it was only after hard fighting by the 1st Marines, 3rd Division, and 187th Airborne RCT that the front was stabilized. There were lesser attacks farther west, toward Seoul, but this was the major threat, and by May 19 it was surmounted. At enormous cost, the Communists had again run out of steam.

In fact, they had both exhausted themselves and presented the UN Command with a striking opportunity. Both Van Fleet and Ridgway realized that the enemy forces were vastly overextended, and that their supplies and manpower had been worn down to nothing by the demands of the battle, and by their inability to bring things forward under the frantic pounding of Fifth Air Force. As they had in late summer of 1950, the Communists had gone out on a long limb; now it was time to saw it off.

Van Fleet therefore proposed to Ridgway an attack out of his firm western lines, to head northeast across the peninsula. There was implicit recognition that this was not a MacArthur-like advance to the Yalu. But a realistic assessment of conditions at the moment suggested that the UN forces could well go north again to the Kansas line, could get to the troublesome Hwachon Reservoir, whose dam controlled major rivers in South Korea, and could reach the Iron Triangle, the area between Chorwon, Kumwha, and Pyonggang. Even more important than taking ground itself, there was the chance to cripple the Communist military capacity by destroying it en masse.

On May 20 the drive to the north started. There was plenty of artillery, and the close air support provided by Air Force, Navy, and Marines was impeccable. The Communists stood where they were able to, in narrow defiles or at bridges or river crossings, but they went rapidly back, and by the end of the month, Eighth Army was well above the parallel for most of its length. The weather turned bad in the last week, grounding much of the air support and slowing the tanks and trucks to a crawl. The South Koreans made especially heavy going and had numerous casualties, both to enemy action and to the simple inability of their troops—half-trained recruits and boys—to function in the bad conditions.

Though the Communists fought hard where they could, and resistance steadily stiffened in early June up near the Iron Triangle, there was clear and abundant evidence that they had suffered a major defeat. The advancing troops took large numbers of prisoners, 10,000 by the end of May, and most of them were in deplorable condition, half starved, clad in rags, and suffering from assorted diseases and low morale. Even more significant, perhaps, the advance overran substantial supply points and captured quantities of guns, ammunition, and matériel that never had time to be distributed. This was therefore not just a head-on push, it was a real victory, and Eighth Army knew it. Its troops were on the Kansas line by the end of the month, and reached a forward extension of it, Wyoming, by the second week of June.

They pushed armored patrols into Pyonggang, the northern apex of the Iron Triangle, and just east of the Wyoming line the 1st Marines began to move on a tangled hill mass that acquired the name "the Punchbowl." The North Koreans had lost more than 600,000 casualties since beginning the war, the Chinese half a million more. Van Fleet thought he could keep going, and Ridgway reported to Washington that for at least the next sixty days, the situation should offer "optimum advantages in support of . . . diplomatic negotiations."

The United States government had already decided that it was time to play a more direct role in the negotiation process. Various United Nations initiatives had gone nowhere, and Washington in frustration chose the back-door route instead. Secretary of State Dean Acheson asked George F. Kennan, the great American authority on Soviet Russia, to make informal approaches. Kennan possessed a breadth of vision not often found in official circles, and he knew everything and everyone worth knowing as far as the Russians were concerned. He visited the Soviet ambassador to the United Nations, Jacob Malik, at the latter's home on Long Island. They had two long and wideranging discussions. In the second of them on June 5, Malik said that his government was interested in a peaceful solution to Korea. Since the North Koreans were not going to win, and now the Chinese were not going to win either, it was obviously time for the Communists to cut their losses. That still left the problem of how to go about it.

On June 23, Malik spoke on American radio, saying that the Korean problem should be settled. Official American questions in Moscow elicited the response that yes, indeed, it was time for Korea to be settled, and there should be a military armistice. Unfortunately for Washington, trying to figure out exactly what the Soviets meant at any one moment was like trying to decipher the Delphic oracle. In the *ménage à trois* of North Korea, Communist China, and the Soviet

Union, no one was ever quite sure who controlled whom to what degree; the assumption was that the Russians pulled all the strings, but this was before the days when the United States had become hostage to its own clients, so there was not a clear picture of the other side's situation.

It looked, anyway, as if the Communists wanted to talk. Accordingly, on June 30, General Ridgway, in his capacity as UN commander, broadcast a message saying he was prepared to send a representative to a meeting to discuss the opening of negotiations. Two days later, in a message signed by Kim Il Sung for North Korea and Peng Teh-huai for the Chinese People's Volunteers, the Communists offered "to suspend military activities and to hold peace negotiations." Ridgway, whose reconnaissance told him that the Communists were frantically building up after their beating, vehemently protested to Washington against any suspension of hostilities while the talks were going on, a view which was readily accepted.

It took another week to get liaison officers together to work out the physical details of a meeting, but that was accomplished on July 8, and on July 10 the first meeting between the two negotiating parties took place at Kaesong, the ancient capital of Korea. On the United Nations side, there were hopes abounding for a speedy settlement. The Communists, however, had no intention of acknowledging at the negotiating table any defeat on the field of battle. If fighting them was frustrating, talking with them was to prove even more so. The war which had lasted a year was not even half over.

PART
II
WAR OF POSTS

CHAPTER 9
NEGOTIATING

If the Korean conflict was a strange new phenomenon for Americans, a half war in a world of half measures, negotiating their way out of it was even stranger. The appropriate theme music for the truce talks would have been the same piece to which Cornwallis surrendered at Yorktown: "The World Turned Upside Down." On July 8, when the first liaison teams met to work out details, the Americans had entered the hall and casually sat down, facing south. There was great consternation among the Communists, for it turned out that in Asia, the conqueror traditionally sat facing south; they had intended that the Americans sit facing north. When the full negotiating teams met two days later, the Communists had done their preparation rather better; they provided high chairs facing south for themselves, low chairs facing north for the United Nations. When the UN leader put a small flag on the table in front of him, the Communists bustled around and came in with a big flag to put on their side. So it went; the Americans, extremely conscious of "oriental face," did their best not to make the Communists look like losers, and the Communists did *their* best to *make* the United Nations look like losers. Such little matters seemed almost laughable at first; unfortunately, they were symptomatic of the whole procedure. The American chief delegate, Vice Adm. C. Turner Joy, characterized the Communist negotiating style as insisting that two and two made six, and finally, after exhausting argument, conceding that it made five instead.

The talks opened on July 10 at Kaesong, inside North Korean lines. The United Nations delegation was based at Munsan-ni, twenty-some miles northwest of Seoul near the south bank of the Imjin River. To get to Kaesong they crossed the river, proceeded to a small outpost at Panmunjom, almost ten miles from Munsan-ni, and there passed through the Communist lines to Kaesong, another five miles. In these early sessions the Communists escorted the UN delegation triumphantly from Panmunjom to Kaesong, so later on, after talks had been suspended and were reopened in October, the arrangements were changed. Both Munsan-ni and Kaesong were declared neutral zones, and each was linked by a road corridor to Panmunjom, where the talks were then held. There had been violations by both sides of the original truce zone around Kaesong, either intentional or otherwise, and the second arrangement was both more suitable and, on the UN side, the fruit of hard experience.

The Americans, as they dominated the conduct of the war for the United Nations, also dominated the truce negotiating team. It was led by Admiral Joy, who at the time was Commander Naval Forces Far East. He was supported by officers from the Army, Air Force, and Navy; the Republic of Korea delegate was Gen. Paik Sun Yup, who had successfully commanded ROK I Corps. After ten frustrating months, Joy was relieved to return to the United States, and replaced by Maj. Gen. William K. Harrison. It was actually Admiral Joy who saw the negotiations through to their virtual conclusion, for agreement had been reached on most points by the time of his departure, and fixed positions established on those remaining in contention.

The Communist delegation was led by Gen. Nam Il, who was both Chief of Staff of the North Korean Army and vice-premier of the People's Republic. The two leading Chinese delegates were Lt. Gen. Teng Hua, commander of the 15th Army Group, and Maj. Gen. Hsieh Fang, who was Chief of Propaganda for the Northeast China Military District. Almost all of the Communists had long experience in the political field as well as the military one, while the UN delegates were strictly military professionals. As with the Communist war effort generally, it gradually appeared that though Nam Il was officially in charge, most of the major decisions were made by the Chinese.

In the early days at Kaesong, the Communists took full advantage of the setting to treat the United Nations delegation as supplicants, to act as if they had won the war and were graciously receiving requests for peace. It quickly became apparent that there was a major propaganda battle at play here, as well as the ostensibly more serious task of bringing the war to a conclusion. Both sides strove to present reality clothed in their own garb, but as the Communists controlled the site, as well as firmly controlling their own press, and initially denying access to western newsmen, they scored the more propaganda points. To counter this, Admiral Joy did better in the negotiations, insisting that they were to be purely military in character, and that hostilities would continue while the talks were in progress. That last was a major point; the Communists were frantically resupplying and rebuilding their forces in North Korea, and the UN Command was certain they wanted to regroup under the safety of talks, then open up the war again whenever it should be convenient to do so. The Americans were determined not to alternate carrot and stick, but to apply both, in the form of talks and military pressure, at the same time. Otherwise they saw the war going on intermittently forever.

The history of the armistice talks is long, complex, and enormously repetitive. At the beginning of it, the more pessimistic among the newspaper observers thought it might take six weeks to reach a cease-fire agreement. It actually took two full weeks just to agree on an agenda, or what to start talking about. There is absolutely no doubt that had anyone in authority in the United States realized that the negotiating process would drag on for just over two years, the whole war would have been fought much differently than it was.

In the afternoon session of the first meeting, the Americans proposed an agenda of nine items; the Communists countered with an agenda of five items. The Americans then produced a four-point proposal, and the Communists countered with a different five-point proposition. So it went; by the 19th, Joy wanted simply to walk out, feeling that he was getting nowhere, and that his willingness to remain at the table was only encouraging the opposition to think he would eventually cave in. Ridgway, the Joint Chiefs, and the American government, however, were determined to have the onus for any breakdown in talks rest on the other side. Joy was ordered to keep at it, though Ridgway, at least, told him he might be as rude as he thought the occasion demanded. At some stages, the delegations were reduced to sitting for hours merely glowering at each other across the table.

Eventually, of course, the irresistible and immovable objects wore each other away, and agreement was finally reached, on July 25, on an agenda. Point one was simply that yes, there should be an agenda. The second item was the drawing of a military demarcation line; third was to settle proposals for a cease-fire, including various control and oversight mechanisms. Fourth was the question of disposition of prisoners of war, and fifth was a general grab bag or "recommendations to governments" which should be made by both sides.

As they now did actually have an agreed agenda, they could move on to item two, developing a line of demarcation. On this question there was a fundamental disagreement. Baldly stated, the Communists wanted the line between the two warring parties to be redrawn at the 38th parallel. As the UN forces were now substantially above the parallel and had regained almost all of the former territory of South Korea except the isolated Ongjin peninsula on the west coast and the territory just around Kaesong, a return to the parallel would have represented a major achievement for the Communists; they would, indeed, have gained at the table all they were incapable of accomplishing on the battlefield. For these very reasons, the UN Command was adamant that the demarcation line reflect the current military situation at the time when a cease-fire should be signed. This had been one of the two major points at issue in establishing the agenda itself, for the Communists had wanted to write into the agenda item the provision for demarcation at the parallel, in effect leaving little further to be discussed.

When the meeting opened on July 27, to discuss the line, the Communists began by demanding the 38th parallel. Admiral Joy countered with a ploy of his own; he said that the UN forces were well above the parallel on the ground, but, he added, they also had absolute superiority both at sea and in the air. Therefore, as the line should recognize the total military reality of the situation, the Communists ought to accept a line where the front now was, plus a further twenty miles which the Communists should vacate as a demilitarized zone. In fact, the Americans were prepared to settle for much less than that, actually for the old Kansas-Wyoming line, but they were definitely not prepared to agree to a return to the 38th parallel.

The Communists reacted to Joy's bland proposal with near-paroxysms of outrage. There was no progress for several days, until, on August 23, the Communists charged that UN planes had bombed the site of the talks, and broke off negotiations. Actually there had been a number of violations of the talk site, by both sides, though this particular one seems to have been a fabrication. Not until October 25 did the full delegations meet again, by which time they had moved the talks from Kaesong to Panmunjom.

However, during the intermission, the Communists apparently realized that they were not going to get the 38th parallel. On the 26th, each side presented the other with a proposal that was based essentially on the line of contact. There were still several days of bitter argument, and an especially sore point was the possession of the city of Kaesong itself. The ancient capital was important simply because of its history; additionally, it was below the 38th parallel, and it was, at the moment, in Communist hands. They were determined to retain it. Eventually, in return for territory in the central sector, they did so. The Americans were more interested in the security of the Kansas line than they were in the psychological advantage of Kaesong.

The Communists next announced they wanted a line based on the *current* line of contact, so that no matter what might happen between that time and the final armistice, the line as of early November would be definitive. Ridgway strongly protested against this, saying that it would totally nullify any military pressure the UN might subsequently exert. In Washington, however, there was desperate anxiety for a truce; the American newspapers were openly criticizing the government for its quibbling, and most editorial opinion favored giving almost anything to get a cease-fire. While item two was under discussion, there were 60,000 UN casualties, and 22,000 of them were American. So Washington backed off again. Ridgway was instructed to set a time limit, thirty days, for the signing of a cease-fire, but provided it was done within that time, the UN would then agree to the current line. The Communists then refused to accept a time limit, so Washington gave up that position too, saying the thirty days might be extended if there were progress on other items. So on November 27 the demarcation-line issue was at last settled. Staff officers drew out the positions on their maps, and there was an enormous sigh of relief.

Everyone had clearly stated that hostilities would continue even while the talks went on, but the agreement on the line was hailed by western papers as virtually the end of the war. This infuriated President Truman, who emphatically announced that the war was not over. It infuriated General Ridgway even more, because he did not see how he could ask his troops to fight and die in a war their country thought was over, for pieces of ground they were going to have to give back at the cease-fire anyway. Admiral Joy was of much the same mind; he had faithfully followed his initial instructions, vigorously defended the UN position, and then been ordered to make what he thought were totally unnecessary and unwise concessions to get an agreement. He was absolutely convinced that the only way to salvage anything out of the talks was to deal from strength, and that any concession made for the sake of goodwill and accommodation was seen by the other side merely as a sign of weakness, and an encouragement to the Communists to push that much harder. Joy wrote that from this time on, the UN team "was constantly looking over its shoulder."

For better or worse, there was now agreement over a demarcation line, so the negotiators moved on to item three, the cease-fire and the control mechanisms for it. Much of the work on this topic was eventually handled by subdelegations who took up specific proposals. However, the simply stated "cease-fire" subsumed a large number of matters. The most notable of these were the questions of maintenance or removal of foreign troops from the peninsula; reconstruction of facilities, including especially transportation systems and airfields; makeup, control, and supervision of inspection teams; and types of permissible inspection and reconnaissance. All of these were unfortunately tied in together; transport and airfield rehabilitation, for example, had an obvious bearing on the capabilities of troops in Korea. What countries made up the inspection teams would have almost as much bearing upon their effectiveness as the degree of freedom of movement they possessed. And to cap it all, everyone disagreed with everyone else on even such basic items as definitions. The United Nations when it talked of using neutral observers thought in terms of Sweden, Switzerland, or perhaps India; the Communists insisted that neutral observers should come from places like Poland, Bulgaria, and possibly Czechoslovakia. As if that were not enough, Ridgway and Van Fleet often thought one type of control was needed or not needed, while the Joint Chiefs of Staff and the State Department wanted something else. Presumably the Communists had differences between field commanders and political leaders also, they too being human, but if they did, it was not apparent at Panmunjom. Even without that, there was still an *Alice in Wonderland* air about the whole procedure. Figuratively as well as literally, the parties spoke different languages and lived in different worlds.

General Ridgway's problem was that he was constantly pressing Washington to develop a hard and fast set of conditions; his natural inclination was to say, "Look, this is it; this is as far as we go; take it or leave it!" This was certainly what Admiral Joy and his long-suffering colleagues wanted to say. But Washington did not. In Washington there was a desire approaching dementia to have any possible onus for a breakdown in talks be placed on the other side. To this end the government was constantly seeking ways to increase rather than lessen its flexibility. Where Ridgway wanted to ensure the security of his command and the success of his mission, Washington wanted to get out with an agreement, any minimum agreement that the United States could live with. American planners were coming to the painful realization that a military cease-fire might be all they could get in Korea, and that it might have to suffice for the next generation. Farther away from the immediate problems—and the frustrations—of Korea, they could take a longer view than could Ridgway and the men on the spot. Whether that longer view was a wiser one, ultimately, or even immediately in terms of facilitating a settlement, is a matter of argument.

The American position on item three consisted of seven basic points. These were: one, a cease-fire; two, a supervisory commission to carry out the armistice terms; three, no increase of military forces or capabilities by either side once the armistice was signed; four, free access for the supervisory commission and its inspection teams to all of Korea; five, withdrawal of the forces of each side, guerrillas, offshore garrisons, and suchlike, to its own side of the cease-fire line; six, no armed forces to enter the demilitarized zone along the line; and seven, the demilitarized zone to be administered in accordance with the armistice terms. Of these seven points, the Communists soon accepted the first two and the last two, leaving, as expected, three, four, and five at issue. On these argument raged back and forth, both across the table at Panmunjom and, to only a slightly lesser extent, over the communications links between Tokyo and Washington.

In late December the thirty-day provision of item two ran out; still the negotiators talked on. Gradually they whittled away at the points of difference between them, and by mid-February 1952 they were down to a hard core of disagreement on the question of rebuilding airfields in North Korea capable of handling jet aircraft. The Communists insisted that a prohibition on this was an unwarranted interference in the internal affairs of the People's Republic; the Americans, for their part, knowing that air superiority was their real hole card, were not prepared to give it away.

Then in mid-February another roadblock was added to the airfield issue. It had been agreed that a Neutral Nations Supervisory Commission would be set up to monitor the armistice; each side was to nominate three neutral states, and either side's nominees had to be acceptable to the other side. The United Nations put forth Switzerland, Sweden, and Norway; the Communists responded with Poland, Czechoslovakia, and the Soviet Union. At this the Americans balked; they simply would not accept the Russians. The Communists blandly asked why not; the Soviet Union, they said, was not involved in the war and was a member of the United Nations in good standing—what was wrong with it? The embarrassed Americans did not want to say what was wrong with it; they suggested that it was too close to the fighting zone to be regarded as truly neutral, and they hemmed and hawed, but ultimately all they could do was insist on the initial provision that the nominees had to be agreeable to both sides, and that was it. Believing they had a propaganda advantage, the Communists hammered away at the point, but here was another irreconcilable difference, to be placed alongside the airfields.

On the various other matters of item three, agreement was obtained. Railroads could be rebuilt, five ports of each country would be monitored as inspection points, and offshore islands would be evacuated or exchanged. Figures for troop rotation were worked out. The Americans originally wanted to rotate as many as 70,000 men a month, but had to settle for a much lesser figure, about half that; the Communists still insisted the U.S. Army must be running a tourist service to the Far East. But even as all these matters were resolved, the question of the airfields and the role of the Soviet Union loomed larger and larger, two huge potholes on the road toward a settlement. By the coming of spring in 1952, the subdelegations handling these matters were reduced to five- and ten-minute sessions, in which they met only long enough to snarl "no change" at each other before stalking out of the truce tents again.

* * *

Frustrated in its attempts to bring the talks to a successful conclusion, Washington over the winter of 1951–52 tried another tack. This became known as the "greater sanctions" statement, and though its importance ultimately was minimal, it provides an interesting and ironic example of government thinking at the time. By December 1951 the policymakers in the State Department and the Joint Chiefs of Staff were trying to explore ways to bring more pressure on the Communists, particularly the Chinese, to move them toward a truce. The Joint Chiefs favored a naval blockade of China; the State Department thought an "economic" blockade would be better. They were thinking, in other words, of some form of action such as they had recently fired General MacArthur for advocating. Eventually this settled out into a new policy directive, known as NSC 118/2. They then went shopping among their allies for support, and finally ended up by developing the "greater sanctions" statement. They proposed, on conclusion of an armistice, to warn the Chinese not to break it, and to say, "Consequences of such a breach of armistice would be so grave that, in all probability, it would not be possible to confine hostilities within frontiers of Korea." That, they believed, would make the Communists sit up and take notice, and presumably behave themselves for the future. Ridgway thought it was so much nonsense, and when Washington instructed him that he should perhaps be prepared to give more on the airfield issue, because they would be able to fall back on the sanctions statement, he responded with little short of ridicule. In fact, giving up the airfields and making the sanctions statement would be historically equivalent to the British Parliament's repealing the Stamp Act and following it with the Declaratory Act in 1766; it was, as was said of the Holy Alliance in 1815, "a high-sounding nothing." At the end of the war, it was issued, to disappear beneath the surface of world politics without even a ripple.

By the beginning of 1952, sanctions, airfields, and even the question of the Soviet Union's role in Korea were all being overshadowed by a larger problem, one on which the truce talks were finally to hang fire. This was the enormously complex issue of item four, prisoners of war, who had them and how many, how to classify them, and what to do with them. This difficulty, around from the first days of the war, gradually grew worse and worse as time passed.

Soon after the outbreak of the fighting, General MacArthur had announced that prisoners would be treated in accordance with accepted principles; both South and North Korea followed suit. The International Committee of the Red Cross offered to act in a supervisory capacity on the matter, and subsequently did so, reporting violations by both Korean governments as time went on. When the truce talks opened in July, Admiral Joy pressed for an early exchange of POW lists, and for rapid progress on that particular matter of the agenda. The Communists were evasive in their replies, and it was not until December that they could even be prodded to furnish numbers and lists of prisoners. From there on the situation got worse. All through the early months of 1952 the negotiators alternately twisted and turned, or remained adamant, trying to find a formula, or a series of formulas, that would get them out of their several impasses. Nothing seemed to work; neither package proposals nor attempts to work out problems individually made any progress at all.

In February the Communists apparently decided to launch a major propaganda offensive on the world stage, designed to embarrass or pressure the United Nations into giving up. It started in Paris, where the UN General Assembly was meeting. Soviet Ambassador Malik accused the UN forces of firing bullets that spread "toxic gases" in Korea. Later in the month, both the North Korean and Chinese capitals charged that the Americans had "bombed" North Korea with infected insects; they then warmed to the theme, and the UN forces were also assailed for firing artillery shells containing germs, and for dropping from aircraft snails, flies, and rats that were infected with disease. By early March the Chinese were saying that the Americans were spreading bubonic plague, cholera, and typhus over Manchuria and North Korea.

The Americans were seriously alarmed by this, as the Chinese were whipping themselves up into a frenzy, and they were so excited that other nations, particularly some of the Asian ones, were beginning to believe them. In Tokyo and Washington it was agreed that there were several possible explanations: it was a mere propaganda ploy; there was epidemic disease in North Korea, and the UN was being made a scapegoat for it; or the Communists themselves were preparing to launch chemical and biological warfare. None of the explanations was very palatable. The Americans made serious and vigorous denials of all the charges, but Hungary, Poland, Romania, and Bulgaria all protested American actions to the Red Cross. The tirades went on into March and April.

Finally they died down. Both the International Committee of the Red Cross and the World Health Organization offered to investigate the charges, provided they were given access to North Korea and Communist China to do so. But in the face of repeated refusal of access, and insistence that the charges be accepted as true just and only because the Communists said they were true, their credibility took a sharp nosedive, and the campaign was at last given up. Or at least given up as far as the West was concerned. Kim Il Sung's official biography still flatly states that the imperialists unleashed germ and bacteriological warfare against the heroic North Korean people.

Meanwhile, in the hills of central Korea, the Communist and United Nations forces, all the while looking hopefully toward Panmunjom, continued to grind away at each other for nameless pieces of ground and for political advantage.

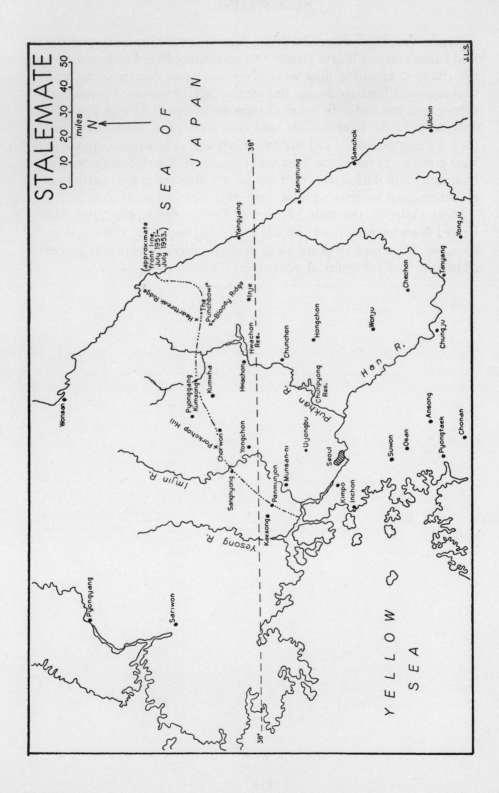

CHAPTER 10
LUNAR BATTLEFIELD

There is a hierarchical order to battles, as to almost everything else. A few are so well known, by virtue of their significance, their climactic nature, their sheer bloodiness, that almost everyone has heard of them. Most people, for example, would recognize the names of Gettysburg, the Somme, or Normandy. At the next level are battles which find their way into the history books, but drop out of common knowledge. The historian, the buff, the professional soldier, will be familiar with King's Mountain, Brandy Station, the Ia Drang Valley; he will be distressed to find the average person may not respond to such names as Chateau Thierry or Guadalcanal. Then there is another stratum where names that were once matters of great importance are all but lost; who now can recite the major battles of the War of the Spanish Succession, or reel off Frederick the Great's victories? Indeed, even whole wars are subject to this pecking order; who now can name Louis XIV's wars? As Robert Southey wrote of the significance of Blenheim, " 'Why that I cannot tell,' said he, 'But 'twas a famous victory.' "

The hierarchical order breaks down for the participants, especially in modern battle. At Gettysburg, before the smoke obscured everything, Gouverneur Warren could stand on Little Round Top and view the entire panorama of the battlefield; a soldier at Gettysburg knew he was involved in something significant. But very few of those who partake of modern battle see much of it. The soldier's recollections of combat are compounds of fatigue, fear, occasional exhilaration, absolute confusion, and noise. Often he does not even see his enemies, and all he can say is "Well, all I know is, it was a hell of a mess." But because of this very fact, that as battles opened out perception narrowed in, the soldier's view of any given battle's significance depends more on proximity than on history. What to the historian is a nameless little company-sized fight is to the participant the place where his best friend got killed, or he himself got wounded, or some incident happened that is forever engraved on his memory.

Almost all of the battles during the last two years of the Korean War fall into this category. To the rhythm of the war, advance and retreat, buildup and consolidation, offense and defense, was now added yet another factor: the pace of the truce talks. All of the major participants, with the possible exception of President Rhee, now tacitly recognized that the war was not going to be "won" in any normal sense of the word. The Chinese no longer could think of driving the United Nations forces into the sea, and the United Nations had stopped thinking of unifying Korea, either by military or by political means. The war was stalled, but it was not stopped. Both sides were now fighting with words. But since words by themselves do not mean a great deal—no matter what the writers of them like to think—they had to be backed up by other, more forceful pressures. The battlefield operations thus became a means of impressing the other side with one's sincerity, one's determination to stay the course and get a favorable settlement. The ultimate proof of determination on a given point is simple: How many lives is one willing to give for it? For two years, the belligerents offered up the lives of their young men on the altar of firm commitments.

If this seems callous and shocking, it is after all what war is about. Any government that goes to war does so, unless it is absolutely frivolous, to make a point, and it makes that point by the expenditure, in greater or lesser degree, of treasure, military skill, and above all, lives. It is more difficult for democratic states to do this than it is for totalitarian ones; democracies have to answer to their citizens, and therefore have to have a general consensus that the war is worth fighting. Totalitarian governments, as long as they can retain control over their subjects, do not have to answer to them, and can do as they please. If the citizens of a democracy withdraw their support from their government, as they did in the case of American action in Vietnam, then they are going to lose the war; that option is not available to the subjects of a dictatorship. Democracies can therefore best fight two kinds of war: little ones, which are simply fought by their professionals, without bothering the ordinary citizen; and great big ones, in which everyone can be caught up in a crusading fervor. They have very real problems trying to fight a middle-sized war, where some go and some stay home. They have even more trouble if they place a very high value on the worth of the individual, while their opponent does not.

Put all these things in the context of the last two years of the Korean War, and it is easy to see that the odds were again with the Communists. They could argue indefinitely, or thought they could; they were perfectly willing to trade manpower with the United Nations and South Korea. They could vacillate, hesitate, stall, change their bargaining position again and again, or remain perfectly unmovable. They had to answer to no one; no *New York Times* or *Washington Post* badgered them to make a settlement; no voters threatened them at the polls if they extended conscription. The United Nations, faced with all these difficulties, had to bring enough pressure to bear, at an acceptable cost, to get a settlement. The UN Command had to demonstrate its determination not to be bullied, and that meant it had to be willing to use its soldiers, and see them killed, for worthless hills. And it had to inflict such disproportionate casualties on the enemy forces that eventually they gave up before it was forced to do so. It was a juggling act of a tall order.

When the talks began in July 1951, the front line stretched across the center of the peninsula. To the south of it, the United Nations deployed some 554,000 men in seventeen divisions. Of these, ten were South Korean, seven were American; there were also a number of independent brigades or battalions. The troops were almost evenly divided; 253,000 were American, 260,000 were Korean, and 28,000 were from other United Nations members.

In support of the ground troops the UN Command still enjoyed total air and sea superiority. The Far East Air Forces were now commanded by Gen. Otto P. Weyland; they provided about 100 B-29s from the Strategic Air Command, based on Okinawa. In the combat area itself, Fifth Air Force, led by Maj. Gen. Frank E. Everest, had seven wings, two in Japan, five in Korea, flying air support, light and night bombardment, and fighter interceptor roles; they also controlled the 1st Marine Air Wing. The Air Force was flying everything from F-51 Mustangs to F-86 Sabres, the best jet in the American inventory. Commanders actually wanted to go back as well as forward, and asked for F-47 Thunderbolts to replace the Mustangs; the old "Jug" of World War II fame was a rugged brute ideal for tactical air support operations.

Offshore the Navy had three major units. Task Force 77 still provided the real muscle, with three fleet carriers, *Princeton, Bon Homme Richard,* and *Boxer,* the battleship *New Jersey,* two heavy cruisers, and eighteen destroyers. Then there was a blockading force, Task Force 95, with two smaller carriers, U.S.S. *Sicily* and H.M.S. *Glory,* plus another eighty lesser ships. Finally there was Task Force 90, the Amphibious Force. None of these faced any real opposition, though there continued to be a mine-warfare threat, and they were always conscious of the Russians not too far away.

On the other side of the line, the Chinese and North Koreans had spent the interval since mid-June rebuilding and resupplying their forces. Their renewed offensive capacity was something that caused Eighth Army heartburn, and made General Van Fleet, and General Ridgway over in Tokyo, especially anxious not to give too much away at the bargaining table. Intelligence estimates put their strength at 460,000 by the middle of July. The North Koreans had twenty-three divisions in seven corps on the line for a total of 210,000 men. The Chinese had forty divisions in fourteen corps-sized "armies," a total of 250,000 men. Eighth Army thought that there might well be elements of six other armies in the north, but lacked sufficient hard evidence to say so with any certainty. On the face of it, the United Nations enjoyed about a five-to-four superiority in manpower, but given the much larger logistical and support tail of the UN forces, the Communists had, as usual, more men at the sharp end of the stick. They did not have anything like the firepower their opponents had; they were weak in both artillery and armor, compared to the UN, let alone the naval capacity.

One thing they did have increasingly was air strength; there were once again ominous signs that the Communists were increasing their numbers of planes, trying to build up their bases south of the Yalu, and getting read to challenge for control of the sky. With something more than 1,000 planes of assorted types available, they posed a real threat, especially as United Nations policy allowed them to stay in sanctuary in Manchuria until they were ready to launch some sort of massive attack.

As the talks opened at Kaesong, there was a good deal of jockeying for position. The Americans had already decided that when the cease-fire came into effect, they wanted to hold the Kansas line as the best possible defensive position. They considered a major advance all the way to the waist of the peninsula, the old Pyongyang-Wonsan situation, but decided it would cost more casualties than it was worth. They therefore estimated that what they needed was a space twenty miles forward of the Kansas line. A cease-fire would probably be agreed along the line of contact; it would most likely call for a twenty-mile-wide demilitarized zone, ten miles of the Communists' territory, ten miles of the UN's. If the line of contact was twenty miles in advance of Kansas, they could give up ten miles for demilitarization, have a ten-mile deep outpost zone, and hold the main position on the Kansas line. Hence Admiral Joy's proposition that the Communists should recognize UN air and naval superiority by giving up twenty miles.

Since the Communists were patently not going to do that willingly, it would be necessary to fight for it, and since they were thought to be preparing an offensive, it would be best to beat them to the draw anyway. All soldiers believe the best defense is a good offense. On July 10, the same day that the talks opened at Kaesong, the government in Washington told Ridgway he could undertake any limited offensives he thought desirable to gain his preferred line.

Between the possibility of a Communist offensive and the fact of the truce talks taking place, a major UN drive was not feasible in the late summer. There was one area, however, where an advance looked particularly desirable. This was a sector in the east, about halfway between the Iron Triangle and the coast and some fifteen miles northeast of the Hwachon Reservoir. Here there was the Punchbowl; the center of this, a valley surrounded by tumbled hills, was about three miles east to west by four miles north and south. In photographs it looks like one of those panoramic scenes that directors of western movies use at the beginning of their films. The valley itself was of no real importance. The rationale for fighting here lay in the surrounding hills, which gave their possessor observation over the UN defenses and supply lines on that segment of the Kansas line.

The hills rose up to about 7,000 feet above the floor of the valley. The most significant of them from the American point of view were the two lying to the southwest and the west, soon to be known as Bloody Ridge and Heartbreak Ridge.

In late July, American troops of the 2nd Division won some hills on the approaches to the Punchbowl, providing a jumping-off place. The weather then turned wet, and it was the second half of August before the battle opened in earnest. South Korean troops of ROK I and U.S. X Corps attacked a J-shaped ridge, therefore known as J-Ridge, on the southeast, while South Koreans of X Corps moved out toward Bloody Ridge. It took eleven days of bitter back-and-forth fighting to gain and hold J-Ridge, which changed hands several times. The South Koreans took it, whereupon the North Koreans mustered a counterattack and took it back again. This seesaw action continued until Van Fleet came over and suggested to the South Koreans better employment of their reserves and supporting fire, and they finally managed to hold on to what they had repeatedly captured.

On the other side of the valley, ROK 5th Division troops had attacked Bloody Ridge simultaneously with the assault on J-Ridge. It took them five days of head-on fighting to get the dominant height, Hill 983—the heights were marked in meters—and then they were pushed off it by the inevitable counterattack. They returned to the attack, now supported by troops of the U.S. 9th Infantry. Still they could not pry the North Koreans out of their deep bunkers and holes. On August 27 the ROKs broke and gave it up, carrying some of the Americans off with them. The attack had been seen as something of a confidence-builder for the South Koreans, but obviously it had not worked that way.

The commander of X Corps, Maj. Gen. Clovis E. Byers, who had recently replaced General Almond, now decided to broaden his assault on the whole area. While the 2nd Division's regiments continued to push against Bloody Ridge, the ROK 5th Division would cut in from the north and west against that part of the valley rim, and the 1st Marines would move up past J-Ridge against the northeast rim. This enlarged drive began on the last day of August. The Marines caught the North Koreans in the middle of relieving units, and took their objectives within a couple of days. The 9th Infantry Regiment of the 2nd Division still could not clear Bloody Ridge. In the first week of September the division, with all three of its regiments up, tried a double envelopment of the whole ridge mass. This finally worked, largely because the North Koreans had evacuated the position; they simply had had enough, and pulled back.

The ridge cost the UN forces 2,700 casualties; they counted 1,389 North Korean dead, and they therefore estimated from that that there had been 15,000 casualties. This ambitious figure was arrived at by assuming that the North Koreans had been able to carry off roughly two dead for everyone left behind, and that they had had two wounded for every one killed. There were actually 264 prisoners, and they at least were easy to count. Given the way the Communists were dug in, estimating casualties was a guessing game at best, and one which unit commanders were disposed to play optimistically. The North Koreans simply did not release figures, and never have, so the UN statistics are the best available. Whatever the losses were on the other side, those on the UN side were enough to make General Van Fleet downgrade his plans for offensives, a decision which the next round, on Heartbreak Ridge, would do more than confirm.

In 1884, the British general Sir Garnet Wolseley airily dismissed the difficulties of getting up the Nile to rescue the famous "Chinese" Gordon with the remark "Rocks are rocks and water is water, wherever you happen to be." Wolseley, incidentally, failed to rescue Gordon. Anyone who had fought in Italy during World War II would have felt instantly at home on Heartbreak Ridge, for the rocks here looked exactly like those of Italy—barren, steep, cold and raw, no cover, no real approaches, a battlefield that might have been on the moon. The ridge ran north and south, rising 1,200 feet between the valleys of the Suipchon River on the west and the Sochon on the east. The North Koreans, having pulled back from Bloody Ridge, were deeply dug in again, and heavily reinforced. They had good lanes of fire and excellent mortar and machine-gun support. There were two divisions of them, and they intended to stay there.

Again it was the 2nd Division that got the nod. After heavy artillery preparation, its 23rd Regiment attacked up the east side of the ridge. The attackers ran into heavy mortar fire from well-hidden bunkers, and by nightfall of the first day, instead of sitting on top of the ridge, they were clinging precariously to a toehold on the lower slopes. The next day, the 9th Infantry, supported by tanks, attacked from the southwest; in two days it got to the southernmost peak of the ridge, but that still left the 23rd stranded. On the 16th the 23rd's infantrymen forced their way to the crest of the ridge, only to be swept away by a mass of North Korean fire. The regiment was now fought out, its line to the rear clogged with litter bearers struggling down against ammunition and ration parties sweating up. The attacks went on for another ten days. The South Koreans got some of the heights across the other side on the Suipchon valley, but that still did little to help the soldiers trying to get Heartbreak. By September 27 the 2nd Division had to call it all off, stop and regroup, and think again.

The second half of the battle was code-named Operation Touchdown. This time X Corps went at it in a big way, with increased artillery support, extra tactical air strikes, and an imaginative use of tanks. This was, of course, hardly tank country; in these mountains, again as in Italy in World War II, the tanks were employed more as mobile artillery than as proper armor. But the roads up the river valleys were carefully and surreptitiously improved by combat engineers, making them passable for the tankers. Reinforcements and replacements brought 2nd Division up to full strength, and for this phase, all its regiments plus the attached French Battalion were employed. The attack opened late in the afternoon of October 5. Under heavy gunfire, plus close air support provided by Marine Corsairs, the 2nd Division attacked up both valleys on either side of the ridge, then swung the regiments up the slopes.

By now the North Koreans were battered and worn, and the three regiments they actually had on the ridge were far understrength, but they were still well dug in and full of fight. It was slow going all the way, with friendly gunfire landing almost on top of the infantry. The Communists had to be rooted out of their holes and bunkers one by one, and few of them surrendered; most fought and died where they were. Gradually, however, the pressure began to tell; the valley attacks disrupted the resupply and the support fire for the units on the ridge, and one by one, the commanding peaks were overrun by the desperate infantrymen. On October 10 the Americans finally got some luck, and a tank breakthrough in the western valley caught the Communists trying to relieve the North Koreans with a new Chinese division. The armor broke this up and reached the little town of Mundun-ni, effectively cutting off the enemy on Heartbreak. Yet it took five more days of close-in fighting, often with bayonets, grenades, and flamethrowers, before the ridge was at last secured. Operation Touchdown was declared over on October 15.

Once again, both sides paid heavily for the readjustment of their lines. In the month it fought for Heartbreak, the 2nd Division had 3,700 casualties. It had mauled four Communist divisions, and estimated they had suffered 25,000 casualties.

While X Corps was fighting for the Punchbowl, I Corps in the west also began to move. It now had five divisions under command: 1st and 9th ROK; 1st Commonwealth, which had reached divisional strength with the arrival of the Canadian Brigade; and U.S. 25th Infantry and 1st Cavalry. The corps commander, Maj. Gen. John W. O'Daniel, known in the Army as "Iron Mike," wanted a general advance to a new line he called the Jamestown line; some miles ahead of Kansas, it would, he thought, provide him with better cover for his supply lines, which ran close behind the Kansas line. The country here was not as bad as in the east. O'Daniel was given permission to go ahead, and on October 3 he launched Operation Commando. This made very decent progress; in most places the Chinese holding this sector of the front went back slowly but steadily. However, in the center of the advance, 1st Cavalry ran into very strong opposition. It was headed for the town of Sangnyong, and as this was a major supply point for the Communists' front, they held hard to it. The hills were here lower than around the Punchbowl, but the enemy was dug in just as deep; it took three days of heavy pounding before the cavalry troopers could even budge the Chinese, and after that, they held hard to every position. The operation did not end until October 19, with 1st Corps forward on the Jamestown line. Next IX Corps, sandwiched between I and X Corps, advanced its line, and the ROKs over on the east coast made a neat little drive ten or so miles farther up the coast.

In these drives, I Corps had more than 4,000 casualties, three-quarters of them in the 1st Cavalry Division, and IX Corps had another 4,000 in its one American and two Korean divisions. It was an expensive way to bring pressure on the Communists, but they in their turn were estimated to have lost well over 50,000 men, as well as substantial amounts of equipment and supplies, all of which had had to be brought forward at heavy costs under the UN air umbrella. To questions about the casualty figures, Van Fleet or Ridgway could only reply that the mission was to keep the pressure on, and it seemed, to some extent, to be working. The Communists had recessed the truce talks in August over an alleged bombing of the truce site. At the end of the first week in October, during the height of the Heartbreak Ridge and Jamestown battles, they suggested they might be willing to talk again, and after two weeks of frustrating meetings by liaison officers, they came back to the table on October 25. As the talks started up again, the battlefield settled down. It was time once more to dig in, to lick wounds, bring up replacements, and speculate as to whether or not this war was ever going to make any progress.

As the second winter of the war came on, there was a chance for tidying up. Some troops were to go home, new ones to arrive. The talks meandered along; agreement on the demarcation line was reached in November, but the December deadline came and went, and no real progress was made.

One of the more cherished aims of the American government was to build up the South Korean Army to the point where it could take over an even greater share of its own defense. This was an extraordinarily difficult task to accomplish. There were, of course, the problems of Korea itself, of a country ravaged not only by the immediacies of war, but by decades of past exploitation as well. It was not, after all, a rich society. There were the losses of huge numbers of young men in the last year and a half, and with them much of the experience, of combat and simply of military service, that went to make an army an effective one, though this could in some measure be balanced by the invaluable knowledge which the survivors now carried with them.

Then in addition to these local impediments, there were also those the Americans labored under, the most important of them the worldwide commitments that the United States had now incurred in its effort to contain Communism. The Americans were stuck with building up not just the Korean army, but also the armies of virtually the entire free world. In October 1949, President Truman had signed the Mutual Defense Assistance Act, pledging military aid to the newly founded North Atlantic Treaty Organization. The United States agreed to provide $1.3 billion worth of military equipment and services to the western European states. Late in 1950, General Dwight D. Eisenhower was named as the first SACEUR, for Supreme Allied Commander Europe, and from 1951 to 1953 the United States distributed $20 billion worth of military funds, supplies, arms, and equipment to its allies.

Meanwhile, at home, the Strategic Air Command was being built up and the Army and the Navy both enlarged. In the first year of the war in Korea the United States drafted 585,000 men and activated 806,000 reserves or National Guardsmen. In the course of the war the U.S. Army's strength nearly trebled, from 591,000 to 1.5 million; the Marine Corps' strength also trebled, and the Air Force and Navy doubled. The rebuilding of American military strength, whose necessity had been recognized but not acted upon just before the Korean War opened, was turned into a reality by the war. It provided the initial impetus to a move that has continued ever since.

Under such circumstances, the Republic of Korea would have been a very low-priority item, except that here was where the war was actually being waged, and it was now imperative that the Koreans wage as much of it as they could handle. From the time the mobile war ground to a halt in July 1951, General Ridgway, and the Korean Military Advisory Group under him, took immediate steps to strengthen U.S. allies and surrogates. An army school system was set up, conscription and replacement services were regularized, and the Republic of Korea Army began to establish the infrastructure that civilians never pay much attention to, but that is a sort of hidden core of what armies are all about. Civilians think military services are for fighting wars, but most servicemen spend only a very small portion of their careers fighting; services are really little societies, more or less self-contained, or at least insulated from the larger bodies that produce them. What military service is *really* about is pension, promotion, social connections, a thousand and one little interrelationships. Service is a way of life, and though its ostensible purpose is to wage war—or to "wage peace" as contemporary public relations people would have us think—war is only an occasional interruption in that way of life.

The Americans had committed themselves to building up a ten-division Korean army. That was all, and perhaps a bit more than all, that General Ridgway thought they could handle; he did not have a great deal of confidence in them or their leadership, and he believed that they would be very hard pressed to produce a competent officer corps for that size army. Early in 1951, President Rhee stole a march by grandiloquently announcing that he wanted a twenty-division army, and moreover that if he got it, all the Americans could go home. This was patent nonsense, and there was good reason to believe that if the Americans equipped twenty Korean divisions and left, they would soon be fighting the equipment they had handed over someplace else, just as they had recently done with all the material given to Nationalist China, which was used against them by the Chinese Communists. General Van Fleet, who was not very acute politically, got trapped into supporting Rhee's ideas, but Ridgway dashed them with cold water. Not only did he think ten divisions and a quarter of a million men were quite sufficient, he thought as well that Korea needed no air force but only a tactical air branch of the army, no marine corps, and only a coast guard instead of a real navy.

In the end, of course, it was not possible to hold to this hard line. When General Ridgway rotated home and was replaced by Gen. Mark W. Clark in May 1952, the latter immediately endorsed a major expansion of the South Korean forces, ultimately to 415,000 men, and he also expressed his thought that of course the Koreans needed an air force and a navy. And as a navy always wants its own army, they got a marine corps too. By the end of the war, the United States was committed to indefinite support of its ally. And the Americans were to discover that they had just barely loosed the latch on this particular Pandora's box.

One of South Korea's immediate problems was the presence of large numbers of Communist guerrillas behind the lines. Many of these had been cut off in the UN drive out of the Pusan perimeter and had been left in the mountains of southwestern Korea, where, like a festering sore, they occasionally broke out and caused a great deal of trouble. The South Korean intelligence estimated that there were perhaps 8,000 or 10,000 of them, and that slightly more than half of them were moderately well armed. Some had descended into mere banditry, but there were several well-armed and competently led groups.

The most important concentration was in the Chiri-san area, mountains almost due west of Pusan and some miles inland from the southern coast. As the front slowed down, Van Fleet released two ROK divisions for antiguerrilla operations, and early in December these moved into the area. Martial law was declared, which gave the government more stringent control over everyone's movement, and in two weeks, working in from a perimeter around the mountains, the ROKs killed or captured something more than 3,000 men in the hills. They then moved north to other areas and repeated the process through the rest of the month, killing or capturing several thousand more. Finally, in January, they went back to the Chiri-san area and surrounded it a second time. Closing the ring, they broke up the last remnants of the guerrillas. The whole drive was known as Operation Ratkiller, and when it was completed in mid-March, nearly 20,000 guerrillas, twice the estimated number, had been killed or taken prisoner. It was, in fact, a major success as a military operation.

The winter brought a general slowdown of operations, while the negotiators at Panmunjom talked, postured, or sulked at each other. There were patrol actions, there were various experiments with artillery fire, but there were no major encounters. It was a static war, with both sides digging, sniping at each other, and improving their positions. Bunkers got deeper, holes were connected up and became trenches, and soldiers concentrated on basics, keeping heads down and bodies warm, and counting days until relief or rotation.

All was not, however, entirely static. The air campaign, which throughout the war had its own particular momentum, went on uninterruptedly, and in 1952 became the major source of pressure for the United Nations. The Communists, on the other side, used in that year a weapon peculiar to their own situation; in January the strange question of prisoners of war began to overshadow everything else.

CHAPTER 11
THE AIR BATTLE

The early prophets of air power repeatedly proclaimed, "The air is indivisible!" Air power, as epitomized in the strategic bomber, was able to leap oceans or mountains at a single stride, and attack, paralyze, and destroy the enemy. His industries, his communications, his population centers, his political structure, all were vulnerable to assault. Air power was the answer to the trench-bound sterility of World War I, and it was in this vein that the air war of 1939–45 was pursued. By the late forties, in the United States, the newly independent Air Force was successfully challenging the Navy's traditional role as the first line of defense. In the phrase popularized by Adm. Sir Herbert Richmond, the air force was now perceived as "the instrument of policy."

Because the early theorists were chiefly interested in the problem of total war, as discussed in the late nineteenth century and practiced in the first half of the twentieth, they did not pay much attention to limited wars. Specifically, they did not ask themselves if some portion of that indivisible air might be politically inviolable. So when it came to fighting a limited war in Korea, the United States was willing to

169

concede certain points to the enemy without ever even challenging them. The war at sea was no contest; the war on the land was doomed to stalemate. The air war thus became the arena where the United States could exert sufficient pressure to win; but it sought victory under self-imposed limitations that made the desired end highly elusive. Being a superpower in a world where you chose not to use that power was a highly frustrating exercise.

Throughout the war, there was an impressive growth of United Nations, mostly American, air strength in the combat area. The 553 combat aircraft with which the Americans began the war eventually became many thousands, though between attrition, rotation, and one thing and another, the strength at any one time was never as great as the combatants would have liked. Far East Air Forces was at its lowest ebb in the summer of 1950, just as the war began. Two years later, in the three summer months of 1952, it reached its operational peak of 1,441 aircraft, including its own planes, plus those of the Navy and Marines and three UN squadrons. There were slightly more than that on hand just after the end of hostilities in July 1953. The trebling of combat aircraft was matched by similar growth of Air Force personnel, from 33,000 in July 1950 to a peak strength of 112,000 at the end of the war.

The actual figure of available aircraft does not mean much, for "combat aircraft" includes everything from the little T-6 spotter aircraft used by the Tactical Air Control Parties, through the jet fighter of one type or another, to the B-29 bomber. For example, there were on average about 100 B-29s available at any given time, ranging from a monthly low of 75 to a high of 120.

As important as the fluctuation in numbers and types available were the geographical constants and constraints of the air battlefield. The immediate combat area was, naturally, the skies over North and South Korea, and the waters adjacent to them. But in fact the theater was larger than that. Far East Air Forces, or FEAF, actually contained three air forces; the Fifth was responsible for Japan and Korea, the Twentieth for Okinawa, Guam, and Iwo Jima, and the Thirteenth for the Philippines. It was, of course, the Fifth that became the combat command for the war, but most of the B-29 bombers were based on, and habitually flew from, Okinawa on their missions to bomb Korea. Throughout the war, there was the constant American fear that someone, probably the Soviets, would enlarge the war by an attack on Japan itself, or that the Chinese would do so by attacking Formosa, within Twentieth Air Force's area. No one was sure what would happen in that case, but it was another of those considerations that kept commanders looking over their shoulders. It might be noted, parenthetically, that while UN commanders chafed under these territorial limits, the Communists accepted limits, too. They never did enlarge the combat area.

At the start of the war, none of the Fifth Air Force units were based in Korea; they were all scattered around Japan instead. Almost all of the early missions, even close air support, were flown from Japan or from the carriers offshore. Then as the Inchon operation and the breakout from the Pusan perimeter provided elbow room, many units were based in Korea itself, and some, before the Chinese intervention, were moved even as far north as Pyongyang. The Chinese changed that, and by the end of 1950 about half of the Fifth Air Force was based in South Korea, around Seoul or down in the Pusan area. Finally, by the time the truce talks began, virtually the entire Fifth was in South Korea, the vulnerability of Japan having to be accepted as the price of putting air pressure on the Communists in Korea.

The greatest constraint on operations was the inviolability of Manchuria. With its short frontier with Korea, the Soviet Union was a less important immediate problem, if potentially a larger long-range one. But Manchuria bedeviled the entire air war. Right from the start the United States government decided that Manchurian—Communist Chinese—airspace should not be entered. There were, of course, inadvertent border crossings during the war, but the restrictions were strengthened periodically. The outstanding example of violations by Americans was the strafing of a Soviet airfield well into Siberia by two overly exuberant Shooting Star pilots, and they were both court-martialed.

The issue naturally became much more complicated when the Chinese entered the war. While they insisted that their forces were only "volunteers," it was very difficult to accept that they could fly from Manchurian bases with impunity, attack UN aircraft across the Yalu in North Korea, and then return home, safe as soon as they reached the river. Such restrictions made sense to Washington and the United Nations, and they were presumably a source of great satisfaction in Peking, but they disgusted and infuriated the men who were shot at and perhaps killed because of them.

As the war passed through its different phases, there was a repeated shifting of boundaries in the air war, not only with air-to-air combat, but also in terms of ground targets. At some periods the bombers were kept many miles below the Yalu; at others they were permitted to hit targets close to the river. As several important hydroelectric complexes were very close to the Yalu or the Tumen, bombing of those specific targets was a matter that had to be cleared all the way to Washington itself.

Fighting a limited war was an exercise that challenged the imagination, and nothing illustrated that better than the matter, which came up several times during the war, of the bridges across the Yalu. These were both numerous and strong, most of them built by the Japanese, and they provided vital avenues of supply for the Communists. They were well defended by antiaircraft batteries, as well as by aircraft operating out of Manchurian airfields just a few minutes' flying time away. Yet when Washington authorized attacks on the bridges, it specified that there was to be no violation of Manchurian territory. This mean the attackers had almost no latitude for their attacks; they *had* to fly certain courses, often at certain heights, to hit their targets. All the Communists had to do was figure out the avenues of attack, line their guns up on them, and let the Americans come in and pay the price. Then, while the bombers or fighter-bombers ran through the shooting gallery, the Communist planes took off in Manchuria, climbed to get the advantage of altitude, swooped over the border, made a diving pass at the Americans that gave them the crucial edge of both height and speed, and fled back across the river again, safe from harm.

This is the most extreme example of tactical restrictions placed on the American pilots, but it is illustrative of the whole. It led General Stratemeyer, then commanding Far East Air Forces, to protest to MacArthur, and caused him to complain to the Joint Chiefs of Staff. There was considerable sympathy for the plight of the combat pilots among the Joint Chiefs, who were all men who knew what it was like to be shot at. They therefore pressed for permission for "hot pursuit," a well-established international principle that allows someone under attack to pursue his attacker across neutral borders for a few miles or a couple of minutes. President Truman was equally receptive, but he would not go alone; the State Department consulted with five of its allies, Britain, Canada, Australia, France and the Netherlands, but they all came back with a strong no. They were too afraid to do anything that might risk enlarging the war, which therefore continued to be waged on Communist terms.

Because of the comprehensive nature of air warfare, it is somewhat difficult to classify or categorize its operations. There is constant overlapping between control of the air and the effects of that on the ground war, between tactical and strategic strikes. In very general terms, however, there were five types of employment for air power. Taken in no particular order, they were supply and logistics, tactical support of ground troops, strategic bombing, air interdiction, and air superiority. Each was dependent upon, and interwoven with, the others, and each had its own vital importance, though some were obviously more dramatic than others.

Air supply and logistics would appear to be the most mundane of the lot, though an aircrew trying to get their overloaded plane on or off a short, muddy strip in the midst of a sudden rainstorm would probably not think of their job as mundane. The airlift capability in the theater became truly enormous as the war went on, and the original provisional Combat Cargo Command evolved into the 315th Air Division, with something more than 200 aircraft in operation. These were largely the standard transport aircraft of the day, from the C-47, workhorse of World War II, through the C-54, C-119 Flying Boxcar, and all the way up to the huge C-124 Globemaster. They carried troops on regular runs, dropped paratroops in assaults, evacuated wounded, and provided rotation service; they also carried supplies and equipment, from much-needed ammunition for local shortages to the famous dropping of the bridges for the Marines coming down from the Changjin Reservoir. This was the sort of work that went largely unnoticed, and mostly unheralded, except during an emergency. But it was also the sort of work, providing the type of flexibility, that kept emergencies from getting out of hand. The bare fact that there were on average twice as many aircraft performing these support services as there were engaging in strategic bombing at any one time is some indication of its importance.

For the combat troops on the ground, air supply was of significant interest at only two times: when they were flown into Korea, and when they were flown out again. What they were much more aware of, and grateful for, was the close air support on the front lines. This went through a dramatic evolution in the course of the war, especially during its early stages. In the first weeks of the war it was pretty haphazard, and friendly troops were often hit by their own aircraft. Support gradually became much more sophisticated, following techniques pioneered by the Marines. Close air support was in constant demand, and there was a good deal of friction over its control, the requests made for it, and the Air Force's ability or inability to fulfill them. Troops on the ground never thought they had all the support they needed; the air people often thought that they were asked to do things that simply could not be done from the air.

One of the problems was simply the type of aircraft available. The post–World War II Air Force had not been especially interested in tactical air support, being more absorbed in the big bomber and the advent of the jet fighter. It was something of a throwback to find that the Mustang, on its way out, was the best weapons system for helping out ground forces, or that the Marines' Corsairs were able to do things that the Air Force could not. It was, as always, the ultimate test of combat that revealed what a given aircraft could or could not do, what needed to be changed and what retained. Initially, for example, commanders thought jet aircraft were unsuitable for tactical air support—they were simply too fast to spot and strike small targets close to friendly forces. Yet the Air Force was necessarily committed to the jet, and eventually both the F-80 Shooting Star, supposed to be purely an interceptor, and the F-84 Thunderjet, ostensibly a fighter-bomber, were used for close support; in fact, they proved more effective at that than at their designed role of air fighting. On the other hand, such types as the famous AD Skyraider, designed as a Navy dive-bomber, were so useful that they soldiered on virtually forever, through Korea, in the sixties with the French in Algeria, then again with the Americans all during the Vietnam War. The jets could patrol over the front lines for only a few minutes; the Skyraider could hang around on call for three or four hours.

Being on call was part of the problem, for in tactical air support the ability to designate a target and then get a plane to hit it while it is still vulnerable is the chief part of the business. Air Force officers and men provided control groups that served with the ground forces and called in air strikes as necessary. The system gradually developed, and the different elements of it made major progress when jobs were temporarily interchanged. An infantry captain who was taken up in a Texan, or better, a jet, got an appreciation of the pilots' difficulties that he had lacked before, while a pilot who did a stint as a ground controller soon appreciated why infantry might be impatient for a strike against a hidden mortar position.

For every action there is a reaction. United Nations air units flew very close to 100,000 tactical air support sorties during the course of the war, divided about half and half between the Air Force on the one hand and the Navy, Marines, and allied units on the other. The Communist response was largely a passive one. They did not enjoy sufficient air superiority that they could use their aircraft in ground support operations. Occasionally they would slip a plane or two across for a strafing attack, and in some areas there were periodic visits from a local "Bedcheck Charlie," sometimes flying little Polikarpov PO-2 biplanes, looking like something that had strayed into the combat zone from an antique air show. But for the most part the Communists improved their antiaircraft capability, to keep the UN fliers at bay, and they dug deeper and deeper, and got better and better at camouflage. While it sounds ineffective, it meant the pilots had to work harder to achieve smaller results. Here again was another microcosm of the war, the expensive and technologically advanced western pilot in his jet aircraft with his bombs, machine guns, and his napalm, versus the Communist infantryman with his rifle, perhaps his light machine gun—and his shovel.

At the other end of the air-war spectrum was strategic bombing, a campaign carried out almost exclusively by the big B-29 Superfortress. This had been the ultimate bomber of World War II, the zenith of grace, power, and destruction. By 1950 the pace of aircraft development was such that World War II's heaviest bombers were now classified as medium bombers, though they remained the largest employed in the Korean War. There were occasional attempts to use them tactically, as in the famous carpet bombing along the Naktong, but they were not designed for that sort of work, and in the Air Force at least it was acknowledged that that was a serious misapplication of the type.

There was also a peculiar problem associated with the proper role of such a weapon. Right from the start of the war, the big bombers started hitting North Korean industrial targets, playing the kind of role the heavy bomber force had done in World War II. Yet even as they did so, the UN Command realized that the destruction of North Korean industry itself could not win the war, for it was Chinese, Manchurian, and Soviet industry that enabled the enemy to keep going. Wiping out every factory in the People's Republic was certainly going to inconvenience the enemy, and might put very heavy pressure on him indeed; it could not make him quit altogether if he did not want to do so.

Nevertheless, the B-29s went after their targets. They were actually more concentrated than a casual glance at the map might suggest. There were four industrial complexes in the northeastern part of the country, Wonsan, Hungnam, Chongjin, and Rashin, though the last of these was only seventeen miles from the Soviet border. Then the capital, Pyongyang, was also a key center. There were various lesser targets around the country. Then there were five major hydroelectric complexes in the northeast, and one more, one of the largest in the world, thirty miles above the mouth of the Yalu, at Supung, or Suiho. Much of the power generated by these systems was exported to North Korea's neighbors. Putting all the information together, the American intelligence teams in the Far East Command produced a priority system aimed at destroying North Korea's war-making capacity first, and then designated to bite deeper and deeper into the country's economic life as the war went on, which in the beginning, of course, no one expected it to do.

In the first few days of fighting, the B-29s were used against troops in the field, dropping fragmentation bombs around the Han River bridges, for example, but the results were marginal. The opening strategic strike was against the railroad yards at Wonsan on July 13, made by groups who had just deployed to the Far East from the United States. Then on July 30 and on August 1 and 2, there were three heavy strikes against the chemical plants around Hungnam. A week later they went back to Wonsan again. The bombing was done visually whenever possible, but the planes could also bomb by radar through cloud cover, so that visibility was not quite the problem it had been during World War II.

Within two months, the bombers were running out of industrial targets. By the time of the Inchon landing the complexion of the war was changing. FEAF now wanted to know whether it should be content with incapacitating North Korea's industry, or whether it should pound the place into the ground. With the plant complexes destroyed, it now turned to the hydroelectric systems, and on September 26 it destroyed the first of these, the Fusen Hydro Plant, which was in the hills in back of Hungnam. At that point, Washington decided to call off the campaign; UN troops were soon to cross the 38th parallel, and the American government was anticipating the unification of all of Korea. Why destroy what the United States would then only have to rebuild?

Though this effort, for reasons cited earlier, could not have a decisive effect on the war, there is no doubt that it was highly successful within its limited possibilities. On the other hand, even though the Americans, enjoying complete air superiority and therefore able to warn civilians of impending attacks, inflicted relatively few casualties in these raids, they attracted a good deal of adverse press reaction, in Europe and especially in Asia. The Communists made free charges of terror bombing, and these were widely accepted in the neutralist press; the official American history of air operations itself felt constrained to deal with such charges. Even though this was before the period when people had begun to question intensely the morality of strategic bombing, there were those who suggested that such heavy bombing might not be the best way to convince people of the desirability of democracy as opposed to Communism.

With the UN entry into North Korea and the subsequent Chinese intervention, the focus of the medium-bomber attacks shifted. They were used for the next several months on interdiction missions against enemy communications and supply points, and it was not until well after the truce talks began that they came back to the strategic role. It was in the spring of 1952 that the Americans began to exert a concerted pressure by air attack on the Communists, in the hope of making them accept terms at the negotiations. Beginning in May, UN air forces mounted massive attacks, with hundreds of fighter-bomber sorties, against all sorts of repair and supply facilities. The newly appointed Commander in Chief Far East, Gen. Mark Clark, wanted to make them pay for the incessant haggling at Panmunjom, and air power was the best way to do it.

With this idea, the FEAF Bomber Command resurrected the question of the hydroelectric plants. This time there was no cavil, and on the afternoon of June 23 a spectacular series of attacks was launched. In the first of these, dive-bombers and F9F Panther jets hit the plant at Supong, deep in the heart of MiG Alley, the pilots' name for heavily defended Communist airspace in northwestern Korea, while Air Force F-86s flew top cover. The Panthers suppressed enemy antiaircraft fire while the Skyraiders hit the hydro plant. There was a major MiG base just minutes' flying time away, and about 250 Communist planes took off in response to the strike, but instead of attacking they flew away from the battle, inland into Manchuria.

The Supong attack was followed that same afternoon by fighter-bomber blows against three other hydroelectric complexes, and these in their turn were succeeded by B-29 attacks during the night. The bombing went on for two days, and when the smoke cleared, analysts studying photographs concluded that North Korea had lost 90 percent of its electrical power capacity. Only two planes had been shot down, both of them Navy, and their pilots were rescued. Not only was North Korea's power grid practically destroyed, but plants as far away as Port Arthur in Manchuria, and even in northern China, were without power for shorter or longer periods. It may well have been the outstanding strategic air strike of the war.

Unfortunately, whatever bargaining leverage all this might have generated at Panmunjom was dissipated by western political reaction. American congressmen wanted to know why this had not been done sooner, to which the administration could only mumble some lame replies, but there was a furor in Britain when the Labour opposition denounced the fact that it had been done at all, and even introduced a motion of censure against the government.

Yet it was clear from this kind of operation that if pressure was to be put on the Communists, air power was the best way to do it; it was expensive in material terms, but it was cheap in manpower. The Far East Air Forces had already mounted several interdiction campaigns against North Korea; from this point on the strategic bombing and the more direct military strikes merged increasingly as the United Nations tried to force an agreement at the table.

Somewhere in the gray area between strategic bombing of industrial targets and the immediate tactical support of troops lay the vast majority of air effort in the Korean War. From the very outset of the conflict until its ambiguous conclusion, United Nations aircraft went after the enemy's communications network and his logistics support system for his armies at the front. It was expensive work, for it risked a highly trained pilot and a costly airplane to bomb a culvert or strafe a truck; it was dangerous, flying at high speed and low altitude into possible antiaircraft traps. And it was repetitive, for the same rail switch or road bridge might well be destroyed today and repaired by tomorrow and destroyed again the next day. But it was a vital part, of halting the Communist drives while they were on the offensive, of preventing buildup of resources when they were quiescent, or simply of making the whole effort so difficult that the Communists would eventually choose to give it up.

This was work for the fighter-bomber types, the Air Force's Mustangs, Shooting Stars, and Thunderjets, the Marines' Corsairs, the Navy's Skyraiders and Panthers. All-weather aircraft such as the Twin Mustang, or night intruders such as the B-26, provided special talents, and the Royal Navy's propeller-driven Fireflies and Sea Furies were also adepts at this type of operation. In many ways this was the worst kind of flying, for overall it was the day-after-day, night-after-night kind of operation that could become almost routine—and then suddenly turn dangerous and kill people.

This interdiction work began in June 1950, and was among the earliest UN responses to the crisis. It gained increasingly in effectiveness, and was particularly useful in taking the impetus out of the Communist attacks. The Communists could bring sufficient supplies forward to mount an offensive, but once they were committed to one, UN airpower was inevitably able to prevent their sustaining it. After ten days or two weeks they would have used up their accumulation, and they would then have to pause and go through the buildup once again. Ironically, the more successful the Communists were, in terms of advancing south and gaining real estate, the more vulnerable they were to wide-ranging fighter-bomber attacks. In that sense, they were up against a law of diminishing returns. Down below the 38th parallel a relatively small advance cost them an inordinate amount of effort.

In spite of the impressive use of interdiction during the first year of the war, it was after the truce negotiations began that it really came into its own. Gen. Otto P. Weyland, who had just assumed command of FEAF, suggested that interdiction could be used as a virtually independent campaign, that the war should not be stalemated, or regarded as such, because the front had solidified, and that air power could be the best means of making the Communists see the light. The final result of his suggestions was a ten-month-long struggle, starting with heavy attacks around Pyongyang, then formalized into Operations Strangle and Saturate.

Strangle actually began in late May 1951, concurrently with the UN drives to the north of that period. It was designed to break down the Communist supply system in the area within 100 miles or so of the front, and featured intensive attacks, day and night, by Air Force,

Navy, and Marine aircraft against rail lines, bridges, road junctions, and supply points. It worked well while the advance was going on, not only preventing movement of material southward, but also keeping the Communists from evacuating material northward out of reach of UN ground troops. However, once the ground pressure eased off, results were less satisfactory; under static front conditions, the enemy had sufficient flexibility to avoid the worst damages the air forces could inflict.

Target analysts then decided that the most profitable attacks would be against the railroad system. From an airman's point of view, the nice thing about railroads is that they are visible, they are stationary—at least the rails are—and they have accessible choke points, bridges, culverts, switches, shunting yards, and roundhouses. The Americans concluded that by putting most of the UN air effort on the railroads, they could make it almost impossible for the Communists to sustain their war effort. Given the concept, this operation too was called Strangle. Launched in the middle of August, it lasted until April 1952.

Unfortunately, it was not as productive, or destructive, as initial projections had suggested it would be. North Korea was divided up, with the Navy hitting targets in the northeast part of the country, the Air Force covering the rest of it, and the B-29s attacking major spots such as the big bridges across large rivers. For the first two months it worked well. There was a noticeable falling-off of Communist rail traffic, and they were obviously having difficulty keeping their front supplied. There were constant breaks of the main lines, and a major reduction in available rolling stock. The night-intruding B-26 bombers found lucrative targets of trucks on the roads, showing that the enemy was forced to seek alternate means of getting material forward.

Gradually, however, the effectiveness of Strangle declined. There were several reasons for this, but the overall one was that the air forces could not apply enough pressure enough of the time to bring North Korea's transport net to a halt. This was particularly true in the face of enemy countermeasures, adopted in a wide variety. One simple explanation was that a railroad, stationary target though it might be, proved pretty hard to break. It took a direct hit by a 500-pound bomb to blow the track apart, and target analysis showed that only about one sortie in four achieved that. The Communists also proved immensely resourceful in repairing roads, and camouflaging what they were doing. For example, bridges were blown, but traffic reports and night reconnaissance revealed that somehow they were still being used; what happened was that the enemy carefully prepared a portable bridge, hid it during the day, and moved it into place and used it during the night. In other places bridges were laid under the water, an old trick from the Naktong days. But the most striking response was simply the huge deployment of skilled and unskilled railway repair crews, with small squads responsible each for its own section of track. At first a single break might take hours or even days to repair. But then observers noted that repairs were being made much more quickly. Next it appeared that even multiple breaks were soon restored, because the North Koreans had put so many workers along the lines they could handle a whole series of breaks simultaneously. This being the case, the Americans concluded, a single break held them up as long as several breaks. Naturally, it did not take too long to go from there to the next stage, that it was not really worth the effort after all.

This was particularly true when the campaign was costly, for not all measures were passive. The Communists also brought in a good deal of antiaircraft artillery, so that raids on crucial targets became pretty chancy; one route in northeastern Korea was named Death Valley by the Navy. Even risking, let alone losing, million-dollar planes and highly trained pilots to blow up a culvert and interrupt rail traffic for two hours is simply not a paying proposition. By early 1952, Operation Strangle was allowed to run down, and though Air Force spokesmen put the best interpretation possible on it, it was clear that its original hopes had not been fulfilled.

In March, after studying what they had done and how the Communists had reacted to it, the Air Force opened Operation Saturate. This was designed not so much to blanket the enemy network as to find certain major sectors and demolish them completely, so that heavy equipment would have to be brought in to effect repairs. There were, after all, fewer heavy repair units than there were peasant workers deployable in North Korea. In late March the fighter-bombers went after one particular strip of line and attacked it repeatedly for two days; it was back in service a week later. They kept on into April, but again with diminishing results and increasing losses to flak. By mid-May, Saturate too was running down.

*   *   *

181

All of these air operations depended upon, and demonstrated, one thing: absolute or nearly absolute control of the skies. Just as the water around Korea belonged to the United Nations, so did the air over it. But that was not a foregone conclusion. The UN airmen always had to be wary of those planes sitting safe across the border in Manchuria, for on several occasions they came south to do battle. In air-to-air combat, there was a strange rhythm whose beat was dictated by the Communists, and which the United Nations never fully fathomed.

Airplane-versus-airplane combat is of course the be-all and end-all of the pilot's existence. Young boys dreaming of flying planes do not see themselves in the cockpit of a maritime patrol plane gazing at endless empty horizons. They visualize themselves taking on the Red Baron or Erich Hartmann or Saburo Sakai. Korea added a new stratum to this sort of fantasy, for it brought the world's first combat between jets, and therefore the world's first jet aces, a group which thirty years later still remains one of the most exclusive in the world.

The North Koreans' air force did not last long. It started out with only about eighty pilots, most of them new. The Communists were flying propeller-driven planes, largely Yakovlev, or Yak, Russian-built fighters, good planes by late World War II standards; the Yak-9 compared in many respects with some of the Spitfire variants. But they were outclassed by the F-80 Shooting Star jets the Americans were flying, and though the North Korean force was not totally destroyed, it was soon hunted from the skies and reduced to little more than a nuisance.

It was another matter, however, when the MiG-15 appeared in the enemy's inventory. Until the first of November the United Nations had it pretty well its own way in the air, and could fly such types as the Texan, Mustang, Corsair, Skyraider, Firefly, or Sea Fury, almost contemporary with the Yak, with impunity, especially when they were covered by the presence of the jet Shooting Stars. But with the Chinese intervention came the MiG. The neat little swept-wing fighter had close to a 100-mile-an-hour speed advantage over the Shooting Star, as well as better dogfighting qualities in several areas. In its first brushes with the Navy, it also showed it could outpace the new Grumman F9F Panther, though the American pilots' skill and experience usually brought them out on top.

November was thus a scary month, while the UN air forces watched, but did not touch, the ominous buildup of Red Chinese air strength across the Yalu. And while the Chinese did that, the Americans undertook a rapid deployment of newer jet types to the theater, in the form of the F-84 Thunderjet, and better yet, the F-86 Sabre. The Thunderjet was a workhorse of the air forces of the fifties, and it eventually equipped many American-supplied countries as well as the USAF itself. But it too had its limitations. A straight-wing fighter, though later variants had a swept wing, the F-84E that fought in Korea still could not match the MiG-15, and it also needed an enormously long runway, in itself a problem in Korea. But the Sabre turned out to be a true classic, the best aircraft in the United Nations inventory, the first American swept-wing fighter. Many of its performance characteristics were still slightly below those of the MiG, but the whole package was a superior airplane, and flown by better pilots using better tactics, it was soon master of all it surveyed.

As Eighth Army retreated south under intense pressure in December 1950, the Air Force and the Chinese mixed it up in the sky along the Yalu. There began to be significant air battles between Communist and UN jets, and aerial victory scores started to climb, though it was not until May 1951 that USAF Capt. James Jabara became the first jet ace in the world, and it was September before he was joined by two others, Capts. Richard Becker and Ralph Gibson. Many Communist planes were destroyed on the ground, both in the early days of the war and later as they tried to deploy south and rebuild their strength inside Korea, but the crediting system of the war insisted on aerial destruction to count toward becoming an ace; that depended not only on skill and luck, but also on the enemy's willingness to come up and fight. Jabara went on to become a triple ace before the war was over. Only one Marine managed to become an ace, Maj. John F. Bolt, just before the end of the war. The sole Navy ace of the thirty-seven the war produced was in quite a different category. Lt. Guy Bordelon was a Corsair pilot from U.S.S. *Princeton,* and the propeller-aircraft fliers were pretty well out of the running. But Bordelon was a specialist in night-flying interception of intruder aircraft, and he got his scores on trainer and ground-strike aircraft flying night heckling missions.

There were several periods of intense air-to-air combat, when the Communists came across the Yalu in force. In the intervals between them, they followed a strange pattern. The Americans finally concluded that what they were actually doing was training classes of pilots. They came across timidly in flights, shepherded by a couple of hotshots who were obviously their instructors. At first they would run at the slightest sign of opposition; then gradually they would become bolder, until they were ready, or thought themselves ready, to dogfight. At this stage they usually paid heavily for premature confidence. Then the cycle would begin all over again, as the now-blooded survivors presumably went off to other duties and a new class came in. It was indeed a strange war.

Though they never approached any real air supremacy, there were a couple of times the Communists reached for it, and for some time in the middle of the war they actually did come close to dominating the area the air forces knew as MiG Alley, which was the diamond-shaped extreme northwest corner of North Korea. Fighting here was almost giving the game away; the Americans had to fly so far, and the Communists were so close to their immune Manchurian bases, that it was highly hazardous, and required precise timing, to work in this area for nominal returns. For that very reason, this was where the Communists were willing to engage; therefore this was where the Americans had to fight them. Again they accepted the disadvantages of the situation, gave the odds to the enemy, and still beat him cold.

Just because air pressure was the Americans' chief means of forcing the Communists into accepting a cease-fire, the airfield issue at the truce talks was one of those to which they clung most determinedly. For if North Korean airfields could be repaired and made serviceable, and above all improved to the point where Communist jet planes could operate from them, then air superiority was going to be that much more difficult, indeed perhaps impossible, to sustain. Accepting the immunity of Manchurian bases was giving away enough already to create very real disadvantages. Eventually, of course, the Americans were prepared to concede on this point too; they had to recognize they could not hope to prevent some long-term rehabilitation of air facilities in the north.

But whatever retreat might be necessary around the table, the war in the air went on. Right until the last moment, the Fifth Air Force, the Navy, and the Marines flew along the Yalu, striking at ground targets and trailing their coats across the sky, daring the Communists to come up and fight. Even on the last day of the war, there was still air activity. This had the effect of demonstrating two paradoxical points. One was that the UN forces had indeed achieved air superiority over North Korea. They could strike, not unmolested, but virtually where and when they pleased. At practically the end of the war, for example, they launched devastating strikes against the irrigation dams in central North Korea. They had already long destroyed the country's industrial capacity; now, hitting at the production of the rice crop, they attacked its very means of subsistence. The first attacks were highly successful; after them the Communists released the water behind the remaining dams, so they could not be effectively blown, but as they needed that water for the rice paddies, even this had its effect, and was just one more added incentive to get a truce signed.

But the second point that these last strikes demonstrate is the simple ability of the enemy to hold out under them. There is absolutely no doubt that air power, or air pressure as it was called during the fighting, was a major instrument of policy in getting the Communists finally to sign a truce. But it was far from the sudden, catastrophic blow that theorists of air power had prophesied. They had seen air power as the means to avoid the long war of attrition, such as they had fought in World War I. Yet World War II had shown that air power raised attrition to another level of destruction, rather than getting rid of it. The Allies bombed Germany and Japan over and over again, attacking their entire society instead of just their fighting forces, and it still took years of intense, costly effort before they collapsed. Nuclear weapons might change that, but no one was yet sure, and they were, of course, not used in Korea. So it was still a matter of attrition, and if, in that process, many areas were to be regarded as sacrosanct for political reasons, then the attrition was going to be a long and painful process. The UN forces could, and did, control the skies over North Korea; they could, and did, bomb it until the cows came home; they could, and did, destroy much of its industry, transport, communications, armed forces, even its agricultural base. But as long as there were numerous other variables, they could not by that alone end the war. That was a lesson still being learned twenty years later, in another war.

Meanwhile the Communists had a weapon of their own to play. Where the United Nations tried air pressure to win the peace, the Communists used the bizarre issue of prisoners of war and propaganda.

CHAPTER 12
THE PRISONER-OF-WAR ISSUE

The negotiators at Panmunjom, stalled on the issue of airfield rehabilitation, turned their attention to item four of the agenda, the
question of prisoners of war. Superficially, this looked as if it ought
to be simple. The United Nations held so many Communist prisoners, and the Communists held so many United Nations prisoners.
They might be exchanged all for all, or one for one, or at any
agreed-upon ratio in between. There was in existence the Geneva
Convention of 1949 Relative to the Treatment of Prisoners of War,
and though not all the major participants had adhered to it—the
United States, for example, had signed but not yet ratified it—all had
announced they would abide by its principles.

Yet for some reason, handling the prisoner-of-war question became more and more tortuous, until it finally was the issue on
which talks were broken off, and the war continued, almost indefinitely. There were holes in the Geneva Convention through
which it was possible to drive a truck—perhaps all the way to
victory.

The first problem was to find out just who held what. When the negotiators met on the prisoner question initially, Chinese Maj. Gen. Lee Sang Cho offered a flat all-for-all exchange; everything else, he said, was merely detail to be worked out. American Rear Adm. R. E. Libby held back; before they got to that, he said, the United Nations wanted to exchange lists of prisoners, and wanted access to POW camps in North Korea for the International Committee of the Red Cross; this was December 1951, and the ICRC had been fruitlessly wooing the Communists since the opening days of the war, even though this access was one of the major points of the convention to which the Communists announced their adherence. From this, which could hardly be considered a high point, things rapidly went downhill.

After a week of haranguing, the Communists finally agreed to provide lists of captives, and four days later they did so. Here came another shock. The Communists admitted to having 188,000 men missing. Fairly early on it had become apparent that substantial numbers of these were actually South Koreans who had been impressed by the North Korean armies during their initial successes. In the summer of 1951, therefore, the UN Command had conducted a thorough screening of its prisoners, and as a result had reclassified them; it now claimed to hold 132,000 more or less genuine POWs, and another 37,000 who were now called "civilian detainees." However they were classified, the UN could account for 169,000 of the 188,000 the Communists counted as missing.

But on the other side it was a far different matter. The South Koreans had listed 88,000 of their men as missing, and the United States 11,500, with the British, Turks, and other UN participants listing a few hundred. The Communists, trumpeting their victories in the first few months of the war, had proudly claimed to have taken 65,000 prisoners, though after releasing the names of 110 they had never announced any more. The list they now submitted to the truce talks held 7,142 South Korean and 4,417 United Nations personnel, of whom 3,198 were Americans, 919 British, and 234 Turks. Of slightly more than 100,000 missing, then, the Communists admitted to holding only 11 percent, and only one-fifth of what they previously boasted of having captured. Clearly something was wrong here, and it only slowly dawned on the UN Command that it was facing the possibility of a major disaster.

Meanwhile, the UN was working its way toward a satisfactory position of its own. To simplify the matter, the question came to center on voluntary repatriation. The Geneva Conventions of both 1929 and 1949 had assumed as a matter of course that prisoners of war would wish to return to their homelands. It happened that World War II had produced contradictory evidence on this matter; large numbers of German POWs, for example, had been forcibly retained in the Soviet Union, and indeed had still not been allowed to go home by 1949. On the other hand, large numbers of Russians, Poles, and other eastern Europeans, who had fought in the German Army, of their own will or otherwise, did not wish to return home to face a victorious Communism, and many of them were forcibly repatriated by the western Allies at Soviet behest. The Geneva Convention, however, was primarily concerned that prisoners should be allowed to return home, and therefore this total repatriation was the point on which it concentrated.

By the summer of 1951, the United Nations was well aware that many of the prisoners it held would *not* wish to return home, either to North Korea or to Communist China. It therefore moved to the concept of voluntary repatriation: every prisoner should be able to go home *if he wanted to do so*. But if he did not, he should not be forced back. This was a good arguing point, for in a *de facto* way the Communists had already accepted it. One explanation for all those missing numbers, they said, was that they had simply been released and allowed to return home or to their own lines after seeing the errors of their ways. In fact, of the 88,000 still unaccounted for, less than 200 had come back through the lines in this fashion, but it still appeared as if the principle had been conceded. Further, the wording of the Chinese proposal for exchanges stated that prisoners should be "released," and then free to return to their homes, so that there was in it an implication of some voluntary quality in their return.

However, when the UN negotiators openly broached the subject of repatriation being voluntary, the Communists flatly refused. They now stood on the rock of Geneva, and having blatantly disregarded it on the matter of inspection of camps, production of lists, and any number of other provisions, they insisted on total repatriation in accordance with the convention; the devil can quote Scripture.

To a rational mind, it would appear that eventually all that can be said on an issue has indeed been said. That, however, does not prevent its being said over again. And again. And again. And again. This the negotiators now did. Some days were different; some days they insulted each other, some days they laughed at each other; some days they reiterated their own positions, and some days they reiterated their attacks on the other's positions. It went on through January 1952, and through February. Each side twisted and turned, but they always came back to, and down to, that hard, inescapable little core of voluntary repatriation. The Communists would not accept a formula that they feared might make them look like fools, repudiated by large numbers of their own soldiers. The United Nations had decided that it would keep fighting rather than force men to return against their will to live under the Communist system.

Though the negotiators must often have felt as if they lived on another planet, none of what they were doing happened in a vacuum. The fighting was, of course, continuing, with variations in tempo, and the POW situation itself was evolving, especially so as the negotiators, in discussing it, focused the world's attention on it. For the UN prisoners in the north, the issue came to center around maltreatment, "brainwashing," and what might be a massive breakdown of morale and conduct. For the Communist prisoners in the south, the question soon was who was holding whom.

Very early in the war, the Communists began broadcasting speeches made by American prisoners, calling on their comrades to stop fighting the capitalists' war. Leaflets preaching a similar message soon appeared, and there was widespread comment on them in the neutralist press. There began to be the suspicion in the United States that something very strange was going on, and no one, at that stage, was quite sure what it was. A peculiarity of the situation was that the issue centered largely on the Americans, and to the end this remained a feature of it. The masses of South Koreans captured disappeared, as it were, into the maw of Asia. The nearly 1,000 British and 200-odd Turks, the only other substantial numbers of western captives, seemed to be getting along all right as far as anyone could tell. But what was happening with the Americans?

Though the captives' experiences varied according to time and circumstance, there were some patterns to them. Given the static nature of the front after early 1951, the vast majority of prisoners were taken either in the North Korean drive south at the start of the war or during the Chinese Communist offensives over the winter of 1950–51. Aside from the odd unfortunate who got caught out on a patrol, most of the prisoners taken after the front stabilized were air crew from planes shot down over North Korea. Many of these were treated extremely harshly, for the Communists wanted them to confess to taking part in germ warfare. Most prisoners, then, were held for almost three years. Those captured by the North Koreans were generally badly treated; the front was fluid, prisoners were a very low priority, and they were routinely beaten, starved, and quite often, as evidence had already shown, simply shot out of hand. The Chinese Communists tended to treat their prisoners better, but by the time they entered the war, camps were already established, and most of their prisoners were captured farther north and did not have to march as far as the earlier ones to reach camp, though they had to do so in far worse weather.

When the prisoners were in permanent camps along the Yalu, the Communists began a campaign of "reeducation." This was widely perceived in the outside world as "brainwashing," though authorities on the matter insist that that was not the case. They define brainwashing as totally erasing the original personality and then constructing a new one, a sort of nonsurgical frontal lobotomy. The Communist reeducation, say the authorities, consisted rather of an intensive process of indoctrination and interrogation.

First of all, any sense of group discipline or solidarity was broken down. Officers and enlisted men were isolated, and the normal military chain of command was broken. Each man was made to feel that he had to take care of himself alone. In the camps the rations were poor, medicines were usually not supplied, wounds were untended, and there was a great deal of disease. The most startling overall statistic in the entire matter was that 38 percent of American prisoners of war died in captivity, compared with a similar figure of less than 4 percent for American prisoners of Germany in World War II.

With their physical condition poor and their morale low, the Americans were subjected to intense and repetitive lectures, classes, and questionings. They were induced to write self-criticizing accounts of their lives and of life in the United States, to spy on each other and to inform. There were simplistic alternations of the carrot and stick, designed to keep them off balance psychologically. Many were led to make condemnatory public statements, just using that as an opportunity to let loved ones know they were still alive, something which the Geneva Convention guaranteed as a fundamental right of prisoners anyway. Under this regime, which was aimed to be destructive of the mind and was incidentally destructive of the body, many collapsed. Large numbers of them simply died; they lost hope, they lost faith in themselves, they sank into apathy and failed to take care of themselves to whatever extent was possible in bad conditions. So, especially in the first winter of captivity, many hundreds just shriveled up and faded into a trance, a coma, death.

Those who survived ran the entire gamut. Some turned into animals, stealing food from their fellow prisoners, beating them, in extreme cases throwing the sick out into the cold to hasten their deaths. Others became "progressives," accepting the Communist teachings and selling out for better rations. The vast majority tried to hold a middle ground, appearing to go along to survive, but basically, in the phrase of the time, "playing it cool." Then at the other end of the spectrum there were the independent, the bloody-minded, the selfless, and some who were just plain heroes, who gave up food or clothing for their friends, who withstood beatings rather than give in, who tried to organize some group effort to stay alive.

When the prisoners were finally released, the first impression was that the breakdown had been nearly complete; the Army organized massive psychological studies and investigations, not only of the conduct of prisoners as a whole, but of each and every individual. The Army concluded that some 425 men might well be tried for acts ranging from giving aid and comfort to the enemy to actual murder. Half of those 425 were already civilians, however, and the other half were gradually weeded down; 35 went before boards of inquiry, and only 14 were finally tried by court-martial. Though the Army took the view that a soldier was still a soldier even when a prisoner, the trials were highly unpopular and widely criticized in the public press.

What did transpire from the studies was that those best able to survive were the men who were mature individuals, with a firm belief in something beyond themselves and their own considerations, whether that something was family, military tradition, or religious faith. It was the young, the immature, the rootless, who sank into apathy, died, or turned their coats. This led to widespread criticism of what was perceived at the time as the materialism and selfishness of American culture, and the lack of discipline in family and society. The survival and better behavior of the British and the Turks was cited as a sort of control group showing what was wrong both with American life and with the U.S. Army, and it was pointed out that American Marines, from an all-volunteer force with an exaggerated esprit de corps, survived better than the soldiers did. The whole matter led eventually to the issuing of a new "Code of Conduct" for American servicemen, which came out soon after the end of the war; and more realistically, to some training as to what might be expected by prisoners in the future and how to withstand it.

Later studies have taken the breakdown theory to task, and have insisted that the crisis was not nearly as bad as it was perceived to be at the time, and that American prisoners in Korea on the whole behaved about as American prisoners have always done, with roughly the same percentages collaborating, resisting, or trying to find some survivable middle ground. These revisionist studies, however, lacking the sensational nature of the original problem, have not attracted as much attention as the earlier charges of disaster. However well or badly American prisoners of war in Korea behaved, there still remained that unanswerable and ghastly 38 percent death rate to add to the whole tragedy of war.

The story of the prisoners in the south is different in most particulars from that of those in the north. The few who were taken in the very early stages of the war were badly treated by the Republic of Korea forces, though this was not so much a matter of policy as exigency; the South Koreans were in almost total disarray, the war was fratricidal in nature, and scores were quickly settled. None of which is to deny that at various points in the war, the ROK and UN forces committed numerous atrocities of their own. But very soon the United Nations began to organize and order affairs, including the regularization of prisoner treatment. Before the landing at Inchon, there were only about 1,000 North Korean prisoners being held, but after it, and the subsequent breakout from the Pusan perimeter, the toll mounted rapidly. Within two months there were 130,000 POWs under UN control, and this placed a huge logistical and control burden on the captors.

Initially the prisoners were held near Pusan, but over the winter they were moved to Koje-do, a good-sized island off the southeast coast about twenty miles below Pusan. Several compounds were constructed here, and the prisoners settled in. Unfortunately, there were difficulties right from the start. First of all, the camps around Pusan had been dominated internally by South Koreans impressed into the North Korean army, who had some hope of release, and who were able to establish a rapport with their guards, also largely South Koreans. But during the move to the island, the prisoners were screened, and many of these South Koreans were reclassified as civilian detainees and segregated until someone should decide what to do with them. Control inside the compounds was therefore assumed by the more militant Communists themselves. On Koje-do, these were soon harassing the South Korean guards, who readily responded in kind. The Americans, ostensibly in command of the whole matter, were very short-handed, largely ignorant of the language, and concerned only that there not be visible waves; guarding POWs was not a high-profile situation for them. The situation got worse as the prisoners began to split into pro- and anti-Communist factions, who fought each other bitterly for control of different compounds. Attempts to introduce education classes and to set up work programs were in some cases successful, and in others only aggravated the situation. Inside the pens there were near-riots, kangaroo courts, and quite often executions. The Geneva Convention, however, was concerned with the prisoners' treatment by their captors, not by each other, and the Americans, hoping vainly that the problem would go away, chose not to exercise any judicial power over the captives.

Instead of going away, the situation got worse. The anti-Communist prisoners became increasingly fearful that they were going to be returned home, and began organizing to resist the possibility. They swore they would fight, and many tattooed themselves with anti-Communist slogans, presumably in the belief that this visible and permanent statement of political principle would prevent their being repatriated to certain punishment. The pro-Communist prisoners, on the other hand, had a communication network that stretched back to Panmunjom, had a fully articulated chain of command, and knew they were in a position to cause a great deal of trouble and embarrassment for the United Nations. In September 1951 they tried and executed fifteen prisoners before a "people's court."

This incident led the Americans to take a more serious look at their problem, but there was relatively little they could do. They did move more troops onto Koje-do, but by the end of the year there were still only 9,000 men, both guards and backup combat forces, to handle well over 100,000 prisoners who were crowded into the several island compounds. Meanwhile, the screening process went on interminably, in response to demands from Panmunjom; it seemed as if one count and classification was no sooner completed than another one was begun, and each changed the categories a little, juggled the figures, and of course excited and scared the prisoners. This sort of thing came to a head in mid-February, when one compound, Number 62, under firm Communist control, refused to be screened. A battalion of American infantry moved in to clear the compound with fixed bayonets; the prisoners responded with rocks, ax handles, and homemade weapons produced in their industrial arts classes. The outnumbered troops resorted first to concussion grenades, and when that failed, opened fire. Seventy-seven prisoners were killed, and twice that number wounded, for one American dead and thirty-eight wounded. In the hopes of avoiding a major propaganda blow, the Army said these were civilian detainees and not prisoners, and that this therefore was an internal matter in South Korea, but obviously that story had holes in it. The Communists cried brutality; the Americans moved in more troops and appointed a new commander, yet another in a long line of officers quickly coming and going. Unfortunately for himself, Brig. Gen. Francis T. Dodd turned out to be the one who had the whole matter blow up in his face.

By early 1952 the guards had virtually lost control of the camps; all they could do was sit around the perimeter and let the inmates fight it out. There had been so many screenings, and so many reclassifications, that it was almost impossible to tell who was what or wanted to do what. For example, there were the Chinese; but some of them were Chinese Communists, and some were Chinese Nationalists who had been taken over at the end of the civil war and incorporated into the new Red Chinese armies with no more than a change of their cap badges. Many of them were still wearing American uniforms that had been originally supplied to

Nationalist China. Some wanted to go home to China, some wanted to go to Taiwan, some did not know where they wanted to go, and many wanted to do only whatever was necessary to survive at the hands of their fellow prisoners. The Koreans were even worse. There were North and South Koreans, but there were Communist North Koreans and anti-Communist ones, Communist South Koreans and anti-Communist ones, pressed men and volunteers. The UN Command believed in fact that there were five different types just of South Koreans held in the camps, including a substantial number who had never been soldiers at all, but who had broken into the camps and stayed there for the rations! If Solomon and Job had had to run Koje-do, their reputations would not be what they are.

At Panmunjom the truce delegates were still hammering away at each other. By April 1952 they had come down to fundamental disagreement on three vital issues: airfield rehabilitation, the membership of the Soviet Union on the Neutral Nations Supervisory Commission, and voluntary repatriation of prisoners of war. The Americans would have liked to lump all three together, and did so in what they called a "package proposal." But the airfields were the only thing they were willing now to give up, and that would leave the Communists surrendering on two of the three issues; they simply were not about to do that.

The problem became even more acute when the results of the latest "final" screening of prisoners became known. Initially the Americans had suggested to the Communists that of the 170,000 or so captives they held, as POWs or civilian detainees, probably about 116,000 would choose to go home to live under Communism. Of the other 54,000, most were in the civilian classification, so the Communists gave up some intimation that they could live with this. Their attitude seemed to be that they cared less how many men were reclassified as civilians than they did that a seemingly large majority of their "soldiers" should want to return to them. It therefore came as a serious shock, and ironically an embarrassment to both sides, when the tally revealed that of the 170,000 total, a mere 70,000 were willing to go home to the brave new world of Communism. When that figure was calmly delivered across the table at Panmunjom, it was met with stunned silence, followed by a request for an immediate recess.

To the Communists such a massive rejection was, of course, a shock, and a grave setback to their attempts to propagandize the rest of the world about the glories of their system. But the UN negotiators, though naturally gratified by this acceptance of western ideas and values, were appalled by what it did for the progress of the truce talks. By this time they were far more interested in ending the war than they were in scoring propaganda points, and anything that introduced a major new disequilibrium into what had become a fine-tuned balancing act was cause for alarm. In this sense, the very success of the democratic appeal was working against the achievement of a truce. The Americans even induced the Communists to promise an amnesty to straying followers, in the hope that that would cause a few more to accept repatriation; but men who were willing to give up home and families because they did not trust the Communists in the first place were not going to be swayed by elegant promises extracted under duress.

It was not all over yet, however. Though both sides were momentarily caught in traps of their own devising, there was still another drama to be played out. In early May the Communists produced a trump card. By then large numbers of the anti-Communist prisoners had left Koje-do and been placed in camps on the mainland. This had obviously eased tensions within the island compounds, but only at the very considerable price of leaving the Communists in almost complete control inside the wire. The UN guards could not even enter the compounds. Meanwhile, Brigadier General Dodd, who was more concerned with alleviating tensions and less with maintaining discipline than he should have been, had developed a pattern of meeting with the prisoners' leaders at the entrance to their camp, to discuss their endless complaints. To show his good faith, which he need not have done, Dodd usually went unarmed and unescorted, leaving his guards several yards behind him. On the afternoon of May 7, when he was conferring with the leaders of Compound 76, Dodd was suddenly grabbed and hustled away inside the fence. He was now a prisoner of his prisoners.

Here was the possibility of a major incident, and the Communists immediately made the most of it. The Americans moved in troops and tanks, but it took some days for the latter to get there. Meanwhile, Brig. Gen. Charles F. Colson was sent down to replace the kidnapped Dodd. The Communists produced a whole series of demands, including among some substantive ones that the UN stop "torture . . . mass murdering, gun and machine gun shooting . . . germ weapons . . . experiment object of A-bomb . . ." and a variety of other things. Here again they were past masters of the carrot-and-stick technique, and every time Colson thought himself ready to solve the matter by force, they were ready for another round of negotiation. Dodd, talking to the outside by telephone, became almost a spokesman for his prisoners. Colson's reply to their written demands was rejected, and was then twice reedited, with Dodd's assistance, until it was acceptable.

What was acceptable to the POWs, inevitably, gave them a major propaganda victory, of the "we have never tortured prisoners and we shall stop doing it in the future" variety. Eventually Dodd was released and the crisis simmered down, but there was absolutely no doubt as to who had scored the points. The Communists' aim in the matter had been to discredit the screening processes that had produced those unbalanced figures, and they had to a certain extent done so. How much that mattered in any long run is problematical. What they had really demonstrated was their ability and willingness to use the Americans' desire to be fair, and above all their desire to be seen to be fair, to make fools of them. Colson and Dodd were both reduced in grade to colonel, and their immediate superior in the chain of command reprimanded, but that did nothing to assuage the defeat; it only acknowledged it.

From then on the emphasis was on control of prisoners rather than wooing them, and the new commander on Koje-do, Brig. Gen. Haydon L. Boatner, soon broke up the compounds and transferred the prisoners into new accommodations where they could be better guarded. The same thing happened at camps around Pusan. Rather late in the day, the Americans had learned their lesson.

But at the truce talks, there was no progress whatsoever. Most of May passed in Communist harangues about the brutality of the United Nations and the untrustworthiness of its figures. Around the world there was a spate of anti-American demonstrations, all of them, of course, purely spontaneous; this period also marked the height of the germ warfare accusations. The chief American delegate, Admiral Joy, went home in late May, turning over his job to Maj. Gen. William Harrison. Joy left with an enormous sigh of relief. Harrison was already conversant with the frustrations of the assignment, and nothing in the next few months changed his mind. Most of the positions were by now so well drawn that there was little room for maneuver. Slowly through May it transpired that the Americans might let airfields go, and the Communists might let Soviet membership on the Neutral Nations Supervisory Commission go, but neither side would move farther on the voluntary repatriation question. In the larger arena, the Americans had tried increasing the pressure by their air attacks, the Communists by their manipulation of the POW issue and propaganda on the world stage. Neither one had exerted sufficient leverage to break the logjam. By the summer of 1952, the delegates were meeting only once a week or once every ten days, to glare at each other. If they could not talk their way out of it, then the fighting must continue.

CHAPTER 13
SEEKING A PRESSURE POINT

Late in 1951 it became apparent that the ground war in Korea was going nowhere. General Van Fleet had developed plans for a series of limited offensives in October, but at that moment the hope of some progress in the truce negotiations led his superiors to cancel them. In November, agreement was reached on the line of demarcation, and the United Nations allowed itself to think this was the beginning of the end. Van Fleet therefore issued a general instruction to Eighth Army that it would respond only to pressure from the Communists, and that there would be no real offensives undertaken. Naturally, the nearer to the shooting this policy got, the more latitude was applied to its interpretation, and on the front line, it was seen as a virtual cease-fire. Van Fleet's candor, for neither the first nor last time, got him in trouble. Ridgway in Tokyo, and the White House in Washington, immediately responded to press questions that of course the war was continuing, and Van Fleet should have kept his mouth shut.

Yet the front *was* quiet. If the UN forces were going only to react to a Communist advance, and the Communists were not going to advance, then there was a *de facto* cease-fire, or at least a marked diminution of the level of hostilities. Van Fleet's problem was the field commander's insistence on calling a spade a spade, when in the world of diplomacy and negotiation a spade might be anything from a spoon to a steam shovel. The winter went by in patrols and artillery duels.

Yet the war had indeed reached a stalemate. The thirty-day deadline after the demarcation agreement came and went, and nothing happened. The negotiators remained high and dry on the rocks of airfields, then the Neutral Nations Supervisory Commission, then increasingly on the POW issue. Winter turned into spring, and still there was no progress at Panmunjom, and little action along the front line.

What the Communists wanted to achieve, and how they proposed to do it, is a matter of some debate. This was the spring of the riots on Koje-do, the spring when the Communists unleashed the wild accusations of germ warfare, the spring of a worldwide "hate America" campaign. When the treaty establishing the European Defense Community was signed, there were violent Communist riots in Paris at the end of May. It was a period of intense tension. The Soviet leader, Joseph Stalin, was in his dotage, and virtually paranoid. Communist leadership everywhere slept with one eye open, and there were purges in places such as Czechoslovakia. In the democratic states, Communist excesses brought reaction rather than victory, and in elections in the early fifties the more conservative parties increased their power. Ironically, this did not always have the results desired by western leaders generally, for these conservatives were accustomed to thinking in traditional terms, rather than along the lines of western European unity stressed by their immediate, centrist, predecessors. Yet the end result was that the Communists' surge declined; they had failed to achieve victory on the battlefield, they had failed to talk their way to it—so far—at the truce table, and now they were failing to shout and demonstrate their way to it in the streets and editorial columns of the world.

But they were still not ready to give up. Perhaps everything would come to him who waited. It is always grossly unhistorical to speak in terms of stereotypes, but both sides in this war, and the larger Cold War, tended to see each other in stereotypical terms; the Americans saw the monolithic "worldwide Communist conspiracy," and the Communists saw decadent, quarreling democracies, dominated by a fickle press and public whose impatience might very well be used against them. If the war could be made to last long enough, and cost enough, then perhaps the chief villains, the Americans, would grow tired of it, give up, and go home.

This perception was perfectly clear to the Americans, and they were quite divided over it. In Washington, there was a constant attempt to restructure negotiating positions in such a way that some agreement could finally be obtained, but the closer one got to the actual truce table, the less this attitude pertained. Admiral Joy, presiding over practically the entire evolution of American proposals, was quite adamant. He repeatedly advised that the United Nations should state its position, say "take it or leave it," and walk out. His view was that the only thing the Communists respected was strength, and that the slightest attempt to be fair, or to be accommodating, or to see the other side's point of view, was regarded merely as weakness to be exploited. If you conceded today that one point might possibly have merit, you would be asked to concede another point tomorrow. Much of the internal history of the last half of the Korean War centers therefore less around the actual fighting and more around the convolutions of developing United Nations policy.

A new element was introduced in May. Gen. Dwight D. Eisenhower resigned his post as Supreme Allied Commander Europe, eventually to run as the Republican candidate for the Presidency; he was replaced by General Ridgway, who was transferred from Tokyo. Ridgway's replacement as Far East commander and Commander in Chief United Nations Command was Gen. Mark W. Clark. One of the more controversial American generals of World War II, Clark had commanded the U.S. Fifth Army in the Italian campaign; in the postwar years, he had held a series of military and occupation commands, in Europe and the United States. Like MacArthur, he was senior to most of his military superiors in the Pentagon, but by the time he arrived in Tokyo, the parameters of the Korean situation were more clearly defined. He therefore presided over the remainder of the war without getting into the major policy arguments of his famous predecessor, though throughout his period of command he argued for an increasingly forceful approach, going so far as to recommend the introduction of Nationalist Chinese formations into Korea and the bombing of Manchuria. In other words he, like every other commander in the area, felt the frustrations of fighting a limited war with limited resources.

Because the war refused to go away. Even if it was not to be pursued vigorously, the front line was still there. It could, and did, flare up when one side or the other wished to make a point. Korea had the character of an international chess match, and the gain or loss of a square, the exchange of pawns, just might occasionally have an effect on the whole. The hills and valleys of central Korea were the squares, and the infantry, artillerymen, and tankers were the pawns. Unfortunately, these pawns bled and died.

Both sides agreed to play by the rules during 1952, and the rules strictly limited what either might do. With a rough balance of forces, neither was going to strike a full-scale blow. Each had something under a million men available. The Communists were estimated to have about 290,000 men manning their front-line positions, 207,000 Chinese and 83,000 North Koreans. Behind them were another 600,000-odd reserve and support troops, including, the United Nations suspected, perhaps 10,000 Soviet or eastern-bloc technical and advisory personnel. The United Nations had just under 700,000 troops in the peninsula. On the line there were almost 250,000, consisting of nine ROK divisions, the Commonwealth Division, the 1st Marine Division, and four U.S. Army divisions. Both sides had spent the previous months digging in and making their defensive positions stronger, so that the front line in Korea was much like the old trench system of World War I days, though not nearly as rigid.

Also similar to World War I was the tempo of action, for there were periodic lulls, punctuated by occasional flashes of action as one side or another decided to improve its position, to probe enemy defenses, or simply to be nasty-minded. May of 1952 was fairly quiet; June was different.

Soldiers are always obsessed with high ground; this is a constant from the earliest days of warfare. When the Greek city-states got together for a battle, they always sought out level ground, for neither side would fight if the other held the higher end of the slope; even a man with a sword or spear has the advantage if he is running downhill. Modern warfare is necessarily more complex, but the principle still holds. High ground now usually means artillery observation, and no one is comfortable if he knows the enemy's artillery controllers are overlooking his position or the approaches to it. In May 1952, Maj. Gen. David L. Ruffner took command of the 45th Infantry Division, holding the right flank of I Corps' line in west-central Korea. The 45th was a National Guard division, and had fought in Italy at Anzio in 1944; most of its Korean War members were too young for Anzio, but the idea of holding the high ground was fixed in the divisional memory. General Ruffner decided he did not like the look of his front line—the Communists were too close, and had observation posts overlooking the whole sector. This was even more worrisome as the enemy artillery had been substantially reinforced during the lull in the fighting. Ruffner wanted to gain some breathing room, and to advance his outpost line forward to get it. The division staff developed Operation Counter to take a dozen forward hills.

The hills stretched in a line from northeast to southwest; the first of them, in the northeast, was called White Horse Hill. White Horse and Arrowhead, the second, were isolated on the northern side of the narrow valley of the Yokkokchon River. The rest of the dozen were on the southern side, and the last two of them were called Porkchop Hill and Old Baldy.

The attack went in on the night of June 6, after several air strikes on the hills during the day. The six northern outposts were quickly seized by the 279th Infantry Regiment, and the 180th moved on the southern hills. Company I of the 180th took Porkchop after a firefight that lasted for nearly an hour, and A Company went up Old Baldy, which it had to overrun, then clear with the aid of an artillery strike. The initial phase of the operation, all in all, went pretty well. Soon the outposts were busy with soldiers digging, signal troops laying wires, engineers making bunkers, and Korean laborers carrying up timber and sandbags. Much of this was done under enemy artillery fire, which provided additional incentive to dig fast and deep.

Over the next several days the attacks by either side continued. The Chinese kept coming back with company-sized counterattacks, trying to push their way onto the hills. The Americans tried to probe forward, in one case down into the river valley. The fighting was especially stubborn around Old Baldy, which was the highest point in the ridgeline, and dominated vistas north and south. It took a major effort by the 179th Infantry, which had relieved the 180th, to clear a Chinese post that was a mere 1,000 feet from the American position on top of the hill. Three companies, supported by two tanks that managed somehow to climb the hill and lend support before being put out of action (one flipped over on the slope, the second threw a track), slugged it out with the Chinese at close range, and finally drove them down the hill.

By the end of the month the Chinese had decided to put some heavy effort into regaining their line. On the night of the 27th, and lasting through the 28th, they launched four separate attacks against the 179th Regiment's all-around perimeter. The first three were in battalion strength, the last was twice that strong. On this fourth try, the Chinese actually broke into the American perimeter, but the soldiers fought on from their bunkers, and called in flares and then their own artillery on the top of the hill, and the Chinese were at last driven off after several hours, with heavy losses. They had another try early in July, then they resigned themselves to giving up the ridgeline.

Such actions were more or less typical of the fighting at this stage of the war, though the battle for Old Baldy was actually on a larger scale than most of the combat. Another element in such positional fighting was the way in which the same battle would be repeated over and over again. The Chinese, for example, took Old Baldy back in mid-July; by that time it was held by the 2nd Division, which had relieved the 45th on the line. The 2nd was able to recapture half of it in its initial counterattacks, and for two or three weeks the Chinese sat on top of the hill. Then in August, the 2nd Division tried again, and took the crest. The Chinese got it back in September, and later in the same month the Americans took it again. As late as March of 1953 they were still at it. There would be a lull, activity would shift to another sector of the front, but then it would return to the Old Baldy–Porkchop area.

It seemed as if some malicious dart player were standing off throwing his darts at the map. Near Panmunjom the Marines fought over Hill 122, which they eventually came to call Bunker Hill. The South Koreans battled in August over Capitol Hill. Some hills had only their height in meters to distinguish them, but others were fought over often enough or had sufficiently distinctive features to gain names and momentary notoriety. Old Baldy, for example, was called that because artillery fire had swept it clean of trees and brush. The contour lines on the map clearly explained the names Porkchop, T-Bone, and Alligator Jaws. Jackson Heights was named after the infantry company commander who first defended it; Jane Russell Hill was a feature with twin peaks. Men came to know, and hate, the horizons that lay before them. After months on the line, they knew where they could walk, where it was necessary to crouch, where the enemy could bring down observed fire, where it was possible to sit and rest and have a cigarette in dead ground. It was all hard-earned knowledge, paid for in fear and sweat and blood, and it was equally hard to convince oneself that it was worth it.

At Eighth Army headquarters, Van Fleet chafed under the burdens of stagnation. He wanted to advance, and he produced plans for another drive that would carry his forces to the waist of the peninsula, taking Pyongyang and presumably forcing the Communists to make the concessions that would end the war. He saw little point in fighting the same battles for the same hills over and over again. But General Clark in Tokyo saw equally little profit in trying a major offensive. The Communists were strong in numbers and artillery, and they were well dug in. There was no sign that Washington would, or indeed could, allocate the forces necessary to give an offensive enough weight to be successful. Clark, indeed, was not even sure that trying to take hills was of any advantage. Though the Communists' casualties were usually thought to be far greater than the United Nations', he could not see that that had any discernible effect upon them. They had the manpower, they seemed perfectly willing to trade it for time, and such trading was merely playing their game. Later he wrote that he thought ten of their men's lives was not worth one of his men's, and he told Van Fleet that any offensive action even at the battalion level must be cleared with Far East Command. So with its costs and objectives firmly limited, the ground war staggered on—from one damned hill to another.

With the ground war slowed to a snail's pace, the tempo of the war in the air increased. As mentioned earlier, 1952 was the year when the United Nations attempted to apply the leverage of air power to achieve a settlement. This was the summer of the attacks against the Communist hydroelectric plants and of the intensified interdiction campaign. The Fifth Air Force maintained its general air superiority, but its reconnaissance planes sighted as many as 500 MiG-15 fighters at one time on bases just across the Yalu. The tempo of combat was very much dictated by the Communists, and they could engage or not as they chose. Most of the time they chose not to do so, but some months were busier than others. Through the summer they also got better radar and ground-control mechanisms, as far as the Americans could tell, for they managed to avoid the F-86 Sabres while still going after the slower or less effective fighter-bomber types, the F-80s and F-84s. For the Americans, coordinating missions at long range between several different types of aircraft, each with different capabilities, was a major exercise in itself, and their success was a remarkable tribute to their staff and planning work. By mid-1952, between buildup of inventory, modernization of aircraft types, and development of both ground-control radar and antiaircraft installations, the Communists held the material trump cards of aerial warfare, yet it was still the United Nations that maintained air superiority.

For the United Nations naval units in the combat area, the war went on routinely. The carriers and cruisers and destroyers rotated into the theater and out of it. Naval and Marine air units flew their missions, while shore-bombardment assignments continued seemingly forever. By 1952 the U.S. Navy had expended as much ammunition against the hills of North Korea as it fired against Japan in all of World War II. The blockade of the port of Wonsan was in its second year, and the commander of the force there was referred to, only half in jest, as the Mayor of Wonsan.

One of the peculiarities of life at sea is that in the midst of apparently suffocating routine, disaster can suddenly strike, the "thunderbolt from the cloudless sky." So there was a slow but constant drain. In April, the cruiser *St. Paul* suffered an explosion in one of her forward turrets, killing thirty sailors in an instant. In August, Typhoon Karen swept through the area, causing damage and leaving mines broken loose in its wake. One of these struck and sank the tug *Sarsi,* the first American ship lost in a year and a half. The destroyer

Barton hit another mine, which blew a hole in her side and killed five more sailors.

The aircraft carriers and battleships made the headlines, but Korea was very much a small ships' war. Destroyers, minesweepers, and assorted patrol craft were busy trying to interdict Communist coastal traffic, as well as shelling road and rail lines near the sea. British and Commonwealth naval forces were used extensively off the west coast; the Canadian destroyer *Iroquois* was hit by shore batteries in October, with three men killed and several wounded. Her sister ship, *Nootka,* sank a large junk being used as a minelayer, in the process coming under attack from several North Korean crew members who had taken to the water, armed with submachine guns and floating on automobile inner tubes! All along the western coast of North Korea, with its multitude of islands, the UN forces played hide-and-seek with the Communists; they held several of the islands, as bases for guerrilla operations, or for advanced radar stations, or to use for helicopter rescue missions.

The largest operation of the year turned out to be a nonstarter. In the fall the Navy suggested that a routine rotation of troops into Korea might be used as an amphibious exercise and deception to scare the Communists and elicit a reaction. A hundred ships were involved, as well as the 8th Cavalry Regiment of the 1st Cavalry Division. On the morning of October 15, the force approached Kojo, an east-coast port about thirty miles above the front line. Guns pounded, fighter-bombers swooped over the beaches, landing craft were launched and formed up, heading for the shore. But the seas were heavy, and no troops were put into the boats. It was all a feint, and it largely backfired. The Communists hardly reacted at all, but the soldiers and sailors involved, who had been led for security purposes to think this was real, were thoroughly bewildered. For many, it appeared a cruel abuse to make men screw their courage to the sticking point, and then tell them it was all a hoax.

The Americans were not the only ones playing games in 1952. Neither for the first nor the last time, they began to have serious troubles with their client. The expansion of the Republic of Korea Army had continued throughout the entire war; there was now actually a preponderance of ROK divisions manning the front line, though they were still strongly dependent upon American support, logistics, advice, and technical arms such as artillery and signals. Indeed, under the semi-static conditions of 1952, the South Koreans were reaching the point where they were actually drafting more men than they needed, but, with the war not decided, no one as yet wanted to scale down the military program.

The trouble was more of a political nature than a military one. From their earliest days in Korea, right after World War II, the Americans had tried to juggle their desire to see a viable government in power, which meant Syngman Rhee, and their desire to have a democratic system, which meant Rhee's opposition. For Rhee's devotion to democracy was of a curiously myopic type; he believed that he, and he alone, represented democracy. All opposition to him he branded as treason; it was as simple as that.

Yet there was opposition to him, and it centered in the National Assembly. From Rhee's point of view, two things made this very bad. One was that the National Assembly, under the constitution, had the power to elect the president of the republic; the other was that elections were due in midsummer. In the summer of 1951 the South Koreans had embarrassed the Americans by demonstrations against the opening of negotiations with the hated enemy; this summer they were going to embarrass them even more. On May 24, President Rhee declared martial law and arrested his leading opponents in the National Assembly.

General Clark in Tokyo and General Van Fleet in Korea both hoped this cup would pass them by; they took the stand that it was a political matter, made what provisions seemed necessary to secure their lines to the front, and otherwise were more than content to leave the matter to the State Department. The government in Washington was, of course, furious. What Rhee wanted, as far as anyone could tell, was to dissolve the National Assembly, elect a new one, and have it provide for a bicameral legislature and popular election of the president, who would, of course, continue to be Syngman Rhee.

American Ambassador Muccio was in Washington when the crisis broke, and after consultations he immediately returned to Korea. President Truman, meanwhile, cabled Rhee and told him in not too disguised language that he was doing himself and his country irreparable damage; the Communists were crowing, and the other United Nations members were asking unfortunate questions such as, at their most basic, whether this government was worth fighting for.

Slowly, Rhee moderated his tone, if not his action. The South Korean Army correctly stood aside, Rhee did not dissolve the Assembly, and the two sides began to negotiate. Eventually, in early July, the politicians reached some sort of compromise; there would be a bicameral legislature, the president and vice-president would be popularly elected, and Rhee was so elected, indefinitely. Presumably, what he offered in return was not to dissolve the Assembly and to let his opponents out of jail. It was the end of July before martial law was lifted, and the entire episode left a very bad taste in very many mouths.

As the face of the war changed, so did the faces of the participants. The Americans had been hard pressed to provide troop strength in the early stages of the war, and even after the first year of fighting, they remained in difficulties. By the fall of 1951 there were still only seven divisions in the United States, and only one of them, the 82nd Airborne, was fully trained; it was regarded as the sole strategic reserve of the United States Army. The other six were in various stages of manning, training, and equipping. In late 1951 a new element was introduced into Korea, with the arrival of the first two National Guard divisions, the 45th and the 40th. These had been called up early in the emergency and sent to Japan, where they completed their training while bolstering the garrison there. General Ridgway had wanted several times to use them as replacements for his formations in Korea, but the Army, always sensitive to the political clout of the National Guard, had balked at breaking them up and using them as less than full divisions. Finally in December the 45th moved to Korea, exchanging support and heavy equipment with the 1st Cavalry, which then went into garrison in Japan. Then after the turn of the year the 40th carried out the same exchange with the 24th Division.

These were the largest rotations of formations in the war; other nations went through the same process on a smaller scale, the French, Australians, Ethiopians, and others taking out old and bringing in new units of battalion size. The other side of the process was the rotation of individuals, and this became an item about which commentators had mixed opinions.

At the end of World War II the United States Army had worked out a point system for troop rotation; a soldier got so many points for periods of service overseas, so many more for service in a combat zone, for actual combat, for medals, and so on. This was designed to ensure that those who had done the most fighting got home first, and though there were occasional inequities, by and large it had worked pretty well.

This policy was employed only for getting the troops home; for the actual duration of the war, a soldier sent overseas to combat stayed there until he was killed or wounded or the war ended. For Korea, however, the Army adopted a policy of troop rotation in March 1951; it was an attempt to spread the burden of danger more equitably, a response to the fact that this was after all a limited war, being waged at any given moment by an amazingly small portion of the total potential manpower pool of the United States. Most observers concluded that on the one hand it helped individual morale, but on the other it damaged unit cohesion and therefore combat effectiveness.

The magic number was initially thirty-six points. A soldier earned four points a month for front-line service, two a month for service in Korea but not in the combat zone. Thus a rifleman could go back to Japan after nine months, while a supply clerk in Pusan might have to do eighteen months. There were several changes in the accounting system during the course of the war, but these were only variations on the theme. The general principle of rotation was accepted, eagerly by the troops, more reluctantly by their commanders. For the drawback to it was that at any given moment, lesser or greater numbers of seasoned soldiers were going out of Korea and raw replacements were coming in. It took time for these to get acclimatized, to find their way around a battlefield, and to become useful soldiers. Fortunately, the static front gave them time to do this, for the most part, but there were occasional examples of large-scale rotation seriously lessening the effectiveness of some units in the Army.

By 1952, though, it had all become a matter of routine. Soldiers came in, did their time, and went home. Officers rotated in and out of Korea at different levels; career officers, in particular, believed they had to serve their time in combat, for the sake of their records, and there was a certain air, in some quarters, of going to Korea "to get your ticket punched." Few were as keen as some of the pilots who, on becoming aces or getting near that status, tried to avoid orders home so they could increase their scores. For most of the men involved, the war was a frustrating, inconclusive affair, something that had to be done. It seemed as if it might go on forever.

CHAPTER 14
THE WORLD STAGE

Before Mark Clark left the United States to take up his command in the Far East, he was invited to New York for an interview with the Secretary-General of the United Nations, Trygve Lie. Clark did not want to go—he was busy—so initially he declined. There was then an exchange between the United Nations and the government of the United States, the result of which was that Clark made a hurried trip from Washington to New York. As it turned out, Lie did not want too much, simply to give Clark his blessing and to remind him that he was in command of a unique multinational force. Clark, who had already commanded in Italy troops from more nations than were represented in the UN force in Korea, was slightly amused by this, and off he flew to Tokyo.

This totally insignificant little incident graphically illustrated the ambiguous relationship between the United States and the United Nations. The latter, ostensibly the parent organization, was in fact more a stepchild of the former. The Americans may have been ever so slightly uncomfortable bossing the United Nations; they were far less comfortable on the rare occasions when the United Nations tried to boss them.

Not, indeed, that that happened very often. For practical purposes the United Nations, having given its blessing to the attempt to resist aggression in Korea, and having recommended—not insisted—that its members assist in that enterprise, had then turned over the execution of the task to the United States. This was in part a result of the fortuitous absence of the Soviet Union from the Security Council at that moment, partly a result of clever and forceful American management of the situation, and perhaps mostly a result of the fact that the United Nations was simply feeling its way here; this had never been done before. Though the Secretary-General was subsequently criticized by some observers for what they saw as his lack of forcefulness, there was very little room for him to maneuver, even on this uncharted ground. After all, as Voltaire said, God is on the side of the big battalions, and the Secretary-General had no battalions at all.

The war was thus seen in a contradictory light. To some it was the United Nations' finest hour, the first and indeed only time that it actually took positive steps to resist aggression, subsequent UN interventions being merely the dispatch of units to observe or supervise a truce, rather than active participation on one side against unlawful acts by another. To others it was merely the tool of the United States, providing an umbrella for what the United States intended to do anyway. And for many Americans, it was simply an organ "full of sound and fury, signifying nothing," which wrangled endlessly, and left Uncle Sam to pay all the bills and do all the dirty work.

If one accepts the premise that the invasion of South Korea was an act of unprovoked aggression, and that all that followed therefore was legitimate, then the simplest way to measure support for the United Nations and devotion to its principles is to look at who contributed what to the effort. There were sixty member states in the organization during most of the Korean War—Indonesia, the sixtieth, was admitted in September 1950. Sixteen of the sixty ultimately sent ground units to Korea; thirty more offered to help in less definite terms, sending food, hospital supplies, Red Cross teams, or other relief items. So three-quarters of the members actively participated to some degree or another; the remaining quarter were largely from the eastern bloc, dominated by the Soviet Union. Some of them too offered aid of a nonmilitary variety, which usually went not to South but to North Korea.

The sixteen who actually sent men to the country did so in interesting ways. At any given point in the war, something around 5 percent of the UN troops were from countries other than South Korea and the United States. Slightly more than half of these were from the British Commonwealth. The majority of the Commonwealth troops were from Great Britain itself, reaching a peak of 14,000 at the end of the war. Australia's force peaked at 2,300, New Zealand's at 1,400, and the Canadians contributed more than 8,000. Supplying such strengths meant, of course, that far more men than that served at one period or another of the war in Korea, and a simple recital of the peak numbers is somewhat deceptive. Canada, for example, sent a total of 21,940 soldiers to Japan and Korea, so, considering replacements, rotations, and the length of time any national contingent was actually in the theater, the overall number of those who served there might be up to three times as high as the strength reported at a specific time. The only other member of the Commonwealth to contribute was India, and while the fighting was on it sent only medical, noncombatant personnel, slightly more than 300 at any time.

Of the other states, Italy, Norway, and Sweden also confined themselves to sending medical units rather than combatants, all less than 200 strong. Combat contributions of battalion size were committed by Belgium, France, Greece, and the Netherlands from Europe, the Belgian force including a forty-man contingent from Luxembourg; given that the armed forces of Luxembourg were only a few hundred strong, that represented proportionately more than a token force. The Philippines, Thailand, and Ethiopia all sent battalions from what would later be called the Third World, and Colombia, also with a battalion, was the only contributor from South America. The last participant was Turkey, which sent a strong brigade and maintained it throughout most of the war.

The United Nations forces at sea were rather less mixed. They came from Great Britain and Canada, Australia, and New Zealand, as well as from Colombia, Thailand, and the Netherlands. Denmark sent a hospital ship. Though there were occasional difficulties in integrating different operational techniques, for the most part they all worked well together. This was especially true with the Commonwealth ships, which still were dominated by British traditions and had similar methods of operating. It was not unusual, for example, to see British, Australian, and Canadian destroyers, all of the same or similar classes, tied side by side at buoys in Sasebo when off patrol, all flying the white ensign, and distinguishable from each other only by their different paint schemes and jacks, and all eagerly visited by American sailors because of their beer rations.

The contributing air forces also had a similar homogeneity. In addition to the Royal Navy's air squadrons, flying from their carriers, there were Australian, South African, Greek, and Thai squadrons, the latter two transport units. The Canadians provided a transport squadron for the Pacific Ocean airlift, and a number of Canadian pilots flew combat missions while attached to the U.S. Air Force. The homogeneity came mainly from the types of aircraft employed, for almost all of them were American-built; the Greeks, for example, flew Douglas C-47s, the Australians Mustangs. The only non-American aircraft were the British carrier types, and the British Gloster Meteor jet fighter, flown by the Australians. Ironically, substantial numbers of the American F-86 Sabre were built by a Canadian aircraft company, Canadair, the major foreign licensed constructor. There was also a lot of limited work around the fringes, though the men who were involved in it might justifiably object to such a casual classification. The Royal Air Force, for example, contributed three squadrons of Sunderland flying boats which flew maritime reconnaissance from bases in Japan, and also sent some small flights of artillery spotter aircraft and controllers to Korea.

Reaction to all these contributions from the United States was mixed, especially among the forces themselves. On the one hand, any help was welcome, but on the other, there were problems of diet, of language, even of uniform. Such simple things as the issuing of dark brown American combat boots to British infantrymen, who traditionally wore, and vastly preferred, their brutally heavy black "ammunition boots," could be the subject of comment over beer, or of the exchange of correspondence at the more official level. Special training and reception centers had to be set up, and of course the contingents varied greatly in their readiness for combat. The British arrived in Pusan completely ready to fight; indeed, they had been led to expect by the press reports that they would virtually have to fight their way ashore. Throughout the entire war they enjoyed a fine reputation. Other countries tended to have linguistic difficulties, especially among those who spoke more esoteric languages. The Americans gradually came to believe that the battalion-sized units were too small to be worth the effort, and they would have preferred regimental- or brigade-strength formations, complete with supporting arms. That turned out to be asking too much, and the majority of the contributions remained at the 1,000-man level or below.

The other side of the coin was that the Americans badly wanted UN members to make some contribution, indeed, any contribution at all, just to get them on side; it was rather reminiscent of Foch's idea of the minimal British contribution in 1914: "One British soldier—and we'll make sure he gets killed!" If for military reasons the UN contributions might be a nuisance, for political reasons they were highly desirable. Throughout the war, there was an ongoing push-pull effect between the U.S. Army and the State Department, as the latter tried to pressure friendly governments into making greater troop allocations, and the former tried to hedge such contributions with conditions, even while anxious to have them.

That it was more a matter of politics than of stark military necessity was illustrated by the case of Nationalist China. For here was one state that was as anxious to offer troops as the United States was to have them, and the issue of Chinese Nationalist troops dogged the entire war. MacArthur, of course, had wanted to use them, and Clark, soon after he took command, also petitioned Washington for permission to employ two of Chiang Kai-shek's divisions, though he admitted that his reasons were somewhat mixed. Among other things, he later wrote, he wanted to see "who would defect to whom," and if the Nationalists were going to fall apart, he thought it better they do so in Korea than at some future, more crucial point. With such reasons as those, he patently could not have had too high expectations of the Nationalists, and as Washington was desperately careful not to do anything that might enlarge the scope of the war, the suggestion was quickly quashed. Even had there not been political reasons for refusing the Chinese offer, it would have been very difficult for the United States to accept it on other grounds, specifically, the fact that the Chinese had only manpower to offer. They would have had to be equipped and supplied from the ground up by the United States, which was already stretched to supply itself and the South Koreans. What the United States really needed from its friends were fully trained and equipped and battle-ready units, and it was not going to get them.

On that score, its best friend and nearest neighbor, Canada, was a case in point. The Canadian government in 1950 responded to the UN request for assistance by deciding, after much public prodding, to raise the Canadian Army Special Force. Initially this was to be a short-term "soldier of fortune" type of formation, because Canada did not have any regular army units fit for dispatch overseas. Ultimately, however, the distinction could not be maintained, the CASF was virtually merged with the regular army, and some of Canada's most distinguished regiments served in Korea. The government agreed to raise a brigade-sized force of about 5,000 men. Recruiting opened on August 7, and by the end of the month, 15,000 men had applied for the force, and this in a time of full employment in the country. Though Royal Canadian Navy ships operated off Korea from the early days of the war, the first of these ground units did not reach Korea until December 1950. Their training status had been downgraded after the Inchon landing, and it was thought in the fall they would be needed merely for occupation duties. Then came the Chinese intervention, and they were suddenly needed more than ever. Even so, it was February 1951 before the first unit reached the front line; this was the 2nd Battalion, Princess Patricia's Canadian Light Infantry. Ultimately Canada contributed a brigade to the war, which suffered 1,543 casualties.

The Canadian government at home, however, was rather less concerned with its actual commitment than it was with keeping the American government in line. It tended to see the Americans as dangerously adventurous, and Canadian policy throughout the war was directed toward seeing that the matter was truly run by the United Nations and not by the United States, and toward trying to moderate and mediate conflicting demands and positions. Its success in this was qualified at best, and for Canada, participation in Korea was a major step out of the British orbit and into the American.

The Canadian government was not the only one that saw its role in Korea as being somewhat ambiguous. The major western European states wanted to keep American attention focused where they thought it belonged, on Europe rather than on the Far East. The tightrope they walked was a different one from the Canadian, however: Their problem was that they could not afford to, or would not, defend themselves, and they wanted the Americans to help them do it, yet at the same time they did not want to fall under the dominance of the United States. In this period they were feeling their way toward the European Defense Community and ultimately NATO. Korea was a distraction they neither needed nor wanted, and through most of the war, their efforts too were devoted to keeping the war, and their own contributions, as limited as possible.

They were, of course, busy with their own concerns. The British were watching their empire fall apart in their hands, and they were trying to contain a Communist insurgency in Malaya throughout the period of the Korean War; during its later stages they were also conducting a low-level conflict in Kenya. France had a full-scale war on its hands in Indochina which, like the Peninsular War in Napoleon's day, was sucking the lifeblood out of the country. The Dutch had just given up in Indonesia. And for all of the western Europeans, conditions at home were still bad, the recovery from the most physically damaging of all Europe's wars only in the early stages.

In addition to this, the British tended to have a substantially different view of the Far Eastern scene than the Americans did. They had never developed the avuncular feeling for China that the United States had, and they had not therefore felt as bitter about the Communist victory in the civil war. They had quickly recognized the new regime and had begun trading with it; trade, after all, was what Britain was all about. The British found it hard to understand the American obsession with Chiang Kai-shek and the ongoing insistence that he, and he alone, was the *real* China. They were thus even more insistent than the United States on keeping the war limited, and they vigorously protested anything done without full consultation, such as the bombing of the hydroelectric plants, which they feared might serve to enlarge the war.

*   *   *

American problems with any of these countries, however, paled to invisibility before relations with India. Throughout the entire war, mere mention of India was apt to be met with sustained growls of vituperation in the United States. Yet India pursued a role which it perceived as perfectly correct, and eventually became a major participant in the truce process.

Once regarded as "the brightest jewel in the British crown," India had become independent in 1947. What had been formerly British India fragmented into India and Pakistan, and where there had recently been at least a veneer of order imposed by Great Britain, partition and independence were accompanied by massacre and civil war between Hindu and Muslim. The two successor states fought over Kashmir, and India also invaded and occupied the princely state of Hyderabad in the center of the subcontinent. Yet in spite of this resort to force when it was deemed useful or necessary, the Indian government acted as if it had a corner on the market for righteousness. The first prime minister of the republic, Jawaharlal Nehru, who also held the portfolio of foreign minister, and his acerbic ambassador to the United Nations, Krishna Menon, were always ready to lecture other countries about their shortcomings, though to American eyes they appeared far more conscious of western failings than they did of Communist ones.

If this was resented in the West, it was perhaps only natural; after all, it had not been Russia or the Soviet Union but Great Britain that had ruled India for the last century or more, and most of India's new leaders had learned their political trade agitating against the British. And where the United States wanted a general condemnation of Communist aggression, where the United States, in other words, was cranking up for the ideological heights of the Cold War, the Indians were determined not to have any part of it. Their government decided that the best role for India to play was that of strict neutral. For example, India, as a member of the Security Council, voted for the initial resolution on June 25, 1950, calling on members to assist South Korea in repelling the invasion from the north, but two days later, India abstained from a more strongly worded resolution put forth by the United States, and thus, in the American view, seriously weakened the force of the

UN position. Of the two other abstentions, Yugoslavia's was to be expected; Egypt's was slightly less important, but India's was a clear declaration that a potential great power was determined not to be drawn into the western Cold War camp.

It was John Foster Dulles who later harrumphed, "Neutralism is immoral!" Dulles was such a notable Cold Warrior that his condemnation almost had the effect of making neutralism moral in many liberal eyes, yet it was precisely the Indian kind of neutralism that he was talking about, for India, in its pursuit of an independent policy, refused to make much distinction between those forces fighting in support of the United Nations and those forces fighting against it. This was especially true after Inchon and the crossing of the 38th parallel by MacArthur's troops, for India was one of the most forceful in expressing its reservations about the wisdom, or the justice, of such an act. Throughout the period, India served as the channel by which the Communist Chinese tried to send signals to the West, though without, as events illustrated, much success.

The Indians continued to play a juggling game. In November the Soviets introduced a resolution in the Security Council calling on the United States to cease aggression against China. The Soviet Union voted for it; nine other members voted against it; India abstained. Then the United States introduced a resolution calling on China to withdraw from the Korean conflict. Nine members voted for it; the Soviet Union voted against it; India abstained. In the General Assembly, India took the lead among the smaller African and Asian states, seeking means to get negotiations started, and was instrumental in establishing and taking part in several "good offices" committees that tried to find some solution. By October 1952, when the long-drawn truce negotiations had stalled semipermanently on the question of voluntary repatriation and went into a six-month recess, it was India that suggested the establishment of a repatriation commission formed of neutral nations. This gained wide support in the General Assembly; the resolution passed by fifty-four to five, with one abstention. Even though the Communists opposed it and it lay dormant for another six months, there were contained in it some seeds that might ultimately bear fruit.

The Indians thus went their own way, determined, as most new states have been, to assert their independence of their former masters and their friends. But they were not simply looking backward and shunning the colonial past; they were looking ahead as well, to leadership of the Asian and nonwestern world. India's leaders saw for themselves a great role in the future, and they were assiduously staking their claims to it. If those claims have not been fulfilled, most Indian authorities on the period have argued that their politicians took the right course, however annoying to the United States that might be. The world seen from New Delhi was different from the world seen from Washington.

India was something of a halfway house. The United States had its allies and supporters, with greater or lesser commitment; then it had the neutral states to contend with; finally, in the United Nations it also had the Soviet Union and its satellites, supporters, or clients to argue with. After their absence during the crucial first days of the war, which permitted the United Nations to act at all, the Soviets hastened back to the Security Council. The Communist bloc consistently voted against the rest of the United Nations, and the Soviets played very successfully on the anticolonial wave sweeping the world. As more and more states that had once been part of western European empires gained independence and took their seats in the General Assembly, the Soviets presented the British, and French, and their associates, the Americans, as the grasping villains of the postwar world, successfully camouflaging the fact that they, in the last few years, had gained military, political, or ideological control over a greater number of people than anyone else had in the last century.

The most consistent problem in dealing with the Soviets remained the simple lack of knowledge. What did they want, who was pulling whose strings, what were the lines of command? No one could say with absolute certainty what, for example, was the precise relation between the Soviet Union, Communist China, and the North Korean People's Republic. The whole system remained a tortuous, labyrinthine, closed society, enormously frustrating for policymakers, who had to formulate lines of action on imperfect and incomplete knowledge. What the other side wants or will do in any given case is always a bit of a guessing game, but with the Communists, it was almost a total shot in the dark.

Yet situations are never entirely static, even though this one might have appeared so to American government officials trying to see a way out of the war, or to United Nations negotiators at Panmunjom, going in the fall of 1952 into a long recess. Someday, somewhere, something would change. The United States was determined to stand on the principle of voluntary repatriation, and equally determined not to enlarge the war. But the pressure for a settlement was growing; 1952 was a Presidential election year.

CHAPTER 15
THE HOME FRONT

Historians are still trying to figure out Harry S. Truman and the years over which he presided. During his Presidency, he was highly unpopular, and widely regarded as "a little man"; one current joke about him was "What was the greatest disaster that ever befell the United States?" The answer was "The failure of Truman's haberdashery shop in Independence, Missouri," for that was what had presumably sent him into politics. Yet his was something of a Horatio Alger story, the success of the great American dream. An artillery captain in World War I, later a judge, he was elected to the Senate from his home state in 1934; during World War II he chaired a committee investigating military spending, and gained sufficient prominence to be named as Vice-Presidential candidate when Franklin Roosevelt ran for his fourth term in 1944. The Vice-Presidency has usually been a ticket to oblivion, but Roosevelt died in April 1945, and suddenly the little man from Missouri was the President of the United States. As such he presided over the dropping of the atomic bombs, and the end of the war, the postwar loans to Great Britain and the initiation of the Marshall Plan, the development of the Truman Doctrine, and the beginning of the Cold War. To virtually everyone's surprise, he won reelection in 1948 over the heavily favored Governor Thomas E. Dewey of New York. And in accordance with his oft-quoted desk sign "The buck stops here," he committed United States troops to Korea.

Few of the things Truman did were ever as popular as this last. In mid-1950 the American people were confused, restless, and vaguely angry. The times were somehow out of joint, and the glorious new world that they had crusaded for from 1941 to 1945 had eluded them. The administration was in retreat, the Republican opposition in full cry about the Communist menace and various domestic short-comings. But the move into Korea won almost unanimous support. When announced in Congress, the decision got a standing ovation in the House of Representatives. In the Senate the Republican stan-dard-bearer, Robert A. Taft of Ohio, attacked the administration and especially his favorite target, Secretary of State Dean Acheson, for allowing, indeed encouraging, Korea to happen, but then having made that obligatory statement, he went on to support intervention enthusiastically. White House mail ran ten to one in favor of the decision, and there was a sense throughout the country that at last someone knew what America ought to be doing, and was doing it.

Only on the far left was there criticism, but it was largely ignored by the vast majority of the country. I. F. Stone, the maverick editor of a business paper, charged that the war was a put-up job, started by South Korea and encouraged by the United States. His subsequent book *The Hidden History of the Korean War* became the starting point for later, revisionist views that accepted his ideas in greater or lesser degree. Then on the extreme fringe, the Marxist-Leninists, whose numbers then were smaller than they would later become, made their standard charges about the "Rhee clique" and U.S. im-perialism. Couched in this rhetoric, they had little impact.

It was one thing to approve of taking a stand at last; it was another to go through the agonizing days of midsummer, when nothing seemed able to stop the North Korean advance. Stories of ambushes, defeats, bug-outs, and sudden death dampened American eagerness for the war. In the midst of trauma, the public ignored or forgot that American armed forces have almost always been unprepared for the opening stage of wars, and that that indeed is the almost inevitable consequence of not initiating them. People began to ask where the rest of the United Nations was, and, as it looked as though this might be a real war after all and not the "bandit incursion," the "police action," the President said it was, why had he not gone to Congress for a regular declaration of war? Though no one could fully realize it at the time, that had set a very dangerous precedent for this strange new world.

By the time the fall Congressional elections came around, the Republicans had returned to the attack, and the administration was bitterly assailed. The GOP, having endorsed support for Korea and the United Nations, could not now back away. Republicans could and did attack Truman and his people for getting them into it in the first place. There was near full employment as a result of the war crisis, but there was also substantial inflation, and there were a number of scandals floating about the country that led pundits to bemoan the decline of public and private morality. There were revelations about influence peddlers in Washington, the notorious "five percenters," and questions about whose wives had obtained mink coats and how. Senator Joseph McCarthy was hurling wild charges about Communists in high places, and was gaining a rabid following.

By the time the elections were held, the war at least was going well. The Inchon operation had been a marvelous success, United Nations troops were moving up into North Korea, President Truman and General MacArthur had had their famous meeting on Wake Island. It did the Democrats little good; the results at the polls were just short of disaster, and though the ruling party held its control of both houses of Congress, its majorities sank to invisibility. As the Chinese Communist divisions smashed into the overextended and overconfident UN troops up near the Yalu, it was obvious that it was going to be a bad winter, on Capitol Hill as well as in Korea.

Because it was clearly the area in which the United States was on the defensive, the major battle centered around foreign policy, and through the Christmas season and into the new year, the "Great Debate" was fought out. It began a week before the holiday, when Truman announced that more American troops would be sent to Europe to fulfill the commitments to NATO. The Republicans countered with their vision of "fortress America," and with resolutions that no troops be sent to Europe without approval of Congress. Early in January, Senator Taft attempted to pull all the threads of disillusionment together in a massive and concerted attack on the administration's conduct of foreign policy.

He could not do it. There were too many contradictions to be overcome, and the most fundamental of them was simply reality. The Republicans wanted to return to a more familiar world, to the world not only before 1941, but even before 1914, when the United States lived in happy, carefree isolation, protected from the rest of mankind's tribulations and follies by two great oceans and a substantial navy. The same politicians who condemned the government for "losing China" and allowing the Red menace to gain so much momentum now wanted—what? To retreat before that menace? To let their former and present allies go down the drain? The truth was, they were not sure what they wanted. They were the classic example of a party so long in opposition that opposition had become an end in itself. They did not really know what the Democrats were doing, or what they themselves would do in power; all they knew was that whatever it was, they could do it better. That was not enough; when it got down to nuts and bolts, Senator Taft had to admit that he would send maybe one less division to Europe than Truman was thinking of, and his budget for the future would be $7 billion less than the Democrats'. The difference therefore turned out to be one of degree, and not much of that, rather than fundamental policy, and the Great Debate was not so great after all.

No sooner had the foreign-policy debate begun to run down than the Truman-MacArthur controversy flared up, and the United States was into another round of name-calling and excitement. So they went on, causing consternation and dismay among their allies, and presumably amusement and amazement among their enemies, who had no conception of a free press and no idea of the resilience of free institutions.

The one point on which all sides were agreed, even if they differed in details, was that the United States had allowed itself to become dangerously weak militarily, and that now the armed forces must be strengthened. This was already beginning before the Korean War, but Korea certainly reinforced the idea, and also changed it in favor of the Army. In the five years since World War II ended, the Army had done poorly compared with the Navy, and been a virtual nonstarter compared with the Air Force. The first soldiers in Korea, with their skeleton formations and their outmoded equipment, had paid the price for that neglect, but the very price they paid had alerted American planners, and more important the American public, to the need for a viable army on the ground.

The buildup went on urgently, if not as rapidly as military men would have liked. Reserves were called up, the National Guard divisions activated, the draft put back into operation. Not everyone agreed on the details, of course. There was a move to introduce Universal Military Training, UMT, to call up all young men of a certain age for a certain period of time. This had long been the practice of some European countries, most notably France, but it never caught on in the United States, in spite of some degree of vocal support. The country preferred to stay with Selective Service; college students, for example, continued to receive deferments, and could do their time after they finished their degrees. At a time when there were no loans for university education and not everyone could make enough money to go to college, this contained obvious possibilities for abuse, as would become increasingly apparent in the next war. Though it was occasionally resented in the Korean period, it did not reach crisis proportions, probably because of the relatively low casualty rate of the static-front phase of the war.

There was one peculiar casualty of the war that did not receive as much attention as it deserved. That was racial segregation. In 1950 the United States Army was still divided into black and white units. The government had already decided that such division was inappropriate in the armed forces of the democracy, but though directives authorizing integration had been issued during the late forties, not much progress had been made. Even those commanders who philosophically accepted the idea were reluctant to try it out, and preferred to let sleeping dogs lie.

Black soldiers had always had a mixed reputation in the Army, where they had almost invariably been segregated into their own units and officered by whites. Two hundred thousand of them had fought in the American Civil War, in formations designated as U.S. Colored Troops. In the period of the Indian Wars, two cavalry regiments, the 9th and 10th, had been black, and so had the 24th and 25th Infantry, and all had good records, though they were often discriminated against both by other soldiers and by army officialdom. In World War II, by contrast, the only black division, the 92nd Infantry, had a poor record in the Italian campaign, where it had both black and white officers.

But by 1950, integration was an idea whose time had come. The Air Force, newest of the services, had largely integrated already, but the Army, Navy, and Marines had made relatively little progress.

Then in the summer of 1950, at both ends of the Army's organization, integration became a fact of life. Hard pressed by the number of new recruits, the Army Training Command quietly dropped its former policy of holding sufficient blacks in limbo until there were enough for a training formation and just took men as they came. For the recruits, everything else was so new about military life that this change made very little difference. And on the hills of Korea, the same thing happened. An army that was desperately cannibalizing its units for combat strength could no longer afford to support segregation. Black soldiers were soon perforce fighting alongside white ones, and in combat the color of a man's skin was simply not important. The same thing happened in the Marines, and the Navy, though slower and under less pressure from events, finally integrated as well.

Sad to say, the armed forces received very little credit for this move. The national civil rights movement of the later fifties and sixties won widespread support from white liberals, but they were either unaware, or unwilling to acknowledge, that the services had done a decade earlier what they were trying to achieve. Those people who did notice the change tended to be people so opposed to military service, or to everything else in American life, that instead of giving credit for a forward step, they accused the services of wanting "black cannon fodder." Yet whatever the reasons and however people perceived the event, Jim Crow died on the hills of Korea.

As the war became stalemated, as MacArthur went and Ridgway restored equilibrium and the crisis of Chinese intervention passed, as negotiations opened and then bogged down, the American public became accustomed but not resigned to the fact of war. The early fifties were a strange time; most people were concerned, then as always, with making a living. Suburbs were blossoming on what one authority has nicknamed "the crabgrass frontier." A home of one's own, a relatively new car in the garage, a television—these things seemed within the reach of most people. There were babies and preschool children everywhere, and, so everyone thought, Mom ought to be happy in the kitchen and Dad in the factory or office, while the kids grew up safe and secure. Some social commentators worried about complacency, and materialism, and new-fangled phrases like "consumerism." But the working generation of the late forties and early fifties had grown up in the Depression and matured in World War II, and a house and car and college for the children did not seem unreasonable desires. They had not yet been rejected by Mom, who, it was later discovered, secretly wanted to get out and make another paycheck, or, as Dr. Kinsey revealed, have a little fling; nor by the kids, who, after having grown up in all that security, would throw their parents' values in their faces. It was a comfortable world of family shows on television, Sunday papers, and the trip to the beach.

But the world kept intruding. The damned war dragged on and on, and the boy who used to deliver the papers went off, came home once in olive drab, and then did not come home again. There was the disturbing sense of dark forces looming out there in the night. And there were those who thought the forces had already stolen inside the house. There was Joe McCarthy and the great fear.

One of the most attractive, and persistent, theories of historical causation is the Plot. People always find it easier to believe there is some sinister intelligence at work than to accept that there are vast impersonal forces beyond human control. Evil makes better reading than weakness or mere stupidity. In World War I it was "the merchants of death"; in World War II there was the repeated insistence that Roosevelt knew about Pearl Harbor, but wanted to get the United States into the war. By 1950 there was "the worldwide Communist conspiracy," and the foremost proponent of this in the United States was Joseph McCarthy.

McCarthy was a Republican senator from Wisconsin, and he achieved prominence, fame, and ultimately ignominy by launching one of the most spectacular smear campaigns of modern American history. It began in February 1950 when he announced that he had the names of 200-odd "known Communists" in the State Department. It happened that he could not produce such a list—one reporter said that what he was actually waving in the air was a laundry list—but such was the temper of the moment that he was widely believed. Headlines blared and trumpets roared, and McCarthy, spurred on by the press, made wild and ever wilder accusations, ultimately attacking such hitherto unassailable figures as George C. Marshall himself. The public outcry against Communism was such that several restrictive laws were enacted by Congress, the most important of them the McCarran Internal Security Act, which took substantial chips out of the rights of free speech and assembly; it was passed over a Presidential veto. But McCarthy was not so much a Congressional player as he was a pure and simple demagogue; he used committee hearings, and the press, to hound any individual whom he happened to suspect of Communist sympathies, and he suspected almost everyone. Before the fever passed he had nearly destroyed the Foreign Service, severely damaged the entire State Department, and taken on the U.S. Army as well, while the fallout practically emasculated the entertainment and communications industries. And he did it all with shouting, bullying, and innuendo, with not a shred of evidence; it was a bizarre and scary time in American history.

Against all these events, the war was back-page news. There were artillery duels; there were occasional firefights; hills changed hands; the negotiators at Panmunjom met and did not meet. In August 1952 the Air Force increased the pressure of its attacks, and flew 1,403 sorties against Pyongyang alone. In late September the line flared up, with Communist attacks all along the front, but they got nowhere. In October the Air Force shot down sixty-two MiG-15s, its best month so far in the war. The Communists also launched the biggest attacks of the year, around the Chorwon valley, but could not make any real impression on the UN lines. And that month the truce talks were suspended. General Harrison reviewed the various alternatives his side had offered, all of which had been rejected by the Communists. He said that until they were willing either to accept a UN plan or to produce a reasonable one of their own, there was no sense talking anymore. He was therefore declaring a recess, and he got up and walked out. Finally, after literally hundreds of meetings, after twisting and turning and compromising on this and retreating on that, the UN negotiators had had enough. That was on October 8, and General Harrison had no idea when, or even if, the talks would ever reopen.

The event did not mean a great deal back home, where newspapers had just about given up recording meetings of the truce teams—there were actually 159 plenary sessions, and countless liaison meetings. For the United States, in October, was caught up in one of the greatest election campaigns in history, a campaign in which the whole of the Korean War was a vital part.

Someone quipped that the basic formula of the election campaign was K_1C_2, for Korea, Communism, and Corruption. But in retrospect it seemed less a matter of issues than of personalities, for the opposing candidates were two men, both of heroic mold, whose power to fascinate—and to inspire argument—has hardly dimmed in thirty years. The Democrats nominated the governor of Illinois, Adlai E. Stevenson, and the Republicans chose General of the Army Dwight D. Eisenhower.

Neither one was a foregone conclusion. Stevenson played coy right until the Democratic convention itself, and became the country's most notable noncandidate. There was a host of seekers, most insistently Senator Estes Kefauver of Tennessee, who had made a name investigating organized crime. But the tide went to Stevenson, who finally won the nomination on the third ballot. The governor was a brilliant man, quietly witty, broadly philosophical, a good speaker when he once warmed to the task. He was the darling of the eastern liberal intellectuals, who worked hard for him, but he had several problems. One of the worst was that while he accepted the record of the Democratic Party, he tried to distance himself from the party machine, and from Truman himself; he did not want to be soiled by association with the bosses and the odors of corruption wafting from Washington. He wanted to be like his predecessor from Illinois, Abe Lincoln, but he forgot that Lincoln had been a very clever politician; Stevenson wanted to be a statesman.

But Stevenson's worst problem was that he ran against Dwight Eisenhower. "Ike" was not so much a noncandidate as he was uncertain of his way; his world was the Army, not politics, and he was not even entirely certain he was a Republican. Nevertheless, he let his name be entered in the preconvention primaries, where a bitter fight developed between his supporters and the backers of Senator Taft. Taft was a perpetual bridesmaid, and he was now absolutely determined to be a bride. The fight continued onto the floor of the Republican convention, where the two factions savaged each other over the seating of delegates. Eventually Eisenhower won the nomination on the first ballot, which was almost an anticlimax. The big question was whether or not Taft and his people would splinter off, but eventually they stayed on side—just barely. To get the nomination, Eisenhower accepted help from the West Coast wing of the party, and therefore ended up with Senator Richard M. Nixon of California as a running mate.

The campaign was a bitter roller coaster, as first one candidate and then the other appeared to make progress. Stevenson was a strong early runner, in spite of the Democrats' handicaps. Eisenhower, by contrast, tried to take the high road, standing above partisan politics and producing a series of lackluster speeches that went nowhere. The liberals delighted in Stevenson's brilliance, until it backfired; it was this campaign that produced the term "egghead," the derisory name for anyone guilty of the sin of overintellectualism. A famous photograph of Stevenson with his feet on his desk, and a hole in the sole of his shoe, became an issue: Republicans asked if the fate of the country should be trusted to a man who had his head so far in the clouds that he neglected to get his shoes fixed, while Democrats wore lapel pins in the shape of a shoe sole. Then the Republicans ran into a potential quagmire when it was revealed that Nixon had behind him a political slush fund. Actually, of course, so did virtually everyone else in national politics, but the issue blew up, and Nixon went on national television to produce a bathetic performance about how poor he was, and how his wife wore a good cloth Republican coat. Eisenhower, meanwhile, was forced down off the high ground, and by the time the campaign was nearing its end, all hands were engaged in a regular free-for-all.

Korea remained the major issue, but it was a problem that no one could seem to do much about; it was just *there*. As neither candidate really knew how to get out of it, and neither would disown the commitment, they tended to argue instead over whose fault it was that the United States had gotten into it to begin with. Stevenson was clearly at a disadvantage here, as it was after all his party which was in power. The Republicans could stand off and take free shots at Truman and the Democrats. Somewhat reluctantly—he had, after all, just been Truman's appointee as Supreme Allied Commander Europe—Eisenhower let himself be drawn into this and assailed the administration for its foreign-policy errors. As a result, relations between himself and Truman cooled to the point of freezing during the campaign, and remained that way.

The clincher to the race came in Detroit, on October 24. Eisenhower announced that if elected, he would "forgo the diversions of politics . . ."—an interesting choice of words for a man in his position—"and concentrate on the job of ending the Korean War." He then added, "That job requires a personal trip to Korea. I shall make that trip. Only in that way could I learn how best to serve the American people in the cause of peace. I shall go to Korea."

That did it; the election was all over but the counting. When they got around to that, Eisenhower took all but nine states. Stevenson's nine were in the traditional Democratic bastion, the South, but Ike took Virginia and Tennessee and Florida too; he got almost 34 million votes to Stevenson's 27 million. The troops in Korea had started the war under a commander whose most famous words were "I shall return"; now they had one who got the job by promising, "I shall go."

CHAPTER 16
THE END IN SIGHT

As General Eisenhower was making his "I shall go to Korea" speech in Detroit, the biggest Communist attacks in a year were cresting in the Chorwon valley. On the western hills, seven Chinese regiments had spent three weeks trying to take White Horse Hill away from the ROK 9th Division. It cost the South Koreans 3,500 casualties and the Chinese close to 10,000, but the ROKs, well supported by artillery and air interdiction, held the hill at the end. To the east, on Hill 391, shortly to be renamed Jackson Heights, the U.S. 65th Infantry Regiment took a bad beating and lost the position; it was not a happy affair, and several officers and men were court-martialed. The 65th was basically a Puerto Rican regiment, most of its enlisted men Spanish-speaking, most of its officers English-speaking. More important was the fact that during the previous nine months, 8,700 men had rotated through the regiment; its members felt as if they belonged to a clearing house rather than a real unit. This was an example of the price paid for the rotation policy.

To counter the Chinese initiative in the Chorwon valley, General

Van Fleet wanted to launch an attack a little farther east, in front of Kumhwa. General Clark was reluctant to indulge in swapping hills, but he finally gave approval for Operation Showdown, to be mounted by the U.S. 7th Division and the ROK 2nd Division. Begun on October 14, Showdown turned into a graphic illustration of the difficulties of limiting battles in limited wars. Van Fleet's original concept called for an attack by one battalion from each of the engaged divisions; it should last about five days, and the result would be the seizure of a ridgeline about three miles forward of Kumhwa. Unfortunately, the concept did not take into account the Chinese reaction. They decided that they wanted to keep that hill line, and therefore the little battle stretched on for six weeks. Estimated UN casualties of 200 had swollen to 9,000 real ones, and the Chinese still held most of the hills. True, it had cost them an estimated 19,000 casualties to do so, but once again, the UN Command had to face the hard fact that its enemies were more willing to trade men for landscape than the UN itself was. This was simply a no-win game. By November, both sides were once more acknowledging that, and the front settled down. It was getting cold again, and the troops girded themselves for the third winter in Korea. How long ago MacArthur's jaunty "Home for Christmas!" seemed now.

The next bit of excitement came when the President-elect fulfilled his pledge to visit Korea, though it turned out to be a very small bit indeed. President Rhee wanted to meet with the new leader, indulge in what a later generation would call a "photo opportunity," and sell him on the great mission of uniting all of Korea. Eisenhower gave him an hour. Clark, frustrated by the stalemate, wanted to present his plan for winning the war by a drive to the Yalu; he never got the chance. Instead, Ike put on field gear and went out to talk to line commanders and some of the troops in the field. He ate rations, he watched an artillery barrage, he talked to infantrymen and to a few pilots brought in from the carriers. New lieutenants always want to think about world strategy, but generals like to think about platoon tactics and the state of men's feet; it takes them back to their youth. Eisenhower had a good visit, but looking at the hills of Korea convinced him that the war must be ended; there was just no sense in this endless battle for barren real estate. Whatever Eisenhower was or was not, he was not the man to succumb to some Asian siren song.

Yet for the new American leadership, as for the old, the options remained pretty limited. Cautiously Eisenhower began to explore them. When he got back to Hawaii, traveling by sea, he issued a press statement that implicitly threatened the widening of the war. When he reached the United States, he met with MacArthur, who had publicly announced that he had a plan for ending the war, and that he would present it to the new President (much to Truman's disgust). MacArthur's plan was for Armageddon: a meeting between Eisenhower and Stalin, followed by unification and neutralization of Germany and Korea—or the use of the atomic bomb to create an Asian wasteland. Appalled, Eisenhower thanked him and filed it away.

There were small pressures that both sides would apply. In mid-December the Communists instigated yet another prisoner riot, which resulted in eighty-five of their own people dead, and a good bit of adverse press reaction against the UN. Then, in his first State of the Union Address, Eisenhower announced that he was immediately lifting the blockade of the Formosa Strait by the U.S. Seventh Fleet. The Americans would stop protecting Red China from the Nationalists. The press and the hard-liners in the Republican Party were excited at this, and at last Chiang Kai-shek and his people were to be "unleashed"! This turned out to be a total smoke screen. The fact was, the Truman administration had been permitting, even encouraging, Nationalist raids on the mainland for some time. The second fact was that the Nationalists were barely capable of staging such raids, and certainly not in condition to do anything more substantial. If Red China was to be pushed to the negotiating table, it was going to take a lot more than unleashing the Nationalists to do it.

But there were other means. The new President announced an increase in the buildup of the South Korean Army. And in February, when General Clark reported signs of an impending Communist offensive, Eisenhower and his new cabinet considered the big question: use of the atomic bomb. They decided against it, but they also decided not to give away the hand gratuitously. In any public pronouncements, the President stressed that the situation in Korea was intolerable, that the stalemate could not and would not be allowed to continue, and he explicitly refused to close off any options, including the use of any particular weapons in any particular area. The implication was clear: Let the Communists for once worry about what the other side might do.

The precise relationship between the North Korean regime and the Soviet Union remains murky. One authority maintains that Joseph Stalin, apprised of Kim Il Sung's intention to invade South Korea, came back with a "Do it but I don't want to know about it" type of reply. Yet whether it was coincidence or not, the first big break in the logjam came shortly after Stalin's death. This occurred on March 5. In a dictatorship generally, and in Russia historically, the moment of succession is always a traumatic one; no one is ever entirely certain on whom the mantle of power will descend, nor what the new ruler will do. As the death of Stalin was announced, the United States, almost totally unprepared for this long-awaited event, watched with mixed fear and apprehension for signs of new directions.

During all this time, there had been periodic meetings of the liaison officers at the truce site, even though the negotiations were officially in recess. There were still, after all, day-to-day matters to discuss, and there was still the necessity for either side to have a pipeline to the other. Most of the time the pipe had been full of hot air, denunciations of assorted kinds, but at least it was still there. Then in March things began to happen, in subtle ways.

The origins of the shift went back to December 1952. In the middle of that month, at Geneva, the executive committee of the International Red Cross had passed a motion recommending the exchange of sick and wounded prisoners in Korea, in a separate process that would not prejudice the larger POW question, and would simply be a humanitarian gesture. General Clark had suggested to his Washington superiors that he try such an offer, though he did not think it would elicit much response. They too were pessimistic, but in February they said he might as well try; if nothing else, it would look good on the record. Accordingly, Clark wrote to the enemy commanders, announcing his readiness to participate in the exchange. Nothing happened for almost six weeks, but then a startling letter came back at the end of March. Not only were the Communists ready for the exchange, they were also ready to seek a larger solution to the war.

This little crack in the facade was so unexpected that the Americans were almost completely nonplussed by it. They were further amazed when the Chinese foreign minister, Chou En-lai, released a statement saying that the Chinese were ready to reconsider the POW issue as a whole, and that perhaps the nonvoluntary repatriates should be handed over to a neutral nation for explanations and subsequent disposition. This was a variation on the theme advanced in the United Nations by India months ago, and again the Americans were surprised. The simple fact was that they had been entrenched in their negotiating positions so long that it was now almost inconceivable that there might at last be a way out. Cautiously, like the little bird whose desire for the seeds overcomes its fear of the hand holding them, they began to inch back toward the negotiating table.

It was still not easy. The Americans were insistent upon only voluntary repatriation, while the Communists were under the necessity of avoiding a huge propaganda defeat. They therefore took the view that there were no such things as defection, or nonvoluntary repatriation. Of course all the Chinese and North Koreans held prisoner by the United Nations wanted to return home; some of them, however, had been misled, or intimidated, by a ruthless enemy, and so no longer realized what they *really* wanted. As soon as the truth was explained to them, they would be eager to return to the paths of righteousness.

On April 6 the liaison group met at Panmunjom, and fairly quickly got down to brass tacks on the matter of sick and wounded. Both sides agreed to give these terms a wide interpretation, in the hope of getting a greater number of their people back. On April 8 they exchanged lists of names, but again the United Nations were due for a disappointment. The UN was prepared to release about 700 Chinese and 5,100 North Koreans, while the Communists would provide 450 South Koreans and 150 UN personnel. This seemed a small number to the UN liaison officers, but in fact the Communists were returning a slightly larger percentage of their prisoners than the UN was of its prisoners, so they could not complain too much. By April 11 they had reached agreement on the details of the actual handover, and they set the date for what the Americans called Operation Little Switch. It was to begin on April 20, with the Communists returning 100 a day and the UN 500.

The exchange began on time, and lasted until May 3. In some ways it went better, in some worse, than had been hoped. Prisoners were handed over in batches of twenty-five at a time, so that there was an opportunity for processing and interviewing the men as they crossed the line. The Communists going home were very obstreperous, singing and chanting, occasionally refusing to move, or to eat. The packages of comforts they were given they largely threw away, and they often cut off buttons, belt buckles, and bootlaces, so that when they reached Panmunjom they could present a haggard or mistreated appearance. UN soldiers gave the Communists very little trouble; no one wanted at this stage to jeopardize his chances of getting out. During the process the UN found it had more Communists that actually qualified for release under the definitions being used, so it passed a total of 6,670 people through the line. The Communists too upped their figure, to 684, though the names they had earlier provided suggested there were another 150 or so who might have been released.

If the Communist returnees made trouble for their captors, the tales the UN soldiers had to tell caused a wave of anger in the western world. The American forces mounted a huge study of their prisoners and their behavior, but press interviews were soon followed by widespread stories of physical and mental maltreatment. Like everything else about this strange war, it was enormously frustrating, for the desire to punish the enemy for his abuse conflicted sharply with the desires to get the rest of the prisoners back and to end the war.

In any case, it now appeared possible to make more progress. The Communists had opened up a little, after all, and as a result, full-scale negotiations were resumed on April 26. The only real remaining issue was that of how to handle those prisoners who did not wish to return home. But as the two sides fenced with each other, it developed that there were substantial divergences here. First was the question of which neutral state would hold the non-repatriates; then, where would they be held, for how long, and what would happen to them at the end of the "explanation" period? The UN wanted to name Switzerland as the holding state, to have the prisoners remain in Korea, and to have the explanation period last for no more than sixty days, after which the prisoners would just be freed. The Communists did not want Switzerland, though they would not say what country they did want; they wanted the POWs moved to the neutral state, and they wanted six months to persuade the POWs to return home.

So it went. As before, there was point and counterpoint, offer and refutation. It took another month, though. By May 25 the UN negotiators presented what they said was a "final offer." The major points were a five-nation repatriation commission, with India to supply all the troops and support staff; ninety days for "explanations," plus thirty more to handle the residue of prisoners still undecided; limits on the number of "explainers" and the time they would have access to prisoners; and the presence of commission members during the explanations. The Communists said they would think about it.

Nothing substantial happened for the next two weeks, but a few small wrinkles were gradually ironed out. On June 7 there was a meeting of staff officers to put the finishing touches on the draft agreements, and on June 8 the Communists announced that they would agree to the settlement of the POW question. At long last, after eighteen months of war, the thorny matter of item four was resolved, and the Communists, disguise it as they might, accepted the principle of no involuntary repatriation. The dam was finally broken, and a full truce should now be but a matter of days.

The rest of it should have been easy, but it was not. The six more weeks before the definitive armistice was actually signed saw some of the heaviest fighting of the war. Worse, for the UN side, they not only had to fight the Communists, they very nearly ended up fighting their friends as well.

As the end approached, the Communists naturally attempted to improve their position, both in the air and on the ground. The UN air forces welcomed the opportunity to tangle with the Red planes, for during the winter air intelligence officers had become seriously alarmed at what they perceived as a major rebuilding effort in Manchuria, including large numbers of MiG-15s, and even more ominously, the first appearance of jet bombers, the Il-28, a medium-range aircraft with substantial potential for threatening South Korea. So in the closing months, and weeks, of the war the Air Force's Sabres and the Navy Panthers went after the opposition determinedly. By now it was not just the Communists who were using the skies over North Korea for training cycles; the U.S. Air Force as well employed substantial numbers of pilots who were getting early combat training. Many of the young second lieutenants or ensigns who flew their first live missions in Korea would go on to command squadrons in another war. The last full month of fighting in Korea, June of 1953, saw the highest count of the war, with seventy-four MiGs downed by the Air Force.

At the same time as air-to-air combat peaked, the bombers, from B-29s down to fighter-bombers, kept up their attack on the enemy's ground systems. The B-29s were increasingly vulnerable to more modern Communist countermeasures, and by the end of the war it was becoming obvious that their day was almost over. Newer aircraft types were being introduced into the theater, such as the F3D Skyknight or F-94 Starfire, night or all-weather interceptors that could help out the hard-pressed bombers. The UN air units ended the war as they had begun it, dominating the sky.

On the ground, the pace of action was closely tied to the progress, or lack of it, at the truce talks. The Communists badly wanted to end the war on a winning note, but for once it was they who had to walk a tightrope: They had to gain enough to call it a victory, but not so much as to call forth a vigorous UN reaction, or worse, a breaking off of negotiations. In March, when they first showed some signs of being willing to talk again, they were fairly aggressive, in small company-sized actions along the front. April was wet and muddy, and things slowed down again. Then they resumed their probes in late May and early June, when the final haggling over the POWs was going on.

When the prisoner agreement was reached on June 8, the stage was then set for the Communists to make a major attack, to improve their line just before the truce could be agreed upon. They did this in the center of the Eighth Army line, where the terrain was bad, and they put in a series of drives against the right flank of U.S. IX Corps and all along the front of ROK II Corps. They were trying to flatten out a bulge in the line that ran about fifteen miles east of Kumhwa, over toward Mundung-ni and the old Heartbreak Ridge position. The attacks went on for about ten days before they finally petered out. The South Koreans were pushed back up to a couple of miles in some places; and the Communists, at heavy cost, did manage to improve their lines. It was also obvious that they were not only thinking in tactical terms, they were also testing the ability of the South Koreans to hold their own on the battlefield, and they were sending signals to President Rhee as well. Unfortunately, just then President Rhee was not in a very receptive mood.

The nearer to fruition came the peace talks, the greater grew the frustration of Syngman Rhee. The president of the Republic of Korea had never resigned himself to continued partition of his country; he never ceased to regard the regime of Kim Il Sung as a bunch of upstart bandits. Now, grateful though he might profess to be for the help from the United States, he saw his goal of ultimate unification receding into some impossible future, and he was a bitter man. He had opposed negotiation when it began, and he had resorted to any amount of chicanery to keep himself in power; he was not now about to accept a truce without a last effort to avert it. The Americans were uncomfortably aware that the more concessions they made to gain a cease-fire, the more they alienated the leader of the people they were fighting for.

As a result, they did everything they could to placate Rhee's fears. As the new administration took office in Washington, President Eisenhower made substantial commitments to long-term support for the South Koreans. Economic aid for the next several years was promised, and the Americans agreed to build up the ROK Army to first sixteen and then twenty divisions.

Yet to Rhee and his government, all these things were no more than sugar-coating of the bitter pill; the Americans were still determined to get out of the war. Rhee wanted all the goodies, and he wanted unification—that is, the continuation of the war—as well. He set out to sabotage the peace process. Fifty thousand people in Seoul attended a rally on April 5, to hear their leaders denounce the armistice negotiations and demand unification. Five days later another 50,000 paraded in Pusan, students this time, chanting "Union or death!" and "Go north!" Students are always volatile; they are young, enthusiastic, and excitable. The American commanders in the Korean Communications Zone, the administrative rear area, were seriously alarmed. On April 21, Rhee cabled Washington that he was about to withdraw the ROK forces from the UN Command, and that he might well feel constrained to fight on alone, if he had to.

From this point through May, General Clark and the new American ambassador, Ellis O. Briggs, scuttled back and forth between

Tokyo and Korea and burned up the wires to Washington, trying to keep Rhee in line. But the truce process marched along, almost inexorably now, and Rhee's rhetoric grew more strident; he was actually backing himself into a corner where he would be forced to do something.

Finally, on June 18, he moved. There were about 35,000 Korean nonrepatriates being held in POW compounds, guarded by ROK troops. Rather than see these men turned over to a neutral nations commission, Rhee ordered their release. He bypassed the UN Command channels, and his troops simply opened the gates. Some 25,000 got out the first night, and though the guards were immediately replaced by American troops, 3,000 or 4,000 more got away as well. As they were all Koreans anyway, they simply faded into the country, and relatively few were caught.

There was some consternation in the UN camp. The new Eighth Army commander, Maxwell D. Taylor, who had replaced General Van Fleet in February, was loath to use force to restrain men who were acting because they were, after all, vigorous anti-Communists. At Panmunjom the Communist delegation denounced the whole thing as a put-up job, accusing the UN of bad faith, which was not true, and the South Koreans of wanting to prolong the war, which was. Angrily they broke off the talks once again, staying away from the table for another two and a half weeks.

In fact, though they would not have admitted it, Rhee's action was one way of avoiding the embarrassment for the Communists; better for them to charge that the other side had acted the villain than suffer the public propaganda defeat of more rejection from their former subjects. So on July 8 they announced their willingness to return, and on the 10th the much-interrupted talks resumed once again.

Meanwhile, the Americans came to terms with Rhee. President Eisenhower sent over his Assistant Secretary of State, Walter S. Robertson. The diplomat held out carrots of deals with the United States, while General Clark applied sticks by changing UN troop dispositions, and finally Rhee agreed to behave, in return for American promises to love, cherish, and support Korea for the foreseeable future.

At Panmunjom the Communists now had the initiative, for they were able to represent the UN as unable to control its client, South Korea. What guarantees, therefore, could there be that any truce would work? Patiently General Harrison went over all the old familiar ground, to which the Communists played coy and called for recesses. They were clearly stalling now, though they had a good position on which to do it. And the reason for the stalling was that at this eleventh hour, they opened up the biggest ground operation in two years.

On the night of July 13, six Chinese divisions slammed into the line held by ROK II Corps in central Korea. Attacking in battalion and even regimental strength, they suffered heavy casualties, but after three days of hard fighting, they had pushed the South Koreans back as much as six miles, broken through their line in two places, and threatened to envelop two divisions. The South Koreans retreated below the Kumsong River, but could not quite hang on there either. Clark and Taylor brought in American troops, including the 187th Airborne Regiment from Japan, and set up blocking positions. After the Koreans had ridden out the first storm and pulled themselves back together, they counterattacked back to the Kumsong River, but they could not regain all they had lost, and had to settle for some ridgelines overlooking the river valley. At the same time as all this was fought out, there was a flurry of little actions all along the front, including some bitter company-sized fights over hills that were already designated to be in the demilitarized zone. The UN troops fired off enormous stocks of artillery and mortar rounds, and the Communists, mostly the Chinese, used up a large number of men. Presumably they wanted to be able to claim a victory in the closing days of the war, and they also wanted to demonstrate their willingness as well as their ability to keep on fighting.

But it really was all over now. Liaison officers worked out the details, of the demilitarized zone, of the process for handing over the POWs, of the actual signing. Even this latter was a matter of contention, for who would sign, where, how, and even who would witness the ceremony were all matters that could be manipulated to make one side look like a winner, the other like a loser.

The day finally agreed upon was July 27, the time 10:00 in the morning. The actual ceremony was something of an anticlimax. The press representatives and spectators arrived half an hour early and filed into the conference hall. Then the negotiating teams came in; the Communists were formally dressed in full uniform, the UN members in ordinary undress khakis. Precisely at ten, General Harrison entered the building from his side, and Lt. Gen. Nam Il of the North Korean People's Army from his end. They sat down at the center of their respective tables and signed the copies of the documents in front of them; aides exchanged copies, and they signed again. It was over in twelve minutes. Neither general spoke; neither offered to shake hands. They got up, looked coldly at each other, and walked out. On both sides, the artillery kept banging away for another twelve hours; then the truce came into effect, silence fell along the hills and valleys of central Korea, and the war was over.

There remained the return of the prisoners of war. The exchange began on August 5. The Neutral Nations Repatriation Commission consisted of five members, Czechoslovakia, Poland, Sweden, Switzerland, and India, with India chairing it and providing the troops to do the actual supervisory work. The Indians sent up a unit which was entitled Custodial Force India, which throughout the long and often frustrating proceeding displayed its impeccable British-derived military bearing.

Though the process should have gone smoothly, it did not. The Communists returned 12,757 prisoners, of whom 7,848 were South Koreans, 1,312 were other United Nations personnel, and 3,597 were Americans. Twenty-three Americans and one Briton chose to stay with the Communists, though in later years a few of them, disillusioned, drifted back to their own country. The United Nations turned over to the Communists a total of 75,823 prisoners, about 70,000 of them North Koreans and the rest Chinese. These went home singing and shouting, throwing their American clothing away and celebrating their return to their own people. The problem came not with them, but with 22,604 nonrepatriates, about two-thirds Chinese and one-third North Korean, who did not wish to return home. These were the hard residue of all those non-Communists who had been classified, reclassified, screened and screened again, and who had not ended up as "civilian detainees" or released in Rhee's *coup de main* or anything else. These were the men to whom the Communists proposed to "explain" their situation, after which they would be willing to return home.

It did not work very well. The explanations consisted of each prisoner being marched into a tent and harangued, for up to several hours, by a team of Communist explainers. As it became apparent that most would still refuse to go home, the explanations became longer and louder, until finally the Indians intervened. Even so, the process went on until January 1954, before the Indians in disgust simply declared the game over. At the end of six months, the Communists had won back 628 of the 22,604 remaining prisoners. The rest went off to life in South Korea, or, for the majority, Nationalist China. It was a final victory for the United Nations, but by then, everyone was heartily sick of the entire matter. All most people wanted to do with Korea was forget it.

CHAPTER 17
LESSONS LEARNED AND UNLEARNED

Compared with the two great wars that had preceded it, Korea was a half-war, in which some Americans were all too involved and most were not involved at all. Its conclusion bore out this same elusive quality, for the cease-fire brought not jubilation, triumph, and ease after toil, but rather a mingled sense of relief and frustration, and unhappy awareness that if things were not going to get worse, neither were they going to get much better. Given what the war had cost, it seemed as if the result ought to be more than that.

For the costs of a partial victory were indeed heavy enough. Precise figures are, as always, difficult to obtain, and even more so when dealing with societies that have never opened their books. The best data available suggest that the Communists suffered something between 1.25 and 1.5 million killed, wounded, prisoners, or missing. Numbers for the United Nations are easier to come by, though there are still disparities among different sources. The U.S. Army's official history simply states that the United Nations Command suffered more than 500,000 casualties, of which 94,000 were killed. The Americans' passion for statistics means they kept better records, and among U.S. forces the figures are firmer: 33,629 dead, 103,284 wounded, 5,178 prisoners or missing, for a total of 142,091. Given the relatively small commitment by other members of the United Nations, that means something over 50,000 South Korean soldiers dead. These are all military casualties; in addition, there were hundreds of thousands of civilians killed, wounded, or dying from disease as a result of bombings, dislocations, flight before the enemy, atrocities, breakdown of the economy, or other war-related problems. It is estimated that the total number of casualties may well have reached 3 million or more.

Both North and South Korea were devastated; bridges were down, rail lines broken, tunnels blocked, ports filled with junk, buildings gutted, irrigation and hydroelectric systems ruined. The countryside was barren, and the rebuilding would take years. As monetary costs shade off into other factors, it is hard to say what the war amounted to in dollars, but the U.S. government put the figures at $83 billion by 1956. Much of that was attributable to the overall growth of the American defense establishment, and might therefore be charged to the Cold War rather than specifically to the Korean War. On the other hand, the tale was by no means told in 1956; there were still pensions to be paid, ex-servicemen to be educated under the Korean GI Bill, seriously wounded to be maintained in hospital. Some of those costs will be borne, indeed, until the last Korean casualty is dead.

Material expenditures, which formed a part of this cost, give some idea of the level of both activity and destruction. The U.S. Air Force's official history states, for example, that Far East Air Forces dropped 386,037 tons of bombs and 32,357 tons of napalm and fired 313,600 rockets and 166,853,100 rounds of machine-gun ammunition during the war. The Navy, Marines, and foreign contingents expended proportionate amounts. In return, all UN air units claimed to have destroyed 976 enemy aircraft, 1,327 tanks, almost 83,000 vehicles, and more than 11,000 railway engines and cars, and to have cut Communist rail lines more than 28,000 times. They themselves lost a total of 1,986 aircraft; as usual in a field combat situation, only just more than half were lost to enemy action, the rest to the normal accidents and attrition of flying under adverse conditions.

Ground expenditure was of an equal magnitude. One quartermaster remarked that Korea was an artilleryman's paradise; in June

1953, for example, UN artillery fired the largest single month's toll of ammunition, 2,710,248 rounds of 105mm or larger. Reliance on gunpowder meant the United Nations often fired three or four times as much ammunition as the Communists did, and this lavish type of allotment, in all categories, did much to account for the relatively larger logistical tail required by the UN troops. Higher commanders sometimes complained about what were regarded as excessive calls for artillery support, but there is no such thing as "lavish" or "excessive" support to a man actually under fire. The result was that at the time of its fighting, Korea was second only to World War II itself in costs to the United States.

The political payoff for all this suffering, expense, and effort remained elusive. International ramifications had to be worked out over the next several months and years. One of the provisions of the cease-fire agreement was for a general political conference to follow it, but by the time that actually met, in June 1954 at Geneva, Korea was already being upstaged by the problem of Indochina, and the United States was barely out of one Asian bog before it embarked on the path leading to another, deeper one.

Both North and South Korea remained fixed in political amber. The People's Republic went on as it had before, being neither a republic nor ruled in any real sense by the people. As it stayed firmly under leftist control, so did South Korea under rightist. President Rhee, who ran unopposed, was elected to a fourth term in March 1960, but a month later he resigned after demonstrators were fired on by the police and more than 100 killed. The next year a military junta seized power and declared a complete military dictatorship. Though it promised to restore civilian rule, a strongman, Gen. Chung Hee Park, ended up as president anyway. By then it was 1964, and South Korea's ally and chief supporter, the United States, was getting more and more caught up in Vietnam, the Indochina of ten years previously. The Korean object lesson, of the chances of creating viable democracies in East Asia by military intervention, was obviously lost on Washington.

The effects of the Korean War on the United States, and the armed forces of the United States, are even more difficult to isolate, for much of what happened during this period resulted from the general climate of Cold War, and ongoing hostility between the Americans and their system and the Soviets and their system, and probably would have happened to greater or lesser degree even had there been no war. In that sense, Korea was more a catalytic agent than a cause in and of itself.

The great Greek historian Thucydides, in his classic account of the Peloponnesian War, remarked that a curious facet of long-term hostility was that the opposed parties tended as time went on to become more like each other. In his case, Athenian democracy became imperialistic and authoritarian, while Spartan autocracy became more materialistic. George C. Marshall, some two millennia later, reflected that Americans should contemplate Thucydides, and see if the same things were not happening to them, in the midst of McCarthyism, the growth of what President Eisenhower characterized as a military-industrial establishment, and the development of an American-dominated power bloc.

Korea served to hasten the pace of hostility. The American military buildup gathered momentum from it. Not that this was all bad; in a real world, after all, United States strength had been permitted, even encouraged, to become dangerously weak. The very fact of Korea revealed that such military weakness by one side invited aggression by the other, and that therefore, as long as one side would not disarm, the other must rearm.

The course taken by that rearmament was open to wide divergence of view. The Army was enlarged, which it desperately needed; the Navy had demonstrated the value of versatility and especially of a readily available amphibious capability. The emergence of assorted technological advances, most notably the helicopter, in Korea may have led military theorists astray; there are good grounds for arguing that in the next war, the U.S. Army would have been far better off with more infantrymen to go out on patrol and fewer helicopters to take them out and back—for arguing, in the larger sense, that the United States needed less fancy weaponry and more manpower. That argument might be carried right up the scale, for the new Republican government opted not for the long hard road of compulsory service and a big army, but rather for massive retaliation and the big bomb. Some problems, such as the obligation to serve and defend one's country, do not go away just because a lot of money is thrown at them.

The U.S. Air Force remained the quick fix of military solutions. Here again the lessons of Korea may have been misread. The Air Force's official history of the war concluded with the affirmation that air power superiority had been the decisive factor in bringing the war to an end, and that the "air mission" had been accomplished. This conclusion was highly arguable, and though there is no doubt that air power *could* have won the war—perhaps by starting World War III—it is by no means so certain that it *did* win the war, especially operating under the limitations the United States imposed upon its use. North Korea was devastated by strategic bombing within the first few months of the war, but kept on fighting. Operation Strangle was an embarrassing failure, and indeed, even if it is accepted that air power was the chief means of applying pressure to bring the enemy to a settlement, that rather ignores how long it took to do it. A more determined enemy, less vulnerable to air interdiction, protected by even more stringent limitations which an American government imposed upon its own forces, might prove even more resistant to the pressure of air attack.

In addition to posing questions about the actual combat response and the nature of it, the war also called into question the appropriate relationship between the commander in the field and his military and civilian superiors at home. The most notable example of this was, of course, the famous Truman-MacArthur controversy. But it is interesting to note that one of MacArthur's successors as Far East commander, General Clark, ended up recommending much the same things that MacArthur had wanted to do, and that the American government itself, in its "greater sanctions" statement, proposed doing those same things if the enemy did not behave. It is also revealing that of the other senior commanders, Generals Ridgway and Taylor subsequently left the military service and became both critics and advisers of American policy in that gray area between political and military action. In an era of brushfire wars, low-intensity conflict, and wars of liberation, an era also of increasingly advanced communication, the line between what was political and what was military became ever more difficult to draw—who should produce and control what response? The kind of escalation by minute gradations that characterized the war in Vietnam was well begun in Korea. So was the preoccupation with "sending signals" to the opposition, as well as the uncertainty about whether or not they were being received and correctly interpreted.

In 1950 a country such as the United States was ill suited for the type of limited war that Korea proved to be. It remained difficult to the end to fight a war without trying to win it in the normally accepted sense of the word. A substantial mental adaptation was needed on the part of the public, of government, and above all of the men asked to suffer hardship, and risk or lose their lives, in pursuit of elusive and ill-defined goals. Yet the adaptation was successfully made, and the war, when all is said and done, was successfully waged. The results may have appeared inconclusive; but aggression was at least stopped, the Republic of Korea, with all its imperfections, was preserved, and the cause of collective security through the United Nations, with all the frustrations that that entailed, was furthered, at least a little bit.

The most famous remark about Korea was that made during the MacArthur hearings by General of the Army Omar Bradley; he said it would be "the wrong war, at the wrong place, at the wrong time, and with the wrong enemy." The statement, which was actually made not about Korea but about enlarging the war by attacking China, has come to sum up the public perception of the Korean War, as if it were somehow a lapse of taste or good judgment, which should not have happened, and which everyone would prefer to forget.

But of course it did happen. The crisis did occur, and men made what seemed to them the best response to it they could make under the circumstances as they understood them at the time. Reputations were made and lost; men fought and died. If at the end of it they did not have any final answers or absolute solutions to their problems, that is because final answers and absolute solutions are not part of the human condition.

SUGGESTIONS FOR FURTHER READING

The first glance at a public or university library might indicate that there is relatively little material available on the Korean War, but such a casual look would be misleading. In *The Korean War: An Annotated Bibliography* (New York: Garland, 1986), Keith D. McFarland lists more than 2,300 titles. This book is an absolutely indispensable tool for studies of the war, and the works it covers include everything from contemporary accounts and articles, often little more than propaganda, to doctoral dissertations and serious monographic studies of very specific problems. Most of the following, especially of the background suggestions, will be found in McFarland.

There is a relatively small number of general histories of Korea itself, to serve as background to the war. Useful political material is in Cornelius Osgood, *The Koreans and their Culture* (New York: Ronald, 1951); and Kyang Cho Chung, *Korea Tomorrow: Land of the Morning Calm* (New York: Macmillan, 1956), is a good survey. More recent, and dealing less with the war, are William E. Henthorn, *A History of Korea* (New York: Free Press, 1971), and Ki-baik Lee, *A New History of Korea* (Cambridge, Mass.: Harvard University Press, 1984). Several studies concentrate on the post–World War II period, among them Bruce Cumings, *The Origins of the Korean War: Liberation and the Emergence of Separate Regimes, 1945–1947* (Princeton, N.J.: Princeton University Press, 1981); Wayne S. Kiyosaki, *North Korea's Foreign Relations: The Politics of Accom-*

modation, 1945–1975 (New York: Praeger, 1976); Koon Woo Nam, *The North Korean Communist Leadership, 1945–1965* (University, Ala., University of Alabama Press, 1974); and Robert R. Simmons, *The Strained Alliance: Peking, P'yongyang, Moscow and the Politics of the Korean Civil War* (New York: Free Press, 1975).

In contrast to the list on Korea, there is an overwhelming number of studies of the United States during the era. For general background, there are Arthur S. Link and William B. Catton, *American Epoch: A History of the United States Since the 1880s,* 3rd ed. (New York: Knopf, 1967); Paul K. Conkin and David Burner, *A History of Recent America* (New York: Thomas Y. Crowell, 1974); William H. Chafe, *The Unfinished Journey: America Since World War II* (New York: Oxford University Press, 1986); and the popularly written Eric F. Goldman, *The Crucial Decade: America 1945–1955* (New York: Knopf, 1956). In addition to the autobiographical or biographical material listed below, there are numerous studies of the Truman Presidency, among them Cabell Phillips, *The Truman Presidency: The History of a Triumphant Succession* (New York: Macmillan, 1961); Bert Cochran, *Harry Truman and the Crisis Presidency* (New York: Funk & Wagnalls, 1973); Robert J. Donovan, *Tumultuous Years: The Presidency of Harry S. Truman,* vol. 2., *1949–1953* (New York: Norton, 1982); Alonzo L. Hamby, *Beyond the New Deal: Harry S. Truman and American Liberalism* (New York: Columbia University Press, 1973); and Richard F. Haynes, *The Awesome Power: Harry S. Truman as Commander-in-Chief* (Baton Rouge, La.: Louisiana State University Press, 1963). For the evolution and condition of the American military services during the period there are two books by Russell F. Weigley, *History of the United States Army* (New York: Macmillan, 1967), and *The American Way of War: A History of United States Military Strategy and Policy* (New York: Macmillan, 1973); also Alan R. Millett and Peter Maslowski, *For the Common Defense: A Military History of the United States of America* (New York: Free Press, 1984), and Paul Y. Hammond, *Organizing for Defense: The American Military Establishment in the Twentieth Century* (Westport, Conn.: Greenwood Press, 1977; original ed. 1961).

American foreign policy has received a great deal of study, particularly for this period when the Cold War was beginning; much of it is highly critical of the United States, and some is openly polemical. The basic documentary source is the series of State Department papers, *Foreign Relations of the United States* for various years, printed in Washington by the U.S. Government Printing Office; the most important one on Korea is Volume III of 1950: *Korea* (1976). Useful studies are John W. Spanier, *American Foreign Policy Since World War II* (New York: Praeger, 1960); Henry Kissinger, *Nuclear Weapons and Foreign Policy* (New York: Harper, 1957); John E. Mueller, *War, Presidents, and Public Opinion* (New York: Wiley, 1973); Lisle A. Rose, *Roots of Tragedy: The United States and the Struggle for Asia, 1945–1953* (Westport, Conn.: Greenwood Press, 1976); and Charles M. Dobbs, *The Unwanted Symbol: American Foreign Policy, the Cold War, and Korea, 1945–1950* (Kent, Ohio: Kent State University Press, 1981). Even more specifically directed to Korea are Edward G. Meade, *American Military Government in Korea* (New York: King's Crown, 1951); and Harold J. Noble, *Embassy at War* (Seattle: University of Washington Press, 1975). The most exhaustive, and exhausting, treatment of the actual crisis is Glenn D. Paige, *The Korean Decision [June 24–30, 1950]* (New York: Free Press, 1968). Isidor F. Stone, *The Hidden History of the Korean War* (New York: Monthly Review, 1952), attacks American policy: Joyce and Gabriel Kolko, *The Limits of Power: The World and the United States Foreign Policy, 1945–1954* (New York: Harper, 1972), is a prominent New Left treatment; and Herbert Aptheker, *American Foreign Policy and the Cold War* (New York: New Century, 1962), is a collection of articles by the author, an American Marxist-Leninist.

On the United Nations and world scene, several works may be used with profit. T. R. Fehrenbach, *This Kind of Peace* (London: Leslie Frewin, 1967), is a readable survey of the United Nations; volume 1 of Evan Luard, *A History of the United Nations: The Years of Western Domination, 1945–1955* (New York: St. Martin's, 1982), is more scholarly; the role of the Secretary-General is covered in Stephen M. Schwebel, *The Secretary-General of the United Nations: His Political Powers and Practice* (Cambridge, Mass.: Harvard University Press, 1952). A Canadian view is Denis Stairs, *The Diplomacy of Constraint: Canada, the Korean War, and the United States* (Toronto: University of Toronto Press, 1974); and an Indian view is Shiv Dayal, *India's Role in the Korean Question* (Delhi: Chand, 1959). On American relations with the UN, there is Leland M. Goodrich, *Korea: A Study of U.S. Policy in the United Nations* (New York: Council on Foreign Relations, 1956). Finally, since almost everyone considers American policy to be groping blindly in the period, it is a comfort that in *Soviet Policy in the Far East, 1944–1951* (London: Oxford University Press, 1953), Max Beloff sees the Soviets as not knowing what they were doing, either.

There are several general histories of the war itself available. In chronological order, there are Robert Leckie, *Conflict: The History of the Korean War, 1950–53* (New York: Putnam's, 1962); T. R. Fehrenbach, *This Kind of War: A Study in Unpreparedness* (New York: Macmillan, 1963); David Rees, *Korea: The Limited War* (New York: St. Martin's, 1964); Harry J. Middleton, *The Compact History of the Korean War* (New York: Hawthorn, 1965); Edgar O'Ballance, *Korea: 1950–1953* (Hamden, Conn.: Archon Books, 1969); J. Lawton Collins, *War in Peacetime: The History and Lessons of Korea* (Boston: Houghton Mifflin, 1969); and George Forty, *At War in Korea* (London: Allen, 1982). All are interesting; each has a slightly different point of view. O'Ballance's book is one of a series he wrote on small wars; Collins was, of course, a major participant, and his work is partly historical, partly autobiographical; Rees is generally considered the best of this type. Two recent studies, Callum A. MacDonald, *Korea: The War Before Vietnam* (New York: Free Press, 1987), and Max Hastings, *The Korean War* (New York: Simon & Schuster, 1987), appeared too late to be used in this study.

There are biographies of or autobiographies by virtually all of the chief figures involved in Korea on the western side. Trygve Lie wrote *In the Cause of Peace: Seven Years with the United Nations* (New York: Macmillan, 1954). In addition to the several works on Truman cited earlier, there is his own *Memoirs: Volume II: Years of Trial and Hope* (Garden City, N.Y.: Doubleday, 1956). On the most famous incident of the war there is, among many others, John W. Spanier, *The Truman-MacArthur Controversy and the Korean War* (Cambridge, Mass.: Belknap Press of Harvard University Press, 1959). Dean Acheson wrote *Present at the Creation: My Years at the State Department* (New York: Norton, 1969), while David S. McLellan wrote *Dean Acheson: The State Department Years* (New York: Dodd, 1976). Stephen E. Ambrose's two-volume *Eisenhower* (New York: Simon & Schuster, 1983, 1984) has much useful material, as does Omar Bradley and Clay Blair's *A General's Life: An Autobiography by General of the Army Omar N. Bradley* (New York: Simon & Schuster, 1983). A Canadian view of the political scene is in volume 2 of Lester B. Pearson, *Mike: The Memoirs of the*

Right Honourable Lester B. Pearson (Toronto: University of Toronto Press, 1973).

For those more directly involved in field commands, there are Maj. Gen. William F. Dean, *General Dean's Story* (New York: Viking, 1954); Matthew B. Ridgway, *The Korean War* (Garden City, N.Y.: Doubleday, 1967); Mark W. Clark, *From the Danube to the Yalu* (New York: Harper, 1954); Burke Davis, *Marine! The Life of Lt. Gen. Lewis B. (Chesty) Puller, USMC (Ret.)* (Boston: Little, Brown, 1962); and Maxwell D. Taylor, *The Uncertain Trumpet* (New York: Harper, 1959), and his later *Swords and Ploughshares* (New York: Norton, 1972). Two works on South Korea's president are Robert T. Oliver, *Syngman Rhee: The Man Behind the Myth* (New York: Dodd Mead, 1955); and Richard C. Allen, *Korea's Syngman Rhee: An Unauthorized Portrait* (Rutland, Vt.: Tuttle, 1960). On the North Korean leader there is Bong Baik, *Kim Il Sung: Biography,* 4 vols. (Beirut: Dar Al-Talia, 1973).

Finally, there is a superfluity of volumes on MacArthur. William Manchester, *American Caesar: Douglas MacArthur, 1880–1964* (Boston: Little, Brown, 1978), is highly readable, but it and virtually everything else are superseded by D. Clayton James' definitive three-volume *The Years of MacArthur,* the third of which, *Triumph and Disaster, 1945–1964* (Boston: Houghton Mifflin, 1985), covers Korea.

For land operations, those volumes of the various official histories that have appeared are essential. Especially useful is Roy E. Appleman, *South to the Naktong, North to the Yalu,* vol. 1 of *The United States Army in the Korean War* (Washington: Office of the Chief of Military History, 1961). So are Walter G. Hermes, *Truce Tent and Fighting Front* (1966), and James F. Schnabel, *Policy and Direction: The First Year* (1972) both in the same series. The latter author, with Robert J. Watson, also wrote Volume III, *The Korean War,* of *The History of the Joint Chiefs of Staff* (Washington: Historical Division, Joint Secretariat, Joint Chiefs of Staff, 1978–1979). There is the five-volume *U.S. Marine Operations in Korea, 1950–1953* (Washington: Historical Branch, G-3, Headquarters, U.S. Marine Corps, 1954–1972), by Lynn Montross and others, as well as the more manageable Allan A. Millet, *Semper Fidelis: The History of the United States Marine Corps* (New York: Macmillan, 1980). For specific battles or aspects of the fighting there are many useful studies, for example, S. L. A. Marshall, *The River and the Gauntlet:*

Defeat of the Eighth Army by the Chinese Communist Forces, November, 1950, in the Battle of the Chongchon River, Korea (New York: Morrow, 1953), and *Pork Chop Hill: The American Fighting Man in Action—Korea, Spring, 1953* (New York: Morrow, 1956). John G. Westover, *Combat Support in Korea* (Washington: Center of Military History, reprint 1987), and Russell A. Gugeler, *Combat Actions in Korea* (Washington: Combat Forces, 1954), both have valuable and vivid descriptions. Edwin P. Hoyt has recently produced a three-volume narrative of the war, *The Pusan Perimeter, On to the Yalu,* and *The Bloody Road to Panmunjom* (New York: Stein & Day, 1984, 1985). On Inchon there is Robert D. Heinl, *Victory at High Tide: The Inchon-Seoul Campaign* (Philadelphia: Lippincott, 1968); and on the Chosin (Changjin) Reservoir, Eric Hammel, *Chosin: Heroic Ordeal of the Korean War* (New York: Vanguard, 1981) and Robert Leckie, *The March to Glory* (Cleveland: World, 1960) The ordinary soldier or Marine in Korea is found in Timothy J. Mulvey, *These Are Your Sons* (New York: McGraw-Hill, 1972), Russ Martin, *The Last Parallel: A Marine's War Journal* (New York. Rinehart, 1957); and the more recent Donald Knox, *The Korean War: Pusan to Chosin: An Oral History* (New York: Harcourt Brace, Jovanovich, 1985).

Material on other armies is available but a bit elusive. For the British there are C. N. Barclay, *The First Commonwealth Division. The Story of British Commonwealth Land Forces in Korea, 1950–1953* (Aldershot: Gale, 1954); and Tim Carew, *Korea: The Commonwealth at War* (London: Cassell, 1967). For Australia there is the brief Norman Bartlett, ed., *With the Australians in Korea* (Canberra: Australian War Memorial, 1954); in addition, Robert O'Neill has written the first volume of the official series *Australia in the Korean War, 1950–1953* (Canberra: Australian government, 1981). The official Canadian history is Lt. Col. Herbert Fairlie Wood, *Strange Battleground: The Operations in Korea and Their Effects on the Defence Policy of Canada* (Ottawa: Queen's Printer, 1966); a more narrative work is John Melady, *Korea: Canada's Forgotten War* (Toronto: Macmillan, 1983). There is no full-scale study of either the South or North Korean armies. The Chinese are treated in Samuel B. Griffith, *The Chinese People's Liberation Army* (New York: McGraw-Hill, 1967); and Alexander L. George, *The Chinese Communist Army in Action and the Korean War and Its Aftermath* (New York: Columbia University Press, 1967).

Naval material is sparse. The official history is James A. Field, Jr., *History of United States Naval Operations: Korea* (Washington: U.S. Government Printing Office, 1962). Two semiofficial studies are Commander Malcolm W. Cagle and Commander Frank A. Manson, *The Sea War in Korea;* and on mine warfare, Arnold S. Lott, *Most Dangerous Sea* (both Annapolis, Md.: United States Naval Institute Press, 1957 and 1959). Another official history is Thor Thorgrimsson and E. C. Russell, *Canadian Naval Operations in Korean Waters: 1950–1955* (Ottawa: Queen's Printer, 1965).

On air activities, the excellent and exhaustive official history is Robert F. Futrell, *The United States Air Force in Korea, 1950–1953*, rev. ed. (Washington: Office of Air Force History, 1983). An interesting discussion is in Richard H. Kohn and Joseph P. Harahan, *Air Superiority in World War II and Korea* (Washington: Office of Air Force History, 1983). Three more popular treatments are Gene Gurney, *Five Down and Glory* (New York: Putnam's, 1958), Stanley M. Ulanoff, ed., *Fighter Pilot* (New York: Doubleday, 1962); and Robert Jackson, *Air War over Korea* (London: Allan, 1973).

Several special studies cover various key elements of the war. There are Allen S. Whiting, *China Crosses the Yalu: The Decision to Enter the Korean War* (New York: Macmillan, 1960); and Walter A. Zelman, *Chinese Intervention in the Korean War* (Los Angeles: University of California Press, 1967). On the almost endless truce negotiations, Admiral C. Turner Joy wrote *How Communists Negotiate* (New York: Macmillan, 1955); this was followed by Allan E. Goodman, ed., *Negotiating While Fighting: The Diary of Admiral C. Turner Joy at the Korean Armistice Conference* (Stanford, Calif.: Hoover Institution Press, 1978). William H. Vatcher, who was there as a UN adviser, wrote *Panmunjom: The Story of the Korean Military Armistice Negotiations* (New York: Praeger, 1958; reprint Westport, Conn.: Greenwood Press, 1973). Given the argument over prisoners of war and their behavior, it is not surprising that there are several works on that problem. Eugene Kinkead, *In Every War but One* (New York: Norton, 1959), is the most outspoken critic of prisoner behavior: and Albert D. Biderman, *March to Calumny: The Story of American POWs in the Korean War* (New York: Macmillan, 1963), is the chief revisionist. William L. White, *The Captives of Korea* (New York: Scribner's, 1957; reprint Westport, Conn.: Greenwood Press, 1978), compares prisoner treatment and behavior on both sides. Of several accounts by or about prisoners, examples are

Clay Blair, Jr., *Beyond Courage* (New York: McKay, 1955); Philip Deane, *I Was a Captive in Korea* (New York: Norton, 1953); and Lloyd W. Pate, *Reactionary* (New York: Harper, 1956).

Beyond the materials listed here there are many articles, in both scholarly and technical journals, in the latter on new medical techniques, for example, and in the popular magazines of the day, such as *Collier's* and *Saturday Evening Post*. Reference to these in the back files of a library will provide the reader with the curious juxtaposition of the good life in the United States and an ambiguous war in Korea.

INDEX

INDEX

INDEX

INDEX